Jean Restayn

WWII TANK

ENCYCLOPAEDIA
in color 1939-45

Translated from the French by Sally and Lawrence BROWN

Histoire & Collections

above. **The Japanese Ha-Go tank, had a range of 250 kilometres and a top speed of 45 kph.**

Previous title page. Panzer III Ausf. **A. The tank shown still has its pre- July 1937 camouflage which allows us to believe that it is one of the first three tanks delivered to the 1. Panzerdivision at the end of 1936.**

ACKNOWLEDGEMENTS

The author would like to thank *Histoire et Collections* and in particular Alexandre Thers for his patience, understanding and constant good humour shown during the putting together of this project, which was at times, of a titanic nature.

Thanks also go to Jean Bouchery, Eric Lefèvre and François Vauvillier for their much appreciated help during the final touches to the chapters dealing with the Commonwealth, Germany and France.

Design and lay-out by Thibault PANFILI and Alexandre THERS
© *Histoire & Collections* 2007

ISBN: 978-2-915239-47-8

Publisher's number: 915239

© *Histoire & Collections* 2007

a book published by
HISTOIRE & COLLECTIONS
SA au capital de 182 938, 82 €
5, avenue de la République
F-75541 Paris Cedex 11 - FRANCE
Fax +33 1 47 00 51 11
www.histoireetcollections.fr

This book has been designed, typed, laid-out and processed by *Histoire & Collections* fully on integrated computer equipment.

Pictures integrated by *Studio A&C*

Printed by *Zure*,
Spain, European Union
December 2007

Summary/Chapters

Notes. All tanks on the colour plates are not reproduced at a constant scale.

Tanks. A matter of tactics or strategy ?

BEFORE DISCOVERING the profiles of standard tanks and their variants, it seemed wise, even if the great tank battles took place in their majority on the Eastern Front, to take a brief look at the situation of the armoured units of the three main belligerents on the Western Front where they showed the full measure of their possibilities during the Battle of Normandy in 1944.

Germany

The progress made by the Germans in the domain of large armoured units allowed them to win lightning victories in the first years of the war. Each time, the Panzerdivisionen made up the spearhead of their land forces. As the war went on, the number of these units continually increased; from 10 in 1940, they reached 25 in 1942. However, the shortage of men and materiel, linked to the problems of constantly higher and better quality production in the face of the enormous Allied industrial resources, forced the German army to adopt, in 1944, a new organisation: the latter meant that the Panzerdivision of this period did not have much in common with those that surged through France in 1940. The evolution in combat techniques (increase in anti tank measures, tonnage and the power of tanks notably) also influenced this overhaul. In 1944, the total strength of a division was brought down to 15,600 men in 1941-42 to 14,727. The tank regiment, which formed the framework of the division, now only had two battalions of 48 tanks (compared to three previously), organised into four companies each. One of the two battalions was, in principal, equipped with the Panzer IV, the other with Panthers. In this manner, with a theoretical number of 160 tanks, 28 tank hunters and 30 self propelled guns, the Panzerdivision could pack an impressive punch, albeit slightly inferior to that of 1943.

Globally, what were the intrinsic qualities and flaws of tanks ? They were, generally, superior to those of the Anglo Saxons, the Tiger and Panther, put into service respectively at the end of 1942 and mid 1943, were superior to them in many domains. The Panzer IV, whose design dated from 1938, was showing signs of age, despite the constant improvements made to it, but its armament remained formidable. Even at this time, it still made up the framework of the Panzerdivisionen, but its American *alter ego*, the Sherman, proved itself to be of the same level. Generally speaking, the German tanks had an inferior speed compared with American counterparts. However, the weak mobility of the other components of the Heer, forced them to fight a more defensive war. The German armoured divisions which took part in the Normandy fighting were of two types: those of the army and those of the Waffen-SS. They were of equal strength, in theory, at full strength they had 96 Panzer IV and 76 Panthers.

The danger facing the armoured units that moved up to reinforce the front line was the threat from Allied aircraft, whose attacks soon became much feared. But, the effects of these attacks remained more psychological than materiel. However, the majority of the bridges of the Seine and between Paris and the coast had been destroyed by planes, and the movement of the German divisions was held up. A few units, did, however, manage to quickly reach the front line. The other major problem that these large units faced, was the lack of fuel. The shortage was such, on the Western Front, that training was considerably curtailed for armoured units stationed in France.

Upon arrival in the combat zone, the units hidden away in the bocage, made full use of the topography which favoured ambush but in no case the correct use of tanks. One could say that assault aircraft were not needed, as they were incapable of inflicting materiel losses on armour in order to stop them gaining ground. Making them remain undercover for hours on end meant that they could only be used in small groups, preventing large concentrations which would have allowed large scale actions and even dissuaded some units from reaching the front.

The commonwealth

The British armoured units about to land in Normandy benefited from, for the initial assault, elaborate logistics and deployment doctrine, the fruit of the intelligence drawn from the disastrous attempt to land at Dieppe in 1942.

The British armoured division of the summer of 1944 operated according to the organisation put into place in 1942, which saw the replacement of one of the armoured brigades by an infantry brigade and an important increase in its artillery. The British were now confronted with a serious crisis, they experienced some difficulty in maintaining the level of manpower due to a lack of personnel. The formation of their last armoured division, the 79th, was back in 1942.

In 1943, the official doctrine placed its priority in exploitation, putting the onus on tanks accompanying the infantry. With this rigid and conventional line, they stood apart from the other belligerents. They remained convinced that infantry support tanks in close quarter combat should, above all, have thick armour rather than an increased fire power and speed. Nevertheless, the divisions saw, in 1943, a slight increase in their fire power, notably in a more and more important number of American Shermans, capable along with the Churchill IV and Cromwell IV of firing, as well as anti tank shells, high explosive shells.

The armoured brigade made up the framework of the division. It was equipped with three tank regiments. A fourth armoured regiment, to which was attached an infantry battalion, was called the *Armoured Reconnaissance Regiment*, the reconnaissance being carried out by regimental *troops* or by the army corps reconnaissance regiments attached to the divisions. In this way, with a theoretical number of 244 medium and light tanks, 25 anti aircraft tanks and eight command tanks, the British armoured division, despite its inferior fire power compared to the Germans, was numerically superior. The tanks used in Normandy can be placed into four categories:

- **Combat tanks (Medium):** Their main weaponry was a 75 or 76.2 mm gun (17 pounder) for medium tanks (the British did not have heavy tanks), mounted on a revolving turret. Designed to be as versatile as possible, their objective was to fight enemy tanks, but also to efficiently take on non armoured targets.

- **Infantry support tanks (Infantry Tanks):** They were capable of destroying mines and the majority of obstacles encountered (fortified positions).

- **Amphibious tank:** Its mission was to reach the shore under its own means in order to support the first waves of infantry in mopping up the beaches.

- **Special tanks:** They played a very important role in the actual landing phase, the tricky moment when troops were still on the beach and not positioned inland.

The tanks were, generally, inferior to their German counterparts. The Cromwell and the Sherman formed the backbone of armoured brigades. They were outgunned by, and inferior in armour, to the German medium and heavy tanks, the Panther and Tiger I and II. On the other hand, they performed more or less as well as the Panzer IV which suffered from a lack of mobility and mechanical reliability.

It was only the appearance of the Sherman Firefly that allowed the crews to fight on equal terms, thanks to the long 76.2 mm gun, using the new APDS shell. It did not, however, compare when it came to armour. As for the Churchill, an infantry tank of old design, its main advantage was in its armour. Despite this clear difference in quality, other factors favoured the British: the amount of man power and the rapid replacement of destroyed materiel.

Normandy, a region chosen for an invasion to be led and dominated by armour, did not, however, offer a countryside which favoured large scale mechanised manoeuvre. In consequence, the campaign's strategy seemed to be conditioned by the need, once the landings were finished, to gain the main road junctions in order to create a space which would allow for a great battle. The doctrine aimed at rapidly gaining control of the beaches thanks to the use of special tanks thus gave way to tactics dictated by terrain, the plain to the south of Caen offering the only arena where a great mobile battle could be led by armoured forces. Everywhere else, as long as the Germans could maintain enough forces in the bocage, the advantage was theirs. The British tactical doctrine, different to that of the Americans, often remained rigid and conventional. The tanks often attacked alone, rarely accompanied by infantry, which resulted in heavy losses, as in operation Goodwood. On the other hand, they showed their worth when supported by aircraft, something the enemy could not do with its battered Luftwaffe.

To sum up, the British strategy, although fainthearted, prevented Panzer divisions at Caen from gaining the upper hand. However, with the exception of Goodwood, the British had not often engaged their forces on a vast scale, using only five armoured divisions and eight independent armoured brigades (including Canadian and Polish units), totalling nearly 3,300 Shermans, Churchills and Cromwells, with very important reserves of trained crews.

The United States

Unlike the British, the Americans in 1943-1944, were constantly expanding the process of creating armoured divisions. In 1944, their economic potential was at its height and meant that they played an important role within the Allied coalition. For this reason, all their efforts of production and standardisation revolved around a single tank, the Sherman, which equipped a large number of allied armoured units.

The examination of mechanised performances on the battlefield revealed to the Americans the necessity of making revolutionary changes in the organisation of their divisions, whose number of tanks was too high compared to the infantry and artillery. The Americans based their idea on the assumption that a tank could fulfil the role of assault tank as well as infantry tank by its combination of armour-firepower-speed. Therefore, in 1943, the armoured divisions underwent a profound reorganisation, which saw their size reduced by 3,600 men. There were also reductions in the number of light tanks. The CCA and CCB, the strike force, were made up to control a number of combat units (battalions or companies) and or support units. The major units of the division were three tank battalions, each one with its staff and company staff, three companies of medium tanks, one company of light tanks and a service company. The number of men in a tank battalion was 729. Each tank company, be it medium or light, had 17 tanks - three squads with five tanks each plus two for command. Towards the end of the war, the regulation number of medium tanks was 195. To sum up, the use of tanks with the Americans was based on a close and flexible collaboration with the infantry, resulting in the absence of armoured corps or armies, which differed with the concept used by the Germans.

The armoured materiel used in Normandy was put into two categories.

- **Combat or assault tanks,** whose main weaponry, a 75 mm gun for medium or heavy tanks, was placed on a revolving turret. Designed to be as versatile as possible, their objective was to take on enemy tanks, but also to efficiently take on non armoured targets.

- **Fast reconnaissance tanks**: Their role was the destruction of various obstacles such as machine gun nests and anti tank positions. Versatile and of good performance, easier and less expensive to manufacture, they gradually grew in importance. This offensive weapon saw its role change with the evolution of infantry, and became an increasingly defensive instrument as the war progressed. Used more and more in the role of tank hunter, it also showed here its capabilities, its mobility (unlike tractor drawn artillery), which allowed it to pull back with ease from enemy fire.

Globally, what were the intrinsic qualities and drawbacks of this materiel ? The assault tanks (in this instance the different versions of Sherman, around which all efforts were concentrated) proved themselves capable of fighting on equal terms the Panzer IV, its main rival in the same category. However, the Americans did not have any heavy tanks, and because of this were largely supplanted by the Tiger and Panther, except in the mechanical and mobile domain. The enormous advantage enjoyed by the Americans, and the British, lay in their numbers, an efficient fuel supply, the rapidity in which destroyed materiel was replaced, and air support.

The sectors in which the Americans fought in Normandy turned out to be difficult for their armour: the beachhead exits were either funnelled by marshes or blocked by cliffs, and inland, conditions became more difficult with the bocage.

Whenever possible, the individual commanders were connected to a radio communications network which allowed them to talk directly with one another, each one knowing what was happening and, more importantly, allowing the commander of the force to impose his orders and personality on the battle.

This was particularly important in a mobile mechanised war that soon became the hallmark of the 3rd Army's battle plans and the reason of its continuous successes. These two major characteristics could be described as the ability to "move and fire". Six armoured divisions were thrown into the battle, which amounted to an approximate total of 2,000 Shermans.

Germany

In 1917 - 18, with the British and French using their tanks in mass attacks, the German high command still considered artillery as being the queen of the battlefield. The few German A7V tanks, but above all, the captured British mark I - IV tanks (and a fair number of French FT-17) were not enough to change this point of view. The attempts of far sighted officers to develop and integrate this materiel invariably came unstuck, faced with this stubborn philosophy, which saw the German soldier as the one who should have been able to deal with this new threat, armed with a few improvised anti-tank weapons.

It was only after the world war, and in the somewhat restrictive conditions of the Treaty of Versailles, that Germany got to work with determination.

The first prototypes were given fictitious names "Grosstraktor" or "Neubaufahrzeug"in order to maintain secrecy, before adopting more revealing names such as "Sonderkraftfahrzeug" and finally "Panzerkampfwagen".

Germany, in 1939, did not have at its disposal a powerful armoured force. Out of an impressive total of 2,820 armed panzers, only the Pz III and Pz IV were equipped with decent weapons and armour. But they were rare, 213 Pz IV and 148 Pz III. To this should be added the tanks of the defunct Czechoslovakian army, 202 Skoda 35 (Pz 35(t)) and 98 Skoda (Pz 38(t)). The bulk of the Panzerwaffe was made up of 928 Pz I and 1,231 Pz II, badly armoured and equipped with, at most, machine guns or (and) 20 mm canons. A Panzer I, with its 1.5 mm armour, was at best, usable against infantry or light barricades. However, in no case can we talk here of an armoured tank. Yet these machines made up the bulk of the materiel used by the Germans at the outbreak of war.

It is often put forward that the Panzerwaffe first proved itself during the Spanish Civil War. This is only partially true, as contrary to the Russians, who 'lent' BT and T-26 type tanks with observers and technical advisors as well, the Germans only used Pz I type tanks, which were very inferior to those of the Russians.

The Polish campaign showed the strengths and weaknesses of German armour. For the campaigns of Holland, Belgium and France the following May, the Germans slightly increased the proportions in favour of the Pz III (349 examples) and IV (278 examples). But these still remained in the minority within armoured units, still equipped with the Pz I (523 used out of 1,026) and Pz II (955 used out of 1,079). In 1940, the Pz 35(t) (106 used out of 146) and Pz 38(t) (228 in total), were used by two Panzerdivisionen, being here the 6. and 7. Pz. Div. Apart from the rare Pz IV, these tanks had a weak armament compared to the 45 mm of the French. The armour of French tanks was also very superior compared to that of the Germans. In consequence, the strength of the German tank lay in how it was deployed and not in its construction or its types. The use of new techniques, such as radio and, above all, the interaction of aviation and artillery, were the keys to the success of the Blitzkrieg.

On April 6th, 1941, four PzDiv. (8. 9. 11. and 14.) attacked in the Balkans and conquered Yugoslavia and Greece despite British intervention.

The Russian campaign clearly showed the limitations of armour confronted with the vastness of Russia and the problems of supply. The Germans engaged there, 180 Pz I, 746 Pz II, 106 Pz 35 (t), 772 Pz 38 (t), 955 Pz II, 439 Pz IV, 230 Bef Pz III... a total of 3,198 armed combat tanks of which over half were already obsolete. Only 1,586 were fit for use on September 4th, 1941, 702 had been lost and 542 were undergoing repairs.

With the Eastern Front bogged down and despite the surprising technological evolution of tanks, the mobility of German armour was reduced by the fighting conditions which were imposed more and more by the enemy but also by the increase and the weight of the means engaged. 20 metric ton tanks rapidly doubled or tripled in weight with a non proportional motorisation. The armour lost its manoeuvrability which was the main reason of its success. The reliability of the tanks was also subjected to the consequences, with a proportional increase in breakdowns. The German engineers came up with the sophisticated Panther and Tiger but they were twice or nearly three times heavier than the T-34. The conditions and the means of towing thus became disproportionate and therefore demanded the means to carry it out.

In the West, another problem faced the German armoured units, the Allied aerial supremacy made the movement of tanks difficult. Because of this, the undoubted tactical advantage that the Germans had compared to their enemies, was very reduced by this factor. The armoured branch became more and more bogged down and found itself reduced to a defensive role. The appearance of the formidable Tiger II could not really influence events.

It still remains that these tanks contributed to the founding of the myth of the German armoured army. This myth is too often exalted, as the proportion of these tanks was minimal compared to the other German tanks. Many victories over the T-34, KV or JS were obtained by the Pz III and IV or the StuG III well before the appearance of the Tiger and Panther...

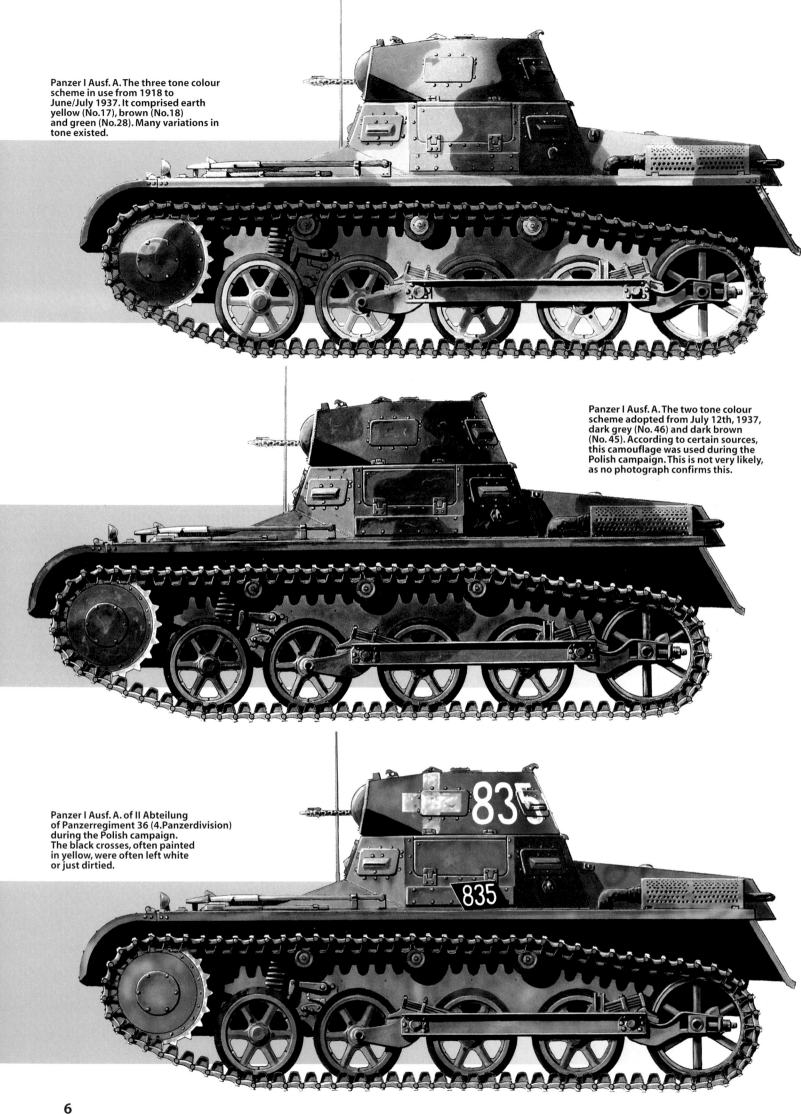

Panzer I Ausf. A. The three tone colour scheme in use from 1918 to June/July 1937. It comprised earth yellow (No.17), brown (No.18) and green (No.28). Many variations in tone existed.

Panzer I Ausf. A. The two tone colour scheme adopted from July 12th, 1937, dark grey (No. 46) and dark brown (No. 45). According to certain sources, this camouflage was used during the Polish campaign. This is not very likely, as no photograph confirms this.

Panzer I Ausf. A. of II Abteilung of Panzerregiment 36 (4.Panzerdivision) during the Polish campaign. The black crosses, often painted in yellow, were often left white or just dirtied.

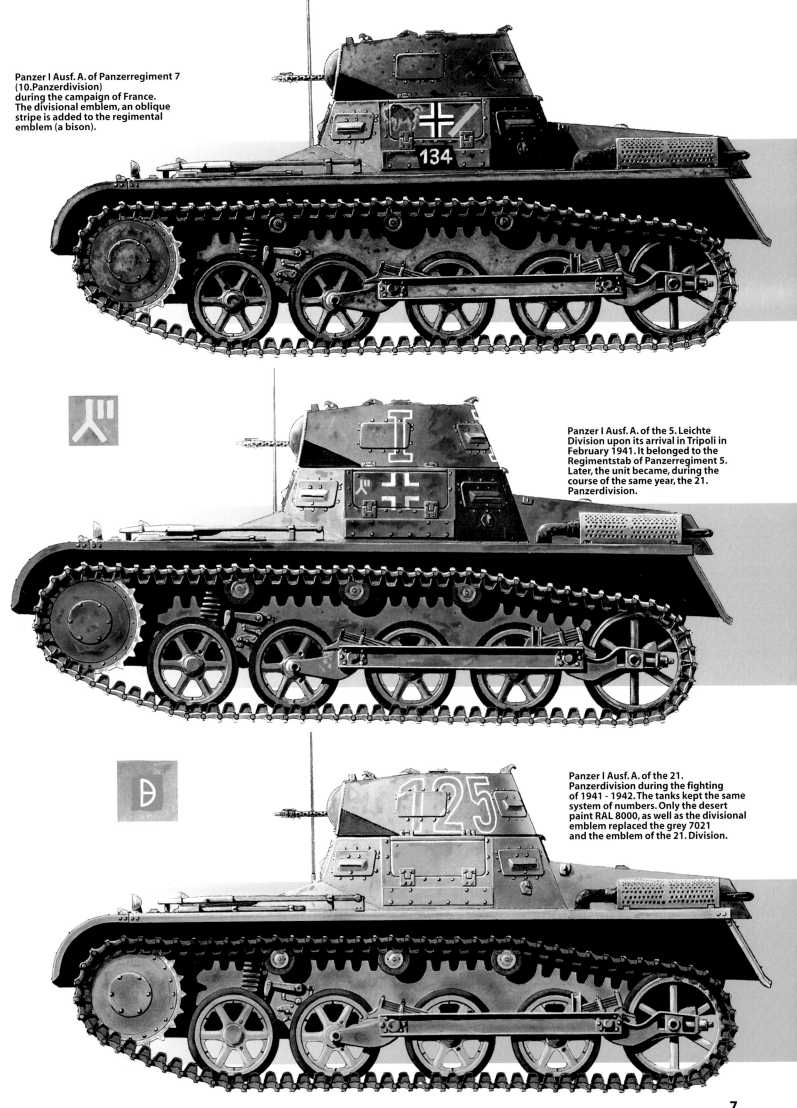

Panzer I Ausf. A. of Panzerregiment 7 (10.Panzerdivision) during the campaign of France. The divisional emblem, an oblique stripe is added to the regimental emblem (a bison).

Panzer I Ausf. A. of the 5. Leichte Division upon its arrival in Tripoli in February 1941. It belonged to the Regimentstab of Panzerregiment 5. Later, the unit became, during the course of the same year, the 21. Panzerdivision.

Panzer I Ausf. A. of the 21. Panzerdivision during the fighting of 1941 - 1942. The tanks kept the same system of numbers. Only the desert paint RAL 8000, as well as the divisional emblem replaced the grey 7021 and the emblem of the 21. Division.

Panzer I Ausf. B of II. Abteilung
of Panzerregiment 1 (1. Panzerdivision)
during the fighting south of Petrikau
on September 4th, 1939.

Panzer I Ausf. B of Panzerregiment 25,
(4. Panzerdivision) during the advance
on Dinant. Note the unusual placement
of the divisional emblem on the upper
armour of the bodywork.

Panzer I Ausf. B of Panzerregiment 36
(4.Panzerdivision), Namur sector
(Belgium) May 17th, 1940.

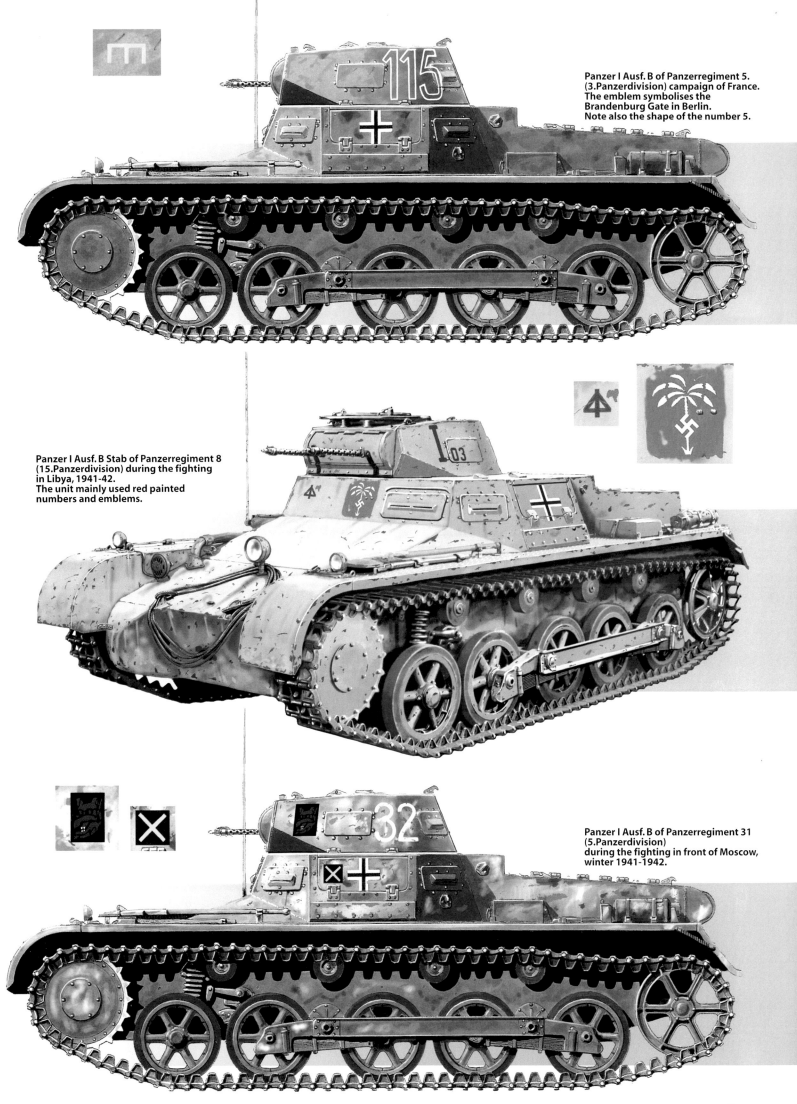

Panzer I Ausf. B of Panzerregiment 5.
(3.Panzerdivision) campaign of France.
The emblem symbolises the
Brandenburg Gate in Berlin.
Note also the shape of the number 5.

Panzer I Ausf. B Stab of Panzerregiment 8
(15.Panzerdivision) during the fighting
in Libya, 1941-42.
The unit mainly used red painted
numbers and emblems.

Panzer I Ausf. B of Panzerregiment 31
(5.Panzerdivision)
during the fighting in front of Moscow,
winter 1941-1942.

Panzer I Ausf. B of Panzerregiment 8 (10.Panzerdivision) in Poland. Only Panzerregiment 8 was used in the campaign. Panzerregiment 7 remained in Germany in reserve.

Panzer I Ausf. A of Panzerregiment 7 (I0.Panzerdivision) campaign of France. Note the oblique stripe emblem of the division and the regiment's bison emblem.

Panzer II Ausf. B of Panzerregiment 25 (7.Panzerdivision) during the preparations and training for operation "Barbarossa".

Panzer II Ausf. A, B or C
of Panzerregiment 1 (1.Panzerdivision)
during the Poland campaign.

Panzer II Ausf. A, B or C
of the 1.Leichte Division during
the Poland campaign.
Panzerregiment 11 would later be
integrated into the 6. Panzerdivision.

Panzer II Ausf. A, B or C
of Panzerabteilung zbV 40,
Norway, 1940.

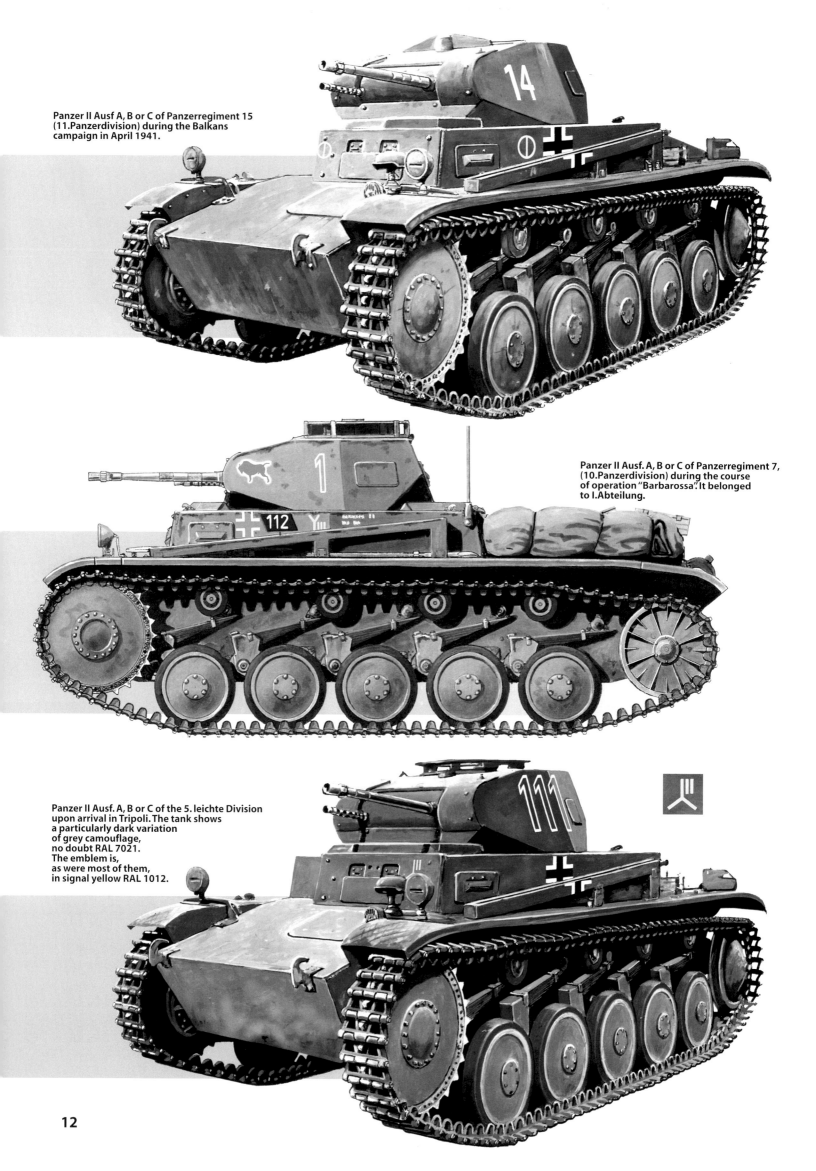

Panzer II Ausf A, B or C of Panzerregiment 15 (11.Panzerdivision) during the Balkans campaign in April 1941.

Panzer II Ausf. A, B or C of Panzerregiment 7, (10.Panzerdivision) during the course of operation "Barbarossa". It belonged to I.Abteilung.

Panzer II Ausf. A, B or C of the 5. leichte Division upon arrival in Tripoli. The tank shows a particularly dark variation of grey camouflage, no doubt RAL 7021. The emblem is, as were most of them, in signal yellow RAL 1012.

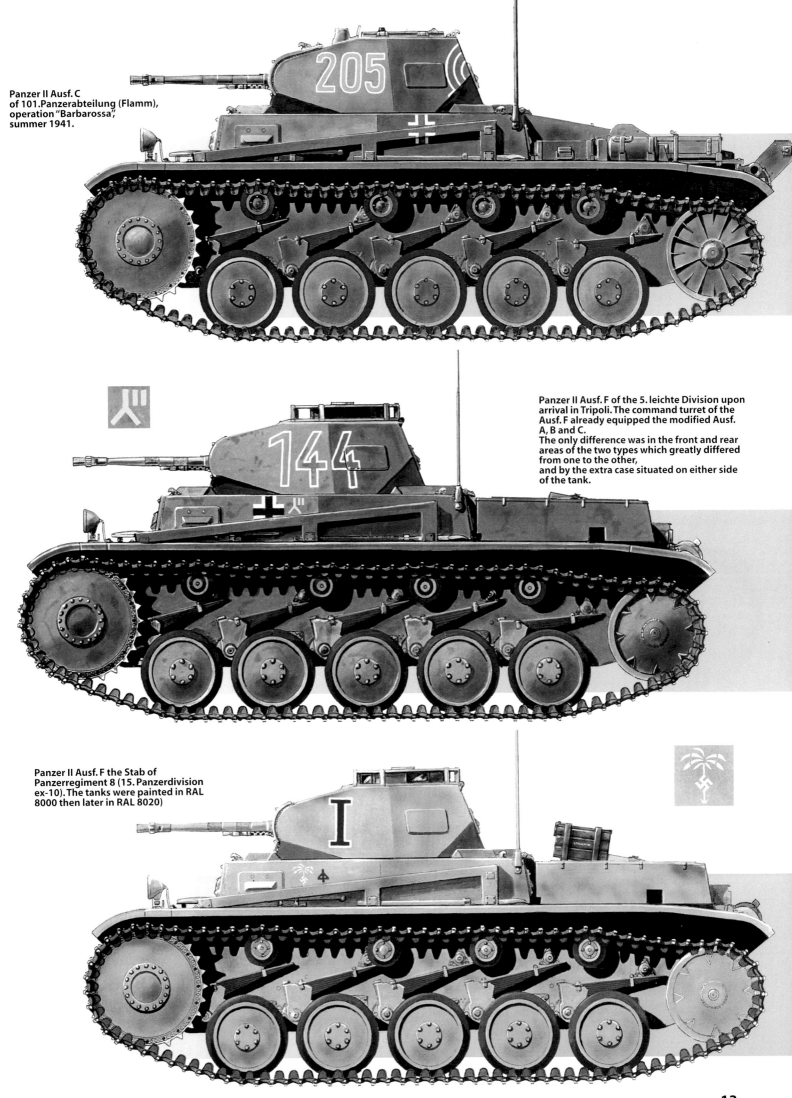

Panzer II Ausf. C
of 101.Panzerabteilung (Flamm),
operation "Barbarossa",
summer 1941.

Panzer II Ausf. F of the 5. leichte Division upon
arrival in Tripoli. The command turret of the
Ausf. F already equipped the modified Ausf.
A, B and C.
The only difference was in the front and rear
areas of the two types which greatly differed
from one to the other,
and by the extra case situated on either side
of the tank.

Panzer II Ausf. F the Stab of
Panzerregiment 8 (15. Panzerdivision
ex-10). The tanks were painted in RAL
8000 then later in RAL 8020)

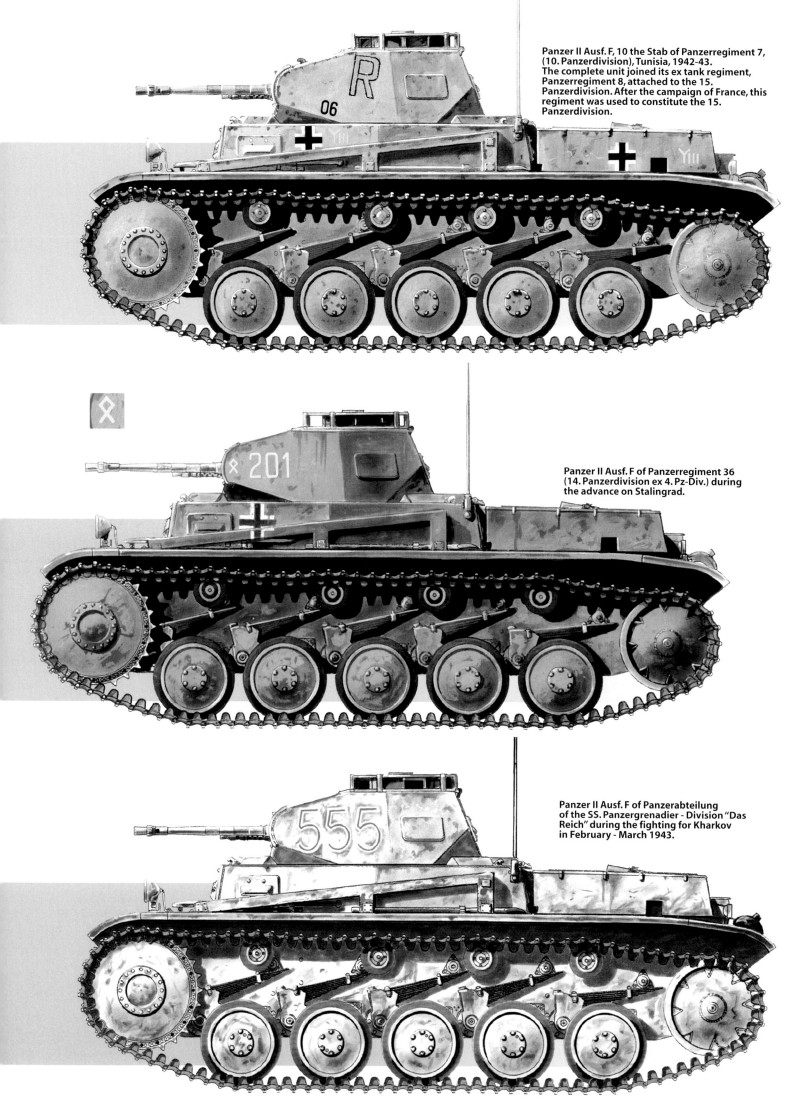

Panzer II Ausf. F, 10 the Stab of Panzerregiment 7,
(10. Panzerdivision), Tunisia, 1942-43.
The complete unit joined its ex tank regiment,
Panzerregiment 8, attached to the 15.
Panzerdivision. After the campaign of France, this
regiment was used to constitute the 15.
Panzerdivision.

Panzer II Ausf. F of Panzerregiment 36
(14. Panzerdivision ex 4. Pz-Div.) during
the advance on Stalingrad.

Panzer II Ausf. F of Panzerabteilung
of the SS. Panzergrenadier - Division "Das
Reich" during the fighting for Kharkov
in February - March 1943.

Panzer II Ausf. D and E of the light platoon of Panzerregiment 35 (4.Panzerdivision) during operation "Barbarossa". Only 43 tanks of this type called 'rapid' were built and later transformed into flame thrower tanks.

The Neubaufahrzeug was the result of an order dating from 1933. Two prototypes and three experimental vehicles were made. The second, equipped with a Krupp turret, served in Norway in April 1940. With a maximum armour of 16 mm, this tank was completely obsolete at the beginning of the conflict.

Two tanks were used in the attack on the Soviet Union as part of Panzergruppe von Kleist. They were lost on June 28th, 1941 close to Dubno.

Panzer II Ausf. L. Luchs Aufklarung Abteilung 4, (4. Panzerdivision), in Russia during the summer of 1943. 143 examples of this type of tank were made. After the 100th, they were equipped with a 50 mm KwK L/60 canon. With the latter, the turret was open.

Another Panzer II Luchs of the 4. Panzerdivision reconnaissance group in the Soviet Union, winter 1943.

Panzer II Ausf. L. Luchs. The two apertures above the driver's vision slit allowed the latter to see in combat when the armoured flap was lowered. The more discreet wire antenna was a great improvement to that of the frame antenna. Normandy, 1944.

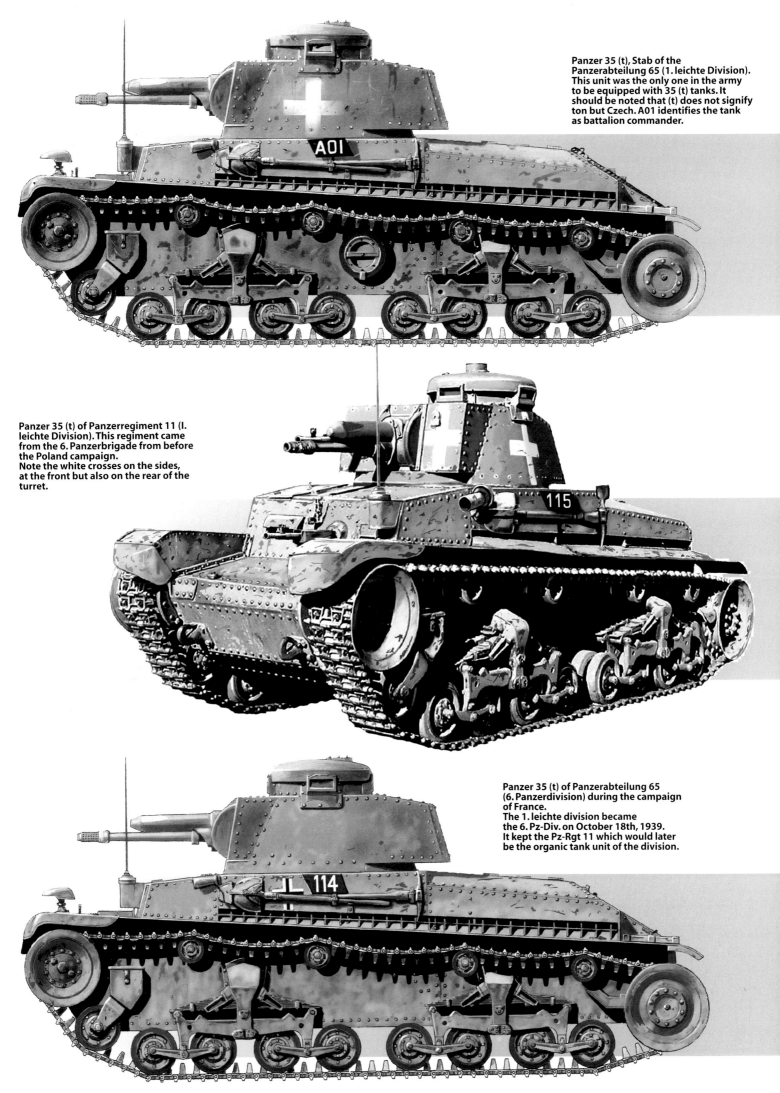

Panzer 35 (t), Stab of the Panzerabteilung 65 (1. leichte Division). This unit was the only one in the army to be equipped with 35 (t) tanks. It should be noted that (t) does not signify ton but Czech. A01 identifies the tank as battalion commander.

Panzer 35 (t) of Panzerregiment 11 (I. leichte Division). This regiment came from the 6. Panzerbrigade from before the Poland campaign.
Note the white crosses on the sides, at the front but also on the rear of the turret.

Panzer 35 (t) of Panzerabteilung 65 (6. Panzerdivision) during the campaign of France.
The 1. leichte division became the 6. Pz-Div. on October 18th, 1939.
It kept the Pz-Rgt 11 which would later be the organic tank unit of the division.

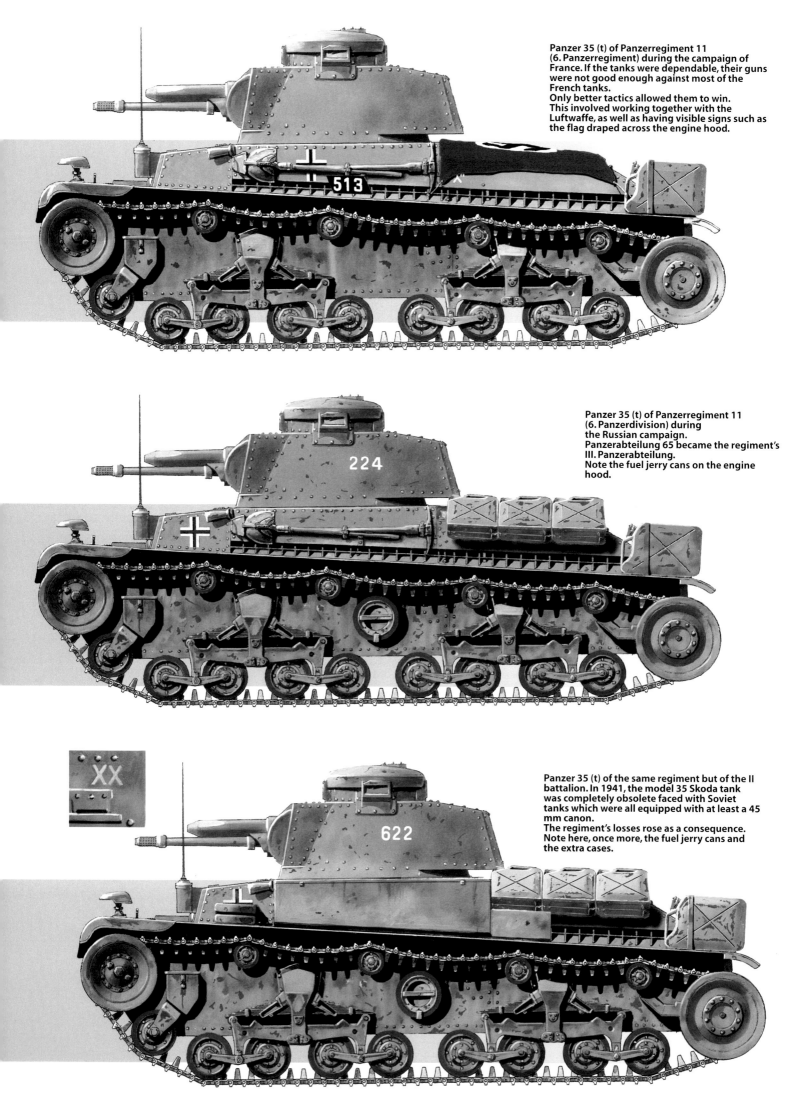

Panzer 35 (t) of Panzerregiment 11
(6. Panzerregiment) during the campaign of
France. If the tanks were dependable, their guns
were not good enough against most of the
French tanks.
Only better tactics allowed them to win.
This involved working together with the
Luftwaffe, as well as having visible signs such as
the flag draped across the engine hood.

Panzer 35 (t) of Panzerregiment 11
(6. Panzerdivision) during
the Russian campaign.
Panzerabteilung 65 became the regiment's
III. Panzerabteilung.
Note the fuel jerry cans on the engine
hood.

Panzer 35 (t) of the same regiment but of the II
battalion. In 1941, the model 35 Skoda tank
was completely obsolete faced with Soviet
tanks which were all equipped with at least a 45
mm canon.
The regiment's losses rose as a consequence.
Note here, once more, the fuel jerry cans and
the extra cases.

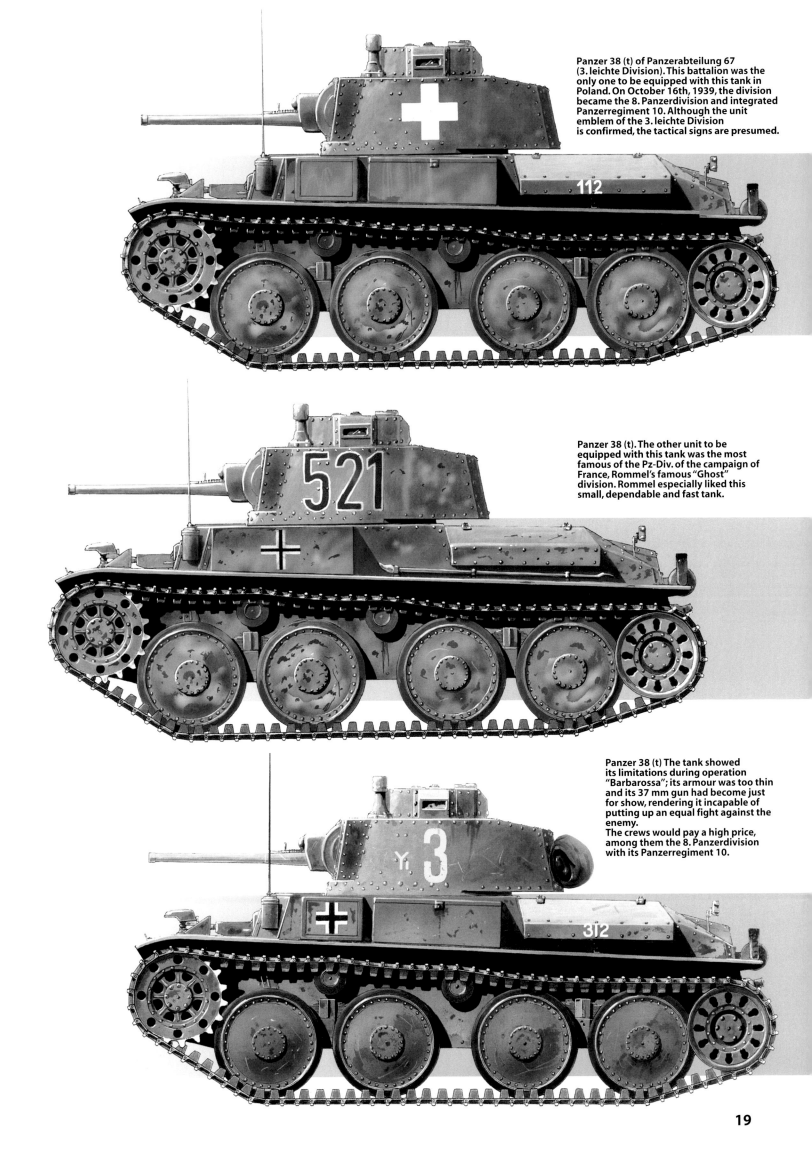

Panzer 38 (t) of Panzerabteilung 67
(3. leichte Division). This battalion was the
only one to be equipped with this tank in
Poland. On October 16th, 1939, the division
became the 8. Panzerdivision and integrated
Panzerregiment 10. Although the unit
emblem of the 3. leichte Division
is confirmed, the tactical signs are presumed.

Panzer 38 (t). The other unit to be
equipped with this tank was the most
famous of the Pz-Div. of the campaign of
France, Rommel's famous "Ghost"
division. Rommel especially liked this
small, dependable and fast tank.

Panzer 38 (t) The tank showed
its limitations during operation
"Barbarossa"; its armour was too thin
and its 37 mm gun had become just
for show, rendering it incapable of
putting up an equal fight against the
enemy.
The crews would pay a high price,
among them the 8. Panzerdivision
with its Panzerregiment 10.

Panzer 38 (t) F. Another unit to be equipped with this tank was Panzerregiment 27. of the 19. Panzerdivision. It is obvious that this tank was used to the fill the more and more numerous gaps in the Panzerdivisionen, German production being unable to equip in good time these new formations.

Panzer 38 (t) F of Panzerregiment 21 (20. Panzerdivision).
This regiment was no exception to the rule. The system of numbering was one or two numbers. The Berlin origin unit emblem is visible.

The last regiment equipped with the Panzer 38 (t) was Panzerregiment 204 of the 22. Panzerdivision. It took part in all the winter fighting of 1941-1942 and was wiped out at Stalingrad.

The 22. Panzerdivision, rebuilt after the defeat at Stalingrad, still received the Panzer 38 (t) but also the Panzer IV F2. After nearly a new year of fighting, it was disbanded on March 4th, 1943. The tank's delivery colour is the basic grey tone with the new colour RAL 8020 or RAL 8000.

Some Panzer 38 (t) remained in combat formations until 1943 and were used as artillery observation tanks in light sections. Some participated in the battle of Kursk. The 20. Panzerdivision kept 10 of these tanks which were sometimes reconverted as ammunition carriers. This one was used in the fighting against partisans in the southern Orel sector.

Panzer 38 (t) F carried on armoured train BP 27 from July 1942 to March 1944.

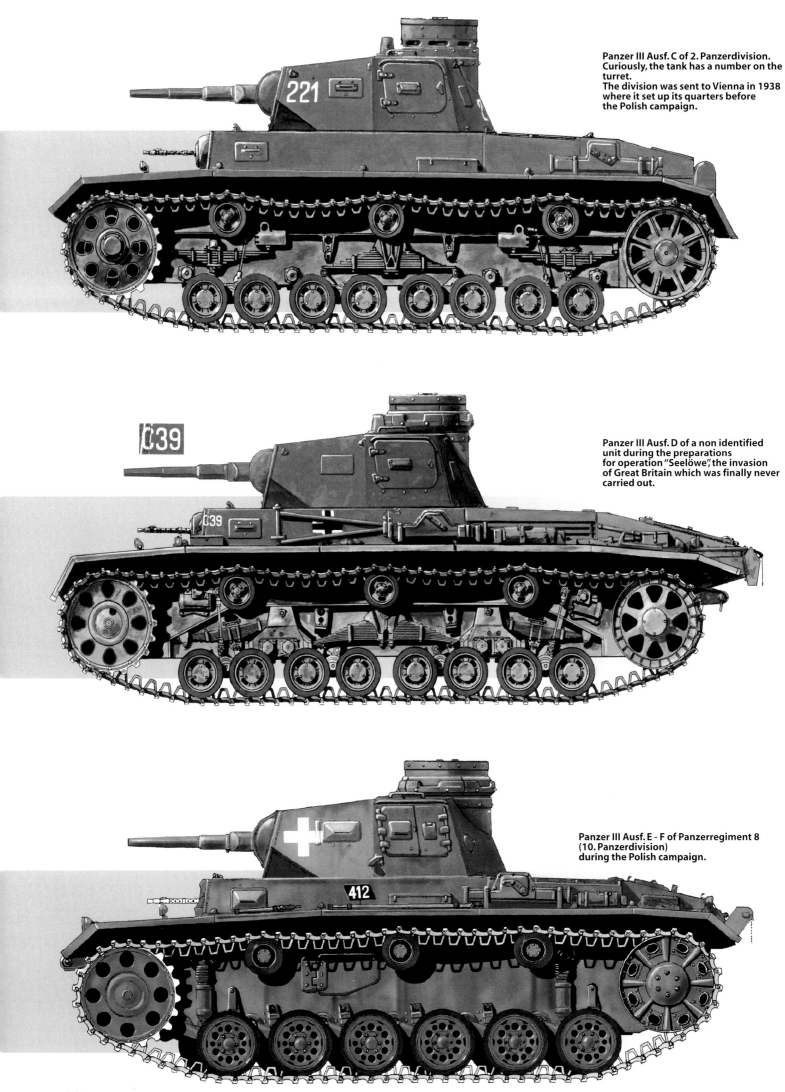

Panzer III Ausf. C of 2. Panzerdivision.
Curiously, the tank has a number on the turret.
The division was sent to Vienna in 1938 where it set up its quarters before the Polish campaign.

Panzer III Ausf. D of a non identified unit during the preparations for operation "Seelöwe", the invasion of Great Britain which was finally never carried out.

Panzer III Ausf. E - F of Panzerregiment 8 (10. Panzerdivision) during the Polish campaign.

Panzer III Ausf. E of Panzerregiment 2
(1. Panzerdivision) France 1940.
The 37 mm gun turned out
to be too weak in the face
of French tanks.
To this handicap
was added a too thin armour.

Panzer III Ausf. E - F of Panzerregiment 3,
(2. Panzerdivision) during
the Balkans campaign in April 1941.
The unit used a system of markings
that used card symbols.
This system had already been partly
used in the Polish campaign.

Panzer III Ausf. E of Panzerregiment 8 (10. Panzerdivision).
We note the diversity of emplacements for the divisional
emblems and those of the von Kleist group.
Campaign of France, May - June 1940.

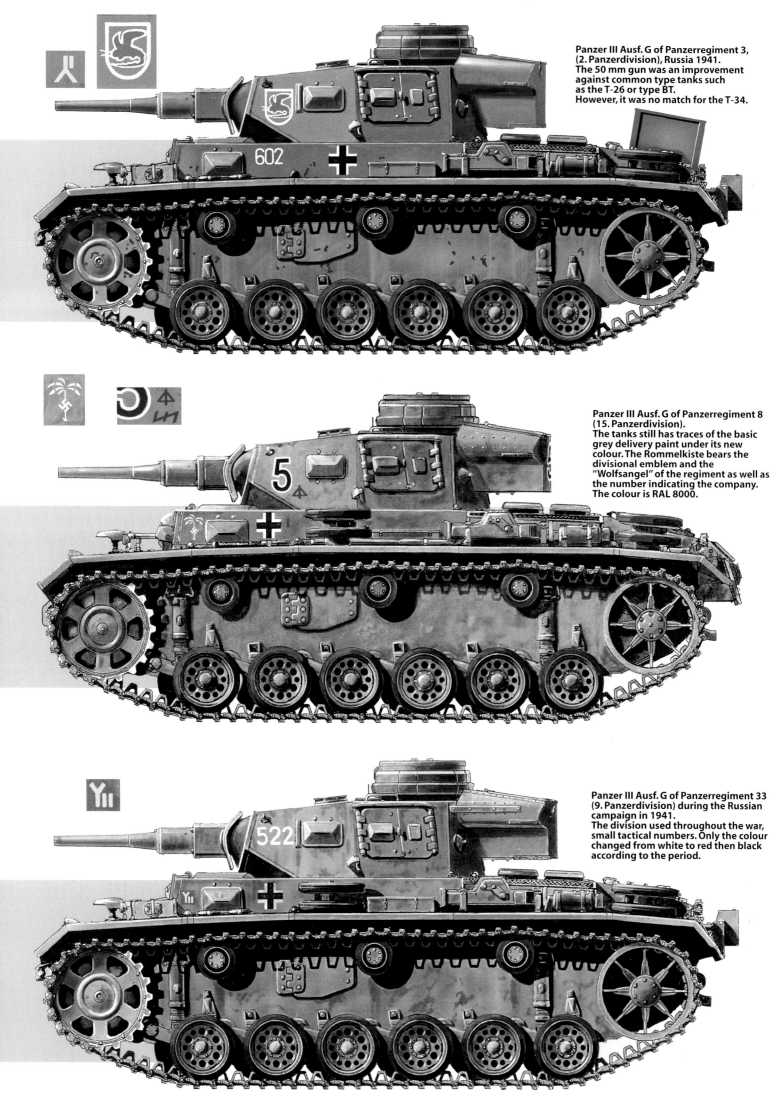

Panzer III Ausf. G of Panzerregiment 3,
(2. Panzerdivision), Russia 1941.
The 50 mm gun was an improvement
against common type tanks such
as the T-26 or type BT.
However, it was no match for the T-34.

Panzer III Ausf. G of Panzerregiment 8
(15. Panzerdivision).
The tanks still has traces of the basic
grey delivery paint under its new
colour. The Rommelkiste bears the
divisional emblem and the
"Wolfsangel" of the regiment as well as
the number indicating the company.
The colour is RAL 8000.

Panzer III Ausf. G of Panzerregiment 33
(9. Panzerdivision) during the Russian
campaign in 1941.
The division used throughout the war,
small tactical numbers. Only the colour
changed from white to red then black
according to the period.

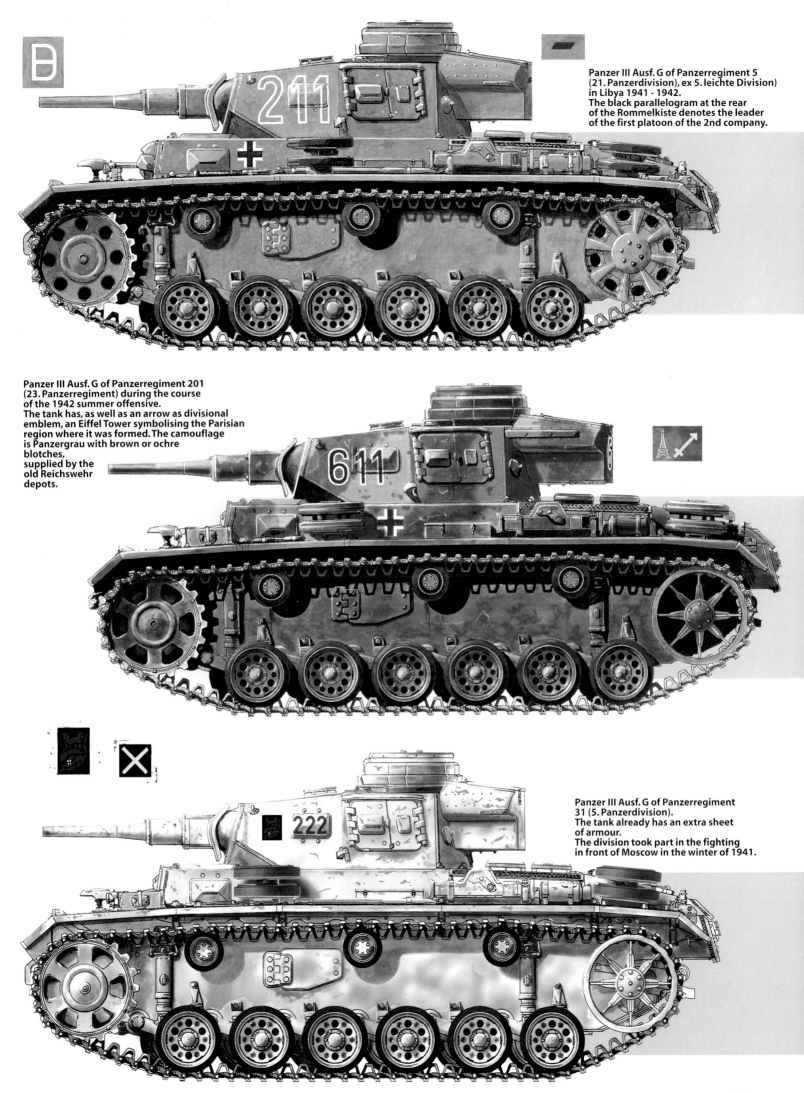

Panzer III Ausf. G of Panzerregiment 5
(21. Panzerdivision), ex 5. leichte Division)
in Libya 1941 - 1942.
The black parallelogram at the rear
of the Rommelkiste denotes the leader
of the first platoon of the 2nd company.

Panzer III Ausf. G of Panzerregiment 201
(23. Panzerregiment) during the course
of the 1942 summer offensive.
The tank has, as well as an arrow as divisional
emblem, an Eiffel Tower symbolising the Parisian
region where it was formed. The camouflage
is Panzergrau with brown or ochre
blotches,
supplied by the
old Reichswehr
depots.

Panzer III Ausf. G of Panzerregiment
31 (5. Panzerdivision).
The tank already has an extra sheet
of armour.
The division took part in the fighting
in front of Moscow in the winter of 1941.

Panzer III Ausf. J of the 15. Panzerdivision. The central region of Tunisia was characterised by very red earth, thus the vehicles naturally took on the colour of the environment.

Panzer III Ausf. J of Panzerregiment 24 (245. Panzerdivision) during the advance on Stalingrad in the summer of 1942. We note that the insignia is painted in white on the front right mudguard and on the case at the rear of the tank.

Panzer III Ausf. J of schwere Panzerabteilung 504, 1st company. The unit fought from its arrival in Tunisia until the surrender in the same country in May 1943.

A Panzer III Ausf. J of the same battalion but in Sicily. Note that it was the Panzer III of the 2nd company that were sent to Tunisia, with of course repainted numbers.

Panzer III Ausf. J of SS-Panzerregiment 3 (SS-Pz. Gren.div. "Totenkopf"), during the fighting for Kharkov in February - March 1943. The tank has the first spaced armoured plating which was supposed to stop Soviet anti tank rifles, capable of piercing the turret and chassis armour.

A Panzer III Ausf. J of Panzerregiment 4 (13. Panzerdivision), on the Russian front in the summer of 1942. Note also the storage case at the rear of the tank. The divisional emblem was often repeated on the front glacis between the machine gun and the driver's vision slit.

A Panzer III Ausf. L of the 10. Panzerdivision. Note the somewhat unorthodox number 3 painted on the turret, indicating the company number, and the absence of a number in front of the small six on the turret.

A Panzer III Ausf. L of the 2nd company of Panzerregiment 7 (10. Panzerdivision) in Tunisia. Note the regimental bison emblem. Here too, the absence of a second number signifying the platoon, indicates without doubt, the company commander.

A rear view of the tank above. On February 20th, 1943, Rommel personally directed the attack led by the brand new 10. Panzerdivision with the aim of capturing the American supply depots of Tebessa.

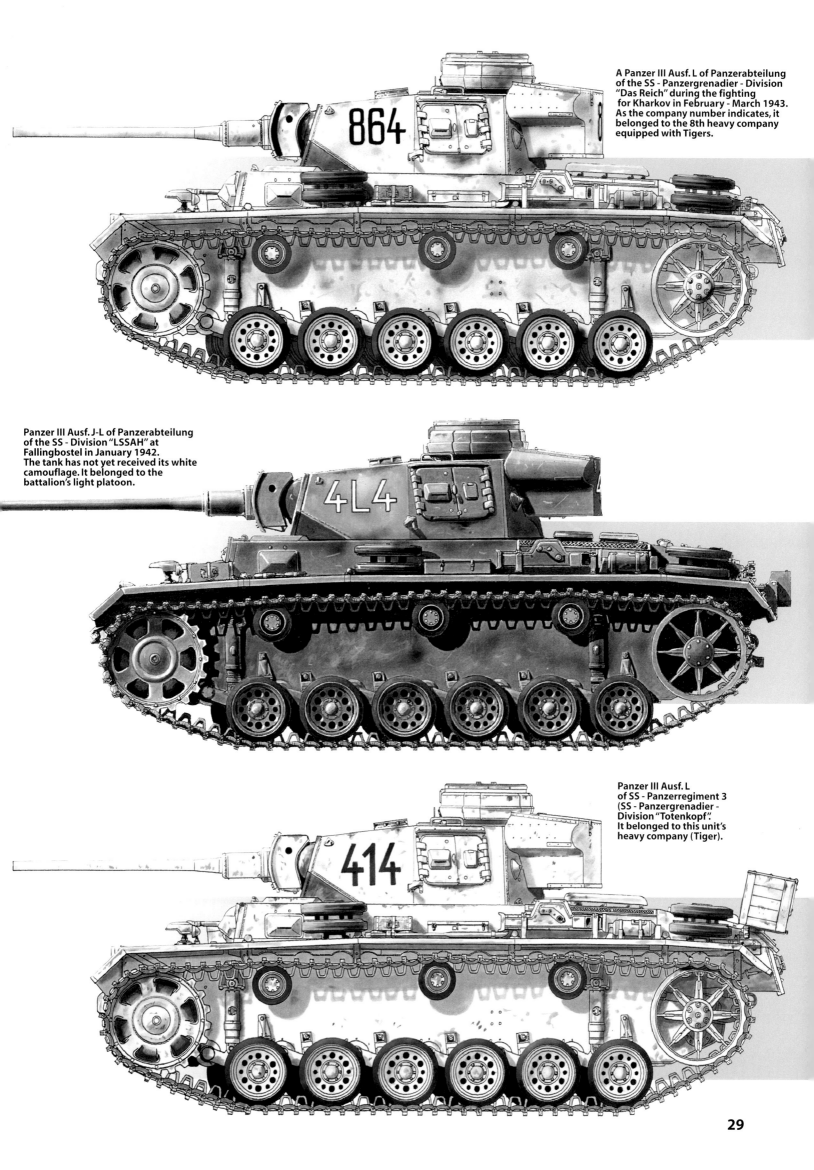

A Panzer III Ausf. L of Panzerabteilung of the SS - Panzergrenadier - Division "Das Reich" during the fighting for Kharkov in February - March 1943. As the company number indicates, it belonged to the 8th heavy company equipped with Tigers.

Panzer III Ausf. J-L of Panzerabteilung of the SS - Division "LSSAH" at Fallingbostel in January 1942. The tank has not yet received its white camouflage. It belonged to the battalion's light platoon.

Panzer III Ausf. L of SS - Panzerregiment 3 (SS - Panzergrenadier - Division "Totenkopf". It belonged to this unit's heavy company (Tiger).

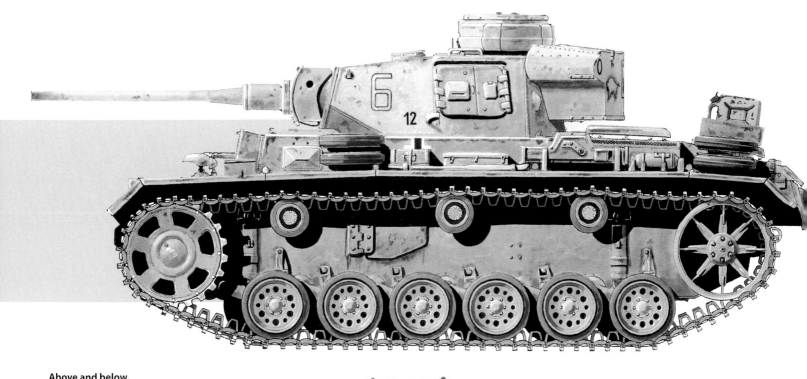

Above and below.
A Panzer III Ausf. L of the 6th company of Panzerregiment 7 (10. Panzerdivision).
The tanks of this company were all lost at sea and the crews were issued with captured American equipment, notably the T-30 and M3 Half Track Tank Destroyer.
The circles at the rear of the tank indicate the platoon leader or the company commander, camouflaged amongst the other vehicles.

Rear view of the Panzer III Ausf. L of the 6th company of Panzerregiment 7.

Panzer III Ausf. J of Panzerregiment 36, (14. Panzerdivision) during the fight for Stalingrad before the winter of 1942 - 1943. The division was, as with the 24th, annihilated.

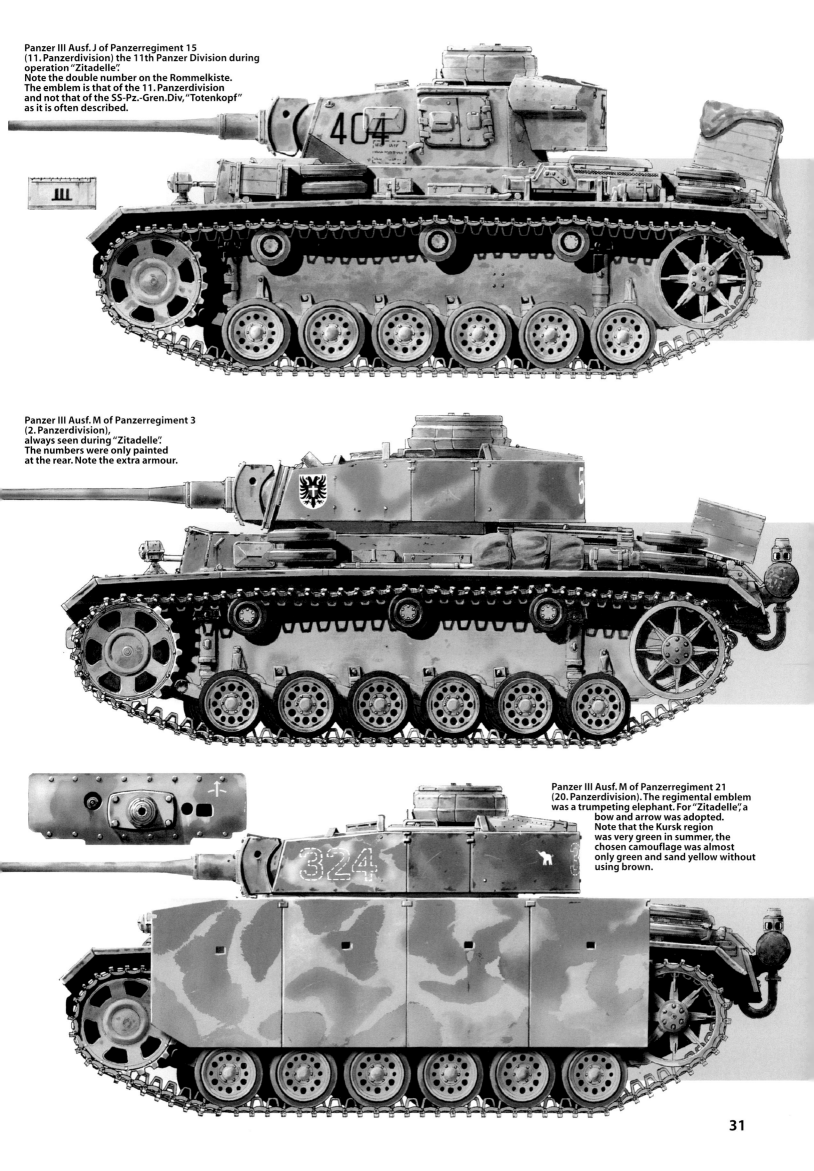

Panzer III Ausf. J of Panzerregiment 15
(11. Panzerdivision) the 11th Panzer Division during
operation "Zitadelle".
Note the double number on the Rommelkiste.
The emblem is that of the 11. Panzerdivision
and not that of the SS-Pz.-Gren.Div. "Totenkopf"
as it is often described.

Panzer III Ausf. M of Panzerregiment 3
(2. Panzerdivision),
always seen during "Zitadelle".
The numbers were only painted
at the rear. Note the extra armour.

Panzer III Ausf. M of Panzerregiment 21
(20. Panzerdivision). The regimental emblem
was a trumpeting elephant. For "Zitadelle", a
bow and arrow was adopted.
Note that the Kursk region
was very green in summer, the
chosen camouflage was almost
only green and sand yellow without
using brown.

Panzer III Ausf. L
of Panzerregiment 15
(11. Panzerdivision).
Note here a very interesting
camouflage for Kursk.
The winter or spring camouflage can be seen
of grey and perhaps green, with wide stripes
of yellow over it. The position of the number
has been lightened with sand yellow which
has remained clean. Kursk, July 1943.

Panzer III Ausf. L of the Panzerregiment
of the SS - Panzergrenadier - Division
"Wiking", during the fighting
on the river Mious in the summer
of 1943. The tank, although obsolete,
was still used for infantry support
or for attacking points of resistance.

Panzer III Ausf. M of Panzerregiment 21
(20. Panzerdivision), during the winter
fighting of 1943 and spring 1944
(operation Hubertus).
Little by little, these tanks were retired and
only used in training schools, or transformed
into ammunition carriers.

Panzer III Ausf. N of shwere Panzerabteillung 501 in Tunisia, November - December 1942. Note the unit insignia on the side of the turret.

Panzer III Ausf. N of schwere Panzerabteillung 501. After being integrated into the 10. Panzerdivision, the numbers were painted in red, even on Tigers. However, it would seem according to some sources that the light platoon had already previously had red painted numbers.

Panzer III Ausf. N of Panzerregiment 3 (2. Panzerdivision) during the battle of Kursk.

Panzer III Ausf. N of Panzerregiment 3 (SS - Pz.-Gren.-Div. "Totenkopf" during operation "Zitadelle". The total German losses were relatively low, not exceeding 310 tanks for the northern and southern sector.

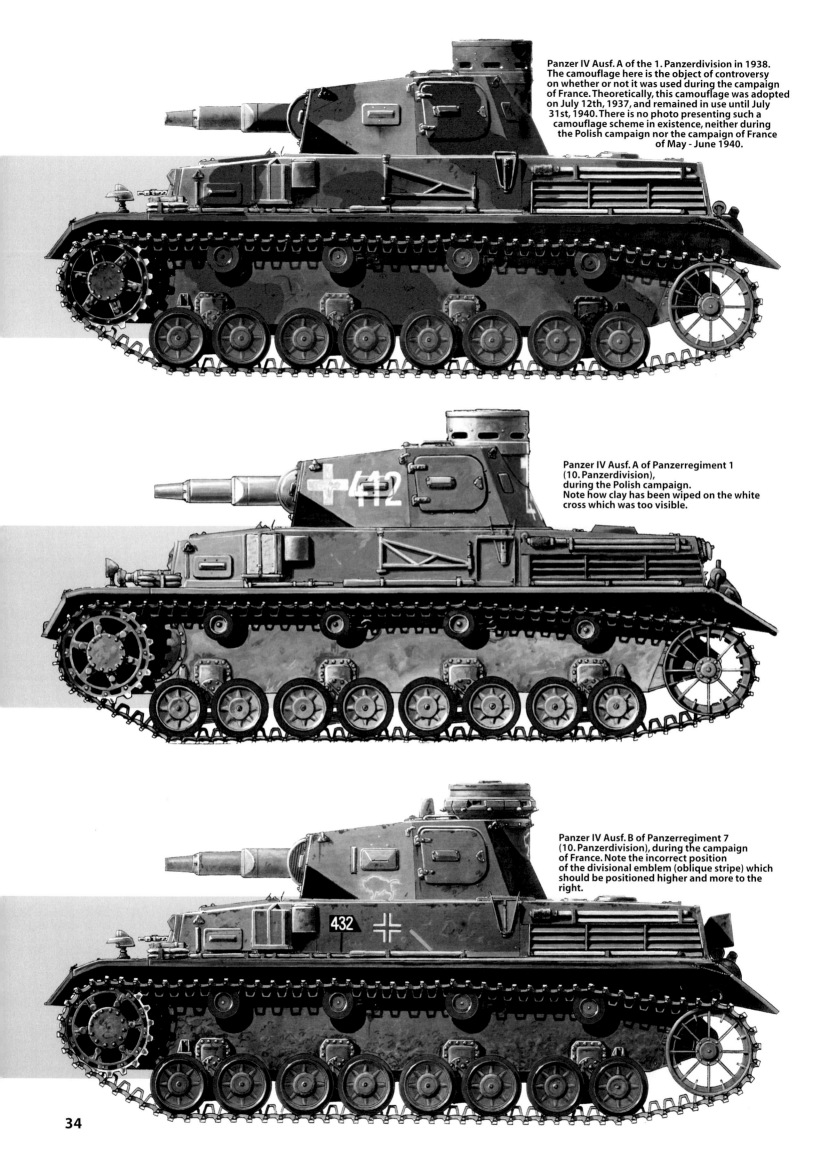

Panzer IV Ausf. A of the 1. Panzerdivision in 1938. The camouflage here is the object of controversy on whether or not it was used during the campaign of France. Theoretically, this camouflage was adopted on July 12th, 1937, and remained in use until July 31st, 1940. There is no photo presenting such a camouflage scheme in existence, neither during the Polish campaign nor the campaign of France of May - June 1940.

Panzer IV Ausf. A of Panzerregiment 1 (10. Panzerdivision), during the Polish campaign. Note how clay has been wiped on the white cross which was too visible.

Panzer IV Ausf. B of Panzerregiment 7 (10. Panzerdivision), during the campaign of France. Note the incorrect position of the divisional emblem (oblique stripe) which should be positioned higher and more to the right.

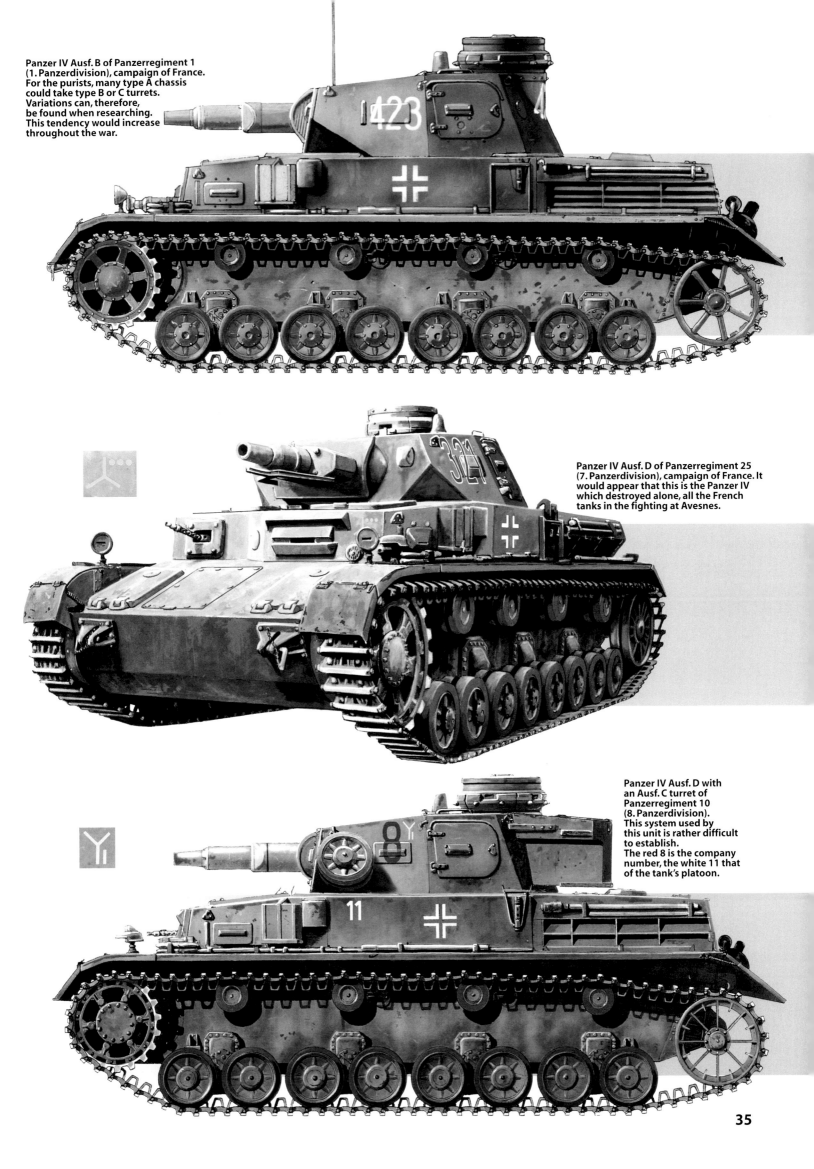

Panzer IV Ausf. B of Panzerregiment 1
(1. Panzerdivision), campaign of France.
For the purists, many type A chassis
could take type B or C turrets.
Variations can, therefore,
be found when researching.
This tendency would increase
throughout the war.

Panzer IV Ausf. D of Panzerregiment 25
(7. Panzerdivision), campaign of France. It
would appear that this is the Panzer IV
which destroyed alone, all the French
tanks in the fighting at Avesnes.

Panzer IV Ausf. D with
an Ausf. C turret of
Panzerregiment 10
(8. Panzerdivision).
This system used by
this unit is rather difficult
to establish.
The red 8 is the company
number, the white 11 that
of the tank's platoon.

Hybrid Panzer IV Ausf. D. The tank bears the emblem of Panzerregiment 7 (10. Panzerdivision), after the campaign of France. It no longer has its divisional emblem and the company number has been moved. Only the regimental emblem remains in its original position on the sides and rear of the turret.

Panzer IV Ausf. D of the 5. leichte Division in March 1941, Libya. The tanks still has its grey camouflage, highly visible in the sands of the Libyan desert. Only the 4th and 8th companies of the Regiment were equipped with the Panzer IV.

Panzer IV Ausf. D of Panzerregiment 7 (10. Panzerdivision), during operation "Barbarossa". The tank is very soberly decorated, the only distinguishing signs are the regimental and divisional emblems at the rear of the Rommelkiste.

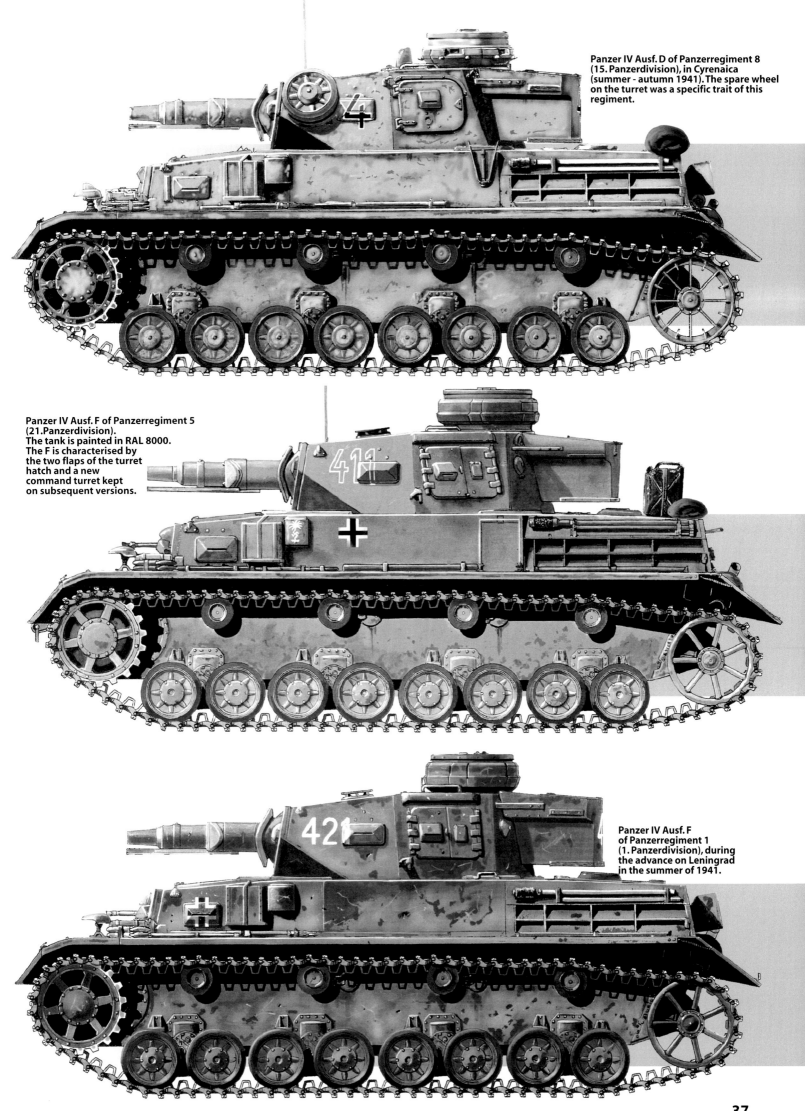

Panzer IV Ausf. D of Panzerregiment 8 (15. Panzerdivision), in Cyrenaica (summer - autumn 1941). The spare wheel on the turret was a specific trait of this regiment.

Panzer IV Ausf. F of Panzerregiment 5 (21.Panzerdivision). The tank is painted in RAL 8000. The F is characterised by the two flaps of the turret hatch and a new command turret kept on subsequent versions.

Panzer IV Ausf. F of Panzerregiment 1 (1. Panzerdivision), during the advance on Leningrad in the summer of 1941.

37

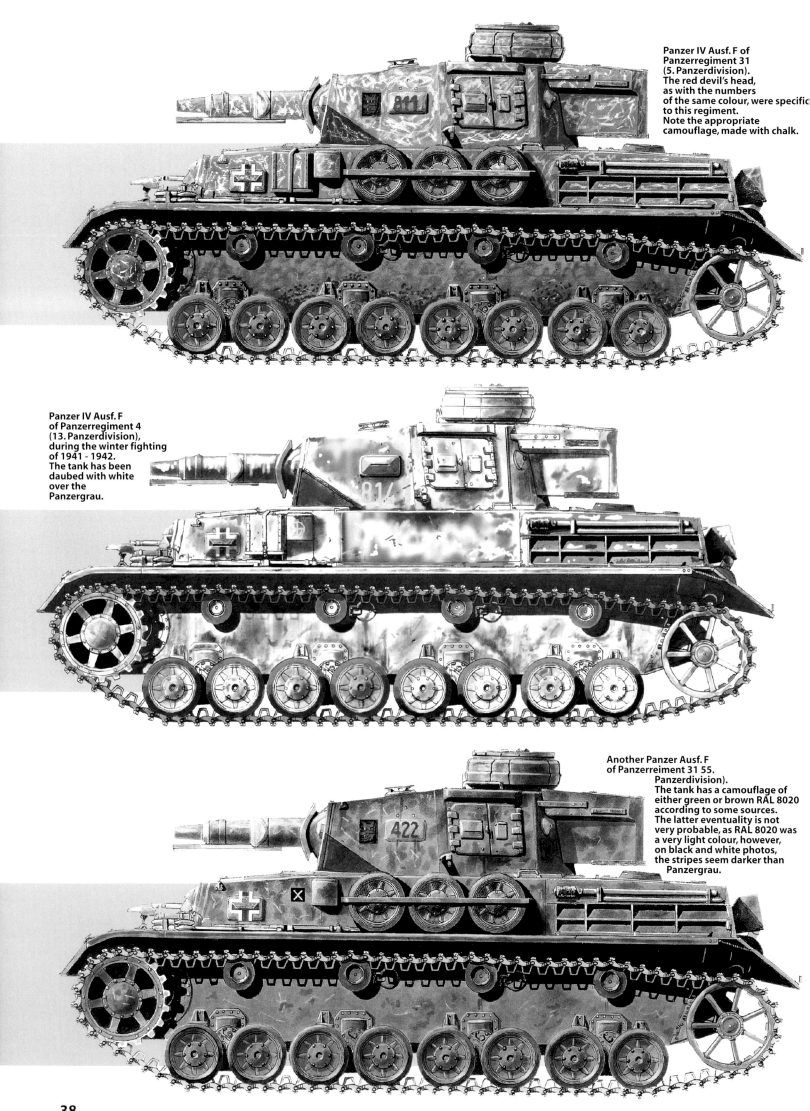

Panzer IV Ausf. F of
Panzerregiment 31
(5. Panzerdivision).
The red devil's head,
as with the numbers
of the same colour, were specific
to this regiment.
Note the appropriate
camouflage, made with chalk.

Panzer IV Ausf. F
of Panzerregiment 4
(13. Panzerdivision),
during the winter fighting
of 1941 - 1942.
The tank has been
daubed with white
over the
Panzergrau.

Another Panzer Ausf. F
of Panzerreiment 31 55.
Panzerdivision).
The tank has a camouflage of
either green or brown RAL 8020
according to some sources.
The latter eventuality is not
very probable, as RAL 8020 was
a very light colour, however,
on black and white photos,
the stripes seem darker than
Panzergrau.

Panzer IV Ausf. F2
of Panzerregiment 5
(21. Panzedivision),
summer 1942.
Note the number 6,
indicating that it belongs
to the 6th company.

Panzer IV Ausf. F2
of the 15.
Panzerdivision.
It has several emblems,
the most interesting
is the clover
indicating
a company platoon,
unless it is an
individual
lucky charm.

Panzer IV Ausf. F2
of Panzerregiment 33
(15. Panzerdivision).
The large number 8
indicates the company.

Panzer IV Ausf. F2 of
Panzerregiment 204
(22. Panzerdivision),
Russia, summer 1942.
The tank is painted in ochre RAL
8020 with grey green RAL 7008
stripes. This is an African type
camouflage also used in
southern Russia.

Panzer IV Ausf. F2 of Panzerregiment 7
(10. Panzerdivision), Tunisia, December
1942. The tank is painted in RAL 8020.
Note the tank tracks supposed to reinforce
the still too thin armour.

Panzer IV Ausf. F transformed into an F2.
The tank belonged to SS-Panzerregiment 2
(SS-Panzergrenadier - Division
"Das Reich"), seen during the preparations
in the month of May for operation
"Zitadelle".
Note the extra rods added
to the side of the vehicle,
indicating that the short
75 mm gun has been
changed to a long gun.

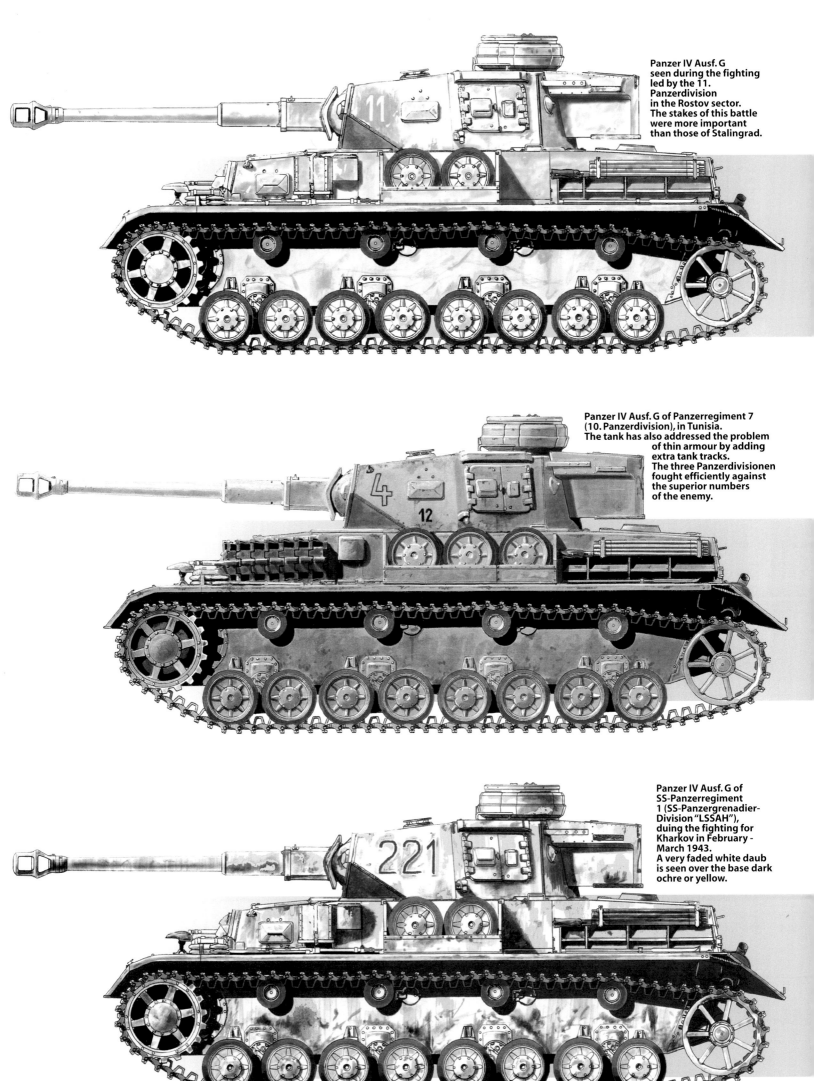

Panzer IV Ausf. G
seen during the fighting
led by the 11.
Panzerdivision
in the Rostov sector.
The stakes of this battle
were more important
than those of Stalingrad.

Panzer IV Ausf. G of Panzerregiment 7
(10. Panzerdivision), in Tunisia.
The tank has also addressed the problem
of thin armour by adding
extra tank tracks.
The three Panzerdivisionen
fought efficiently against
the superior numbers
of the enemy.

Panzer IV Ausf. G of
SS-Panzerregiment
1 (SS-Panzergrenadier-
Division "LSSAH"),
duing the fighting for
Kharkov in February -
March 1943.
A very faded white daub
is seen over the base dark
ochre or yellow.

Panzer IV Ausf. H during the fighting for Caen. The tank does not have any camouflage or Zimmerit anti magnetic coating. It belonged to the 12. SS - Panzerdivision, "Hitlerjugend", the numbers of which were generally quite roughly painted.

Panzer IV Ausf. H of Panzer-Lehr Regiment 130 (Panzerlehrdivision), during the fighting for Villers-Bocage on June 13th, 1944.

Panzer IV Ausf. H of Panzerregiment 1 (1. Panzerdivision), during the winter of 1944-1945 on the Eastern Front. Its gun is still capable of destroying any adversary from a respectable distance.

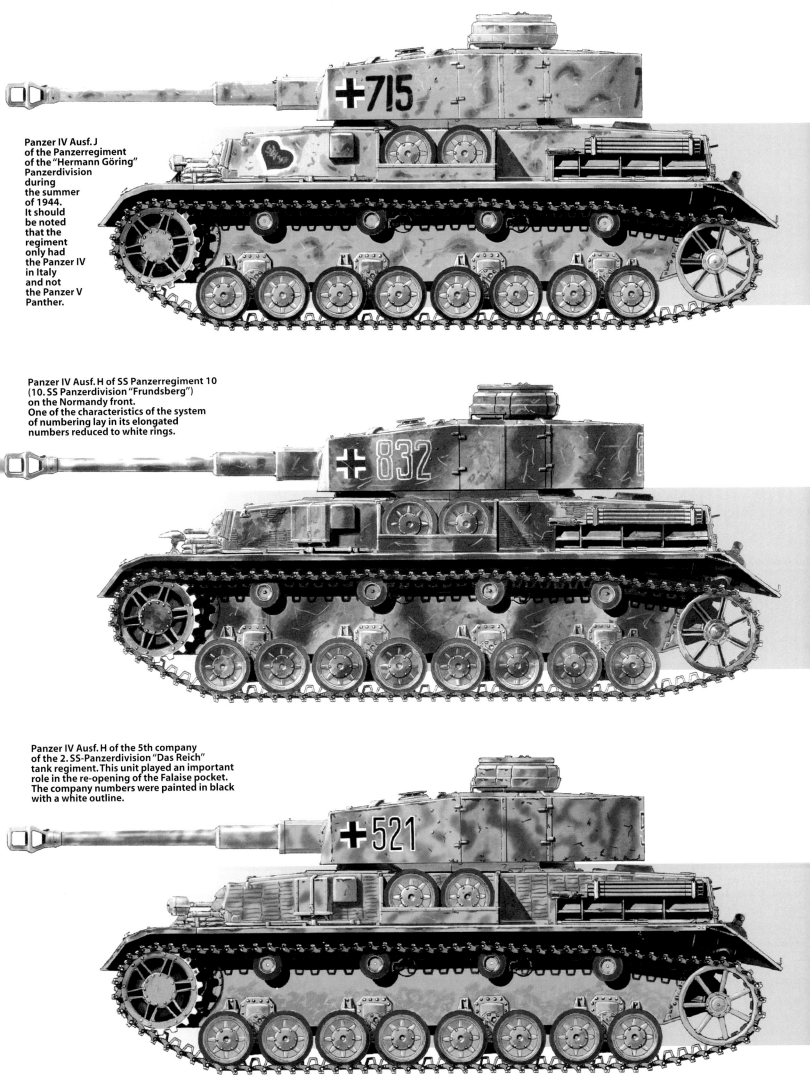

Panzer IV Ausf. J
of the Panzerregiment
of the "Hermann Göring"
Panzerdivision
during
the summer
of 1944.
It should
be noted
that the
regiment
only had
the Panzer IV
in Italy
and not
the Panzer V
Panther.

Panzer IV Ausf. H of SS Panzerregiment 10
(10. SS Panzerdivision "Frundsberg")
on the Normandy front.
One of the characteristics of the system
of numbering lay in its elongated
numbers reduced to white rings.

Panzer IV Ausf. H of the 5th company
of the 2. SS-Panzerdivision "Das Reich"
tank regiment. This unit played an important
role in the re-opening of the Falaise pocket.
The company numbers were painted in black
with a white outline.

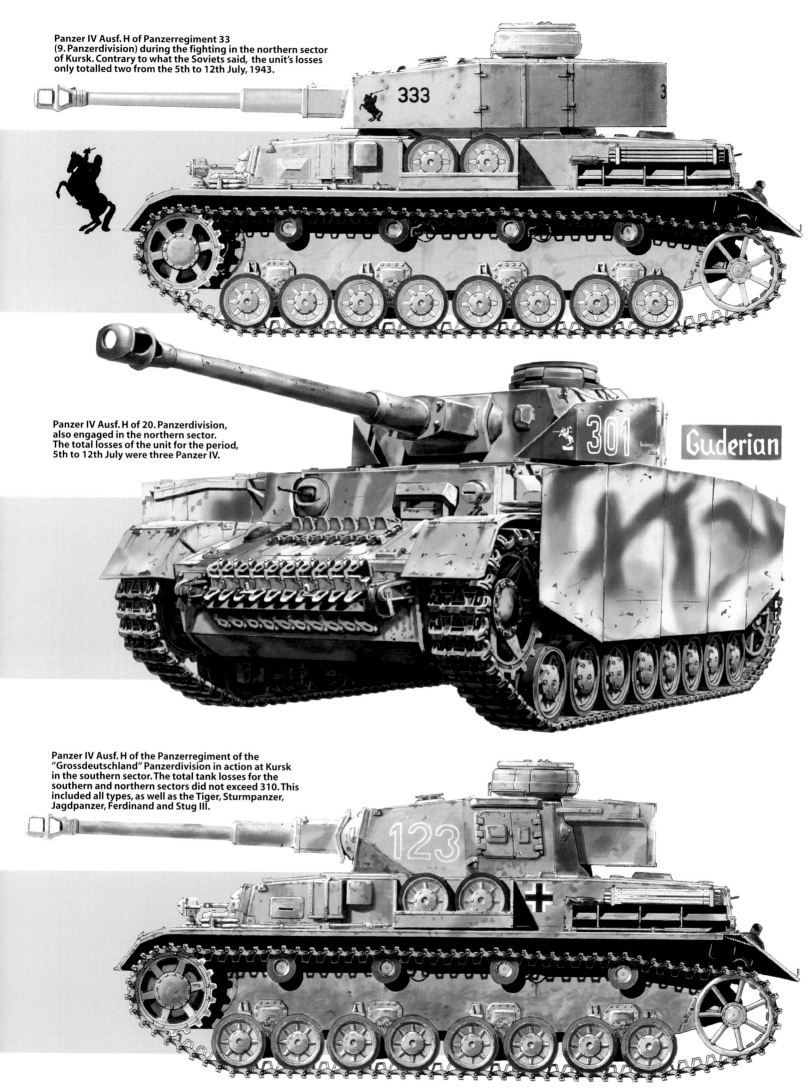

Panzer IV Ausf. H of Panzerregiment 33 (9. Panzerdivision) during the fighting in the northern sector of Kursk. Contrary to what the Soviets said, the unit's losses only totalled two from the 5th to 12th July, 1943.

Panzer IV Ausf. H of 20. Panzerdivision, also engaged in the northern sector. The total losses of the unit for the period, 5th to 12th July were three Panzer IV.

Guderian

Panzer IV Ausf. H of the Panzerregiment of the "Grossdeutschland" Panzerdivision in action at Kursk in the southern sector. The total tank losses for the southern and northern sectors did not exceed 310. This included all types, as well as the Tiger, Sturmpanzer, Jagdpanzer, Ferdinand and Stug III.

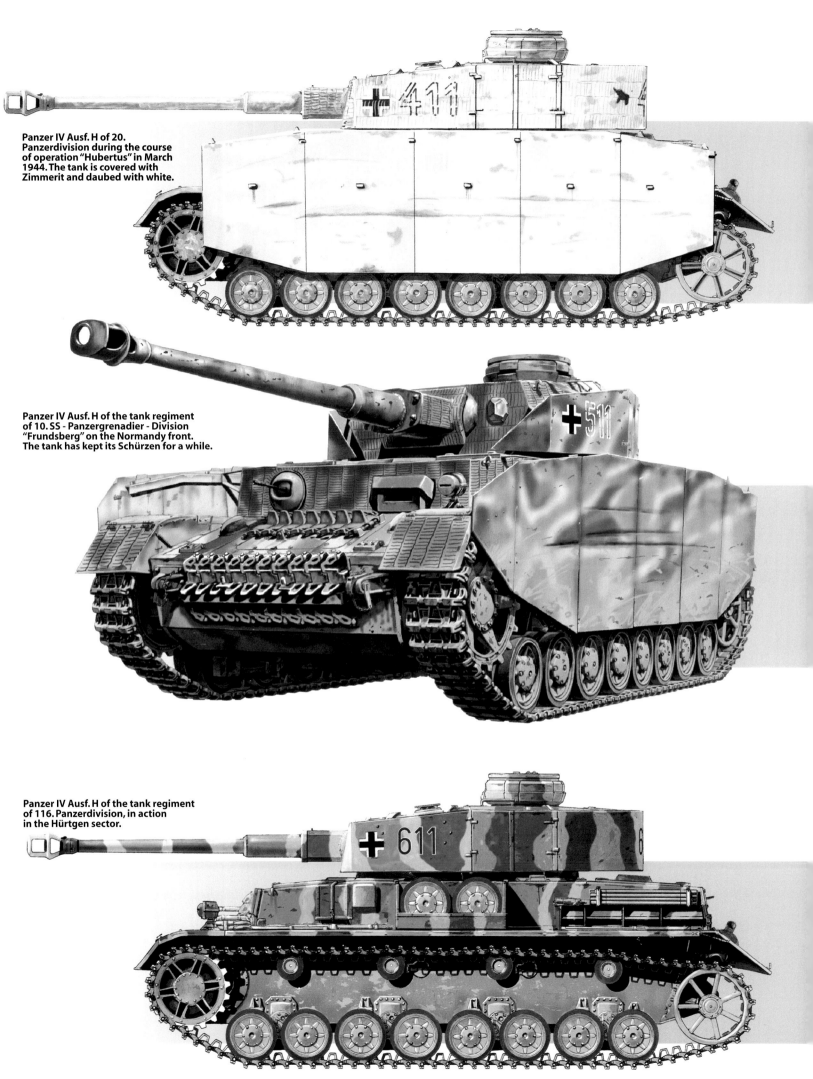

Panzer IV Ausf. H of 20. Panzerdivision during the course of operation "Hubertus" in March 1944. The tank is covered with Zimmerit and daubed with white.

Panzer IV Ausf. H of the tank regiment of 10. SS - Panzergrenadier - Division "Frundsberg" on the Normandy front. The tank has kept its Schürzen for a while.

Panzer IV Ausf. H of the tank regiment of 116. Panzerdivision, in action in the Hürtgen sector.

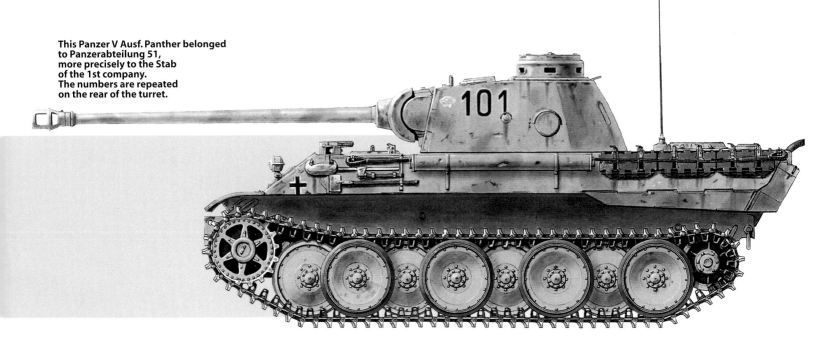

This Panzer V Ausf. Panther belonged to Panzerabteilung 51, more precisely to the Stab of the 1st company. The numbers are repeated on the rear of the turret.

A close up of the emblems used within Panzerabteilung 51. Red identifies the second company, white or yellow the third and black the fourth. The first was just outlined. The colour of the Stab should be green. Note also the difference in sizes of the numbers at the rear of the turrets depending on the companies.

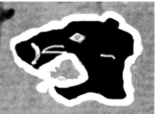

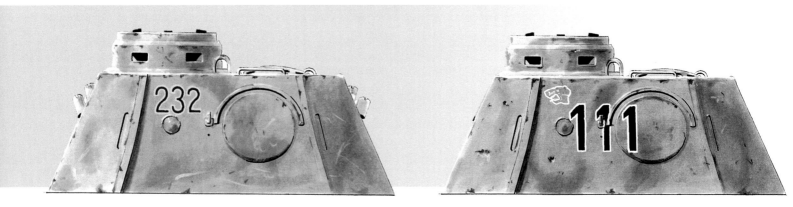

Panzer V Ausf. D Panther of the 2nd company of Panzerabteilung 51. Some tanks kept their smoke launchers, others lost them as the war continued.

Panzer V Ausf. D Panther
of the 3rd company.
The tank does not bear any insignia
but the colour could have been either
white or yellow.

Panzer V Ausf. D Panther of the 4th
company of Panzerabteilung 51.
On the photo used for this illustration,
the tank appears to have a three tone
camouflage scheme.

Panzer V Ausf. D Panther
of Panzerabteilung 52
(Panzer-Brigade 10),
July 1943 during the battle of Kursk.
Mechanical failures were high
at this period as the Panther was
not perfected.
Out of the hundred Panthers
available at the beginning
of the battle, only 15 were fit for
fighting on August 6th, 1943.

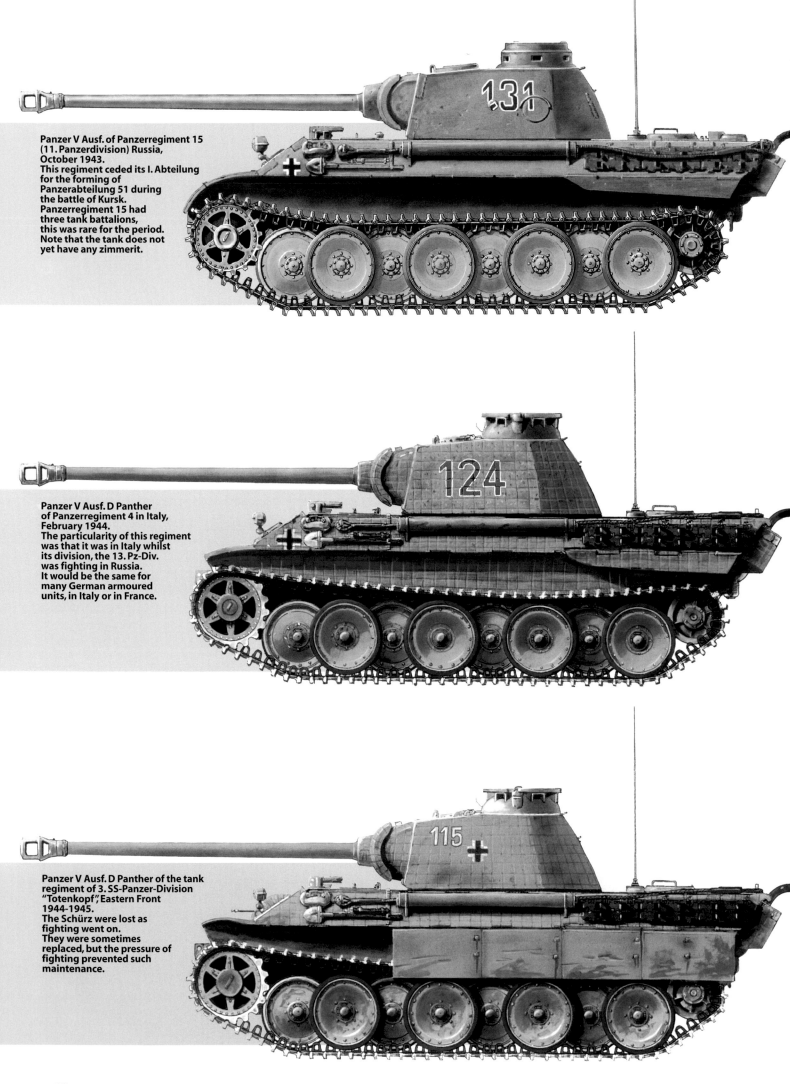

Panzer V Ausf. of Panzerregiment 15 (11. Panzerdivision) Russia, October 1943.
This regiment ceded its I. Abteilung for the forming of Panzerabteilung 51 during the battle of Kursk. Panzerregiment 15 had three tank battalions, this was rare for the period. Note that the tank does not yet have any zimmerit.

Panzer V Ausf. D Panther of Panzerregiment 4 in Italy, February 1944.
The particularity of this regiment was that it was in Italy whilst its division, the 13. Pz-Div. was fighting in Russia. It would be the same for many German armoured units, in Italy or in France.

Panzer V Ausf. D Panther of the tank regiment of 3. SS-Panzer-Division "Totenkopf", Eastern Front 1944-1945.
The Schürz were lost as fighting went on. They were sometimes replaced, but the pressure of fighting prevented such maintenance.

Panzer V Ausf. A Panther of the Panzerregiment of the "Grossdeutschland" Panzergrenadier-Division, Eastern Front. The tank has kept the camouflage characteristic of this unit in summer 1944. The numbers are sand yellow in colour (and not white) outlined in black.

Another Panzer V Ausf. A Panther of the same unit. Note the camouflage which incorporates RAL 6003(olive green) to RAL (brown red). Note that the second sheet of armour on the side is a replacement.

Panzer V Ausf. A Panther of the 20. Panzerdivision, the Koma sector, winter 1944-1945. Only three Panther battalions of the Heer were second battalion within the regiment: the 9th, 20th and 23rd. The small elephant on the rear of the turret is an extra indication.

Panzer V Ausf. A Panther of the Stab of I. Abteilung of Panzerregiment 6
(3. Pz.-Div.). In 1944, the Panzer-Lehr Division received this battalion
to compensate for the absence of I. Abteilung of Panzer-Lehr –Regiment 130.
As for I./Panzerregiment 6, it was taken out in October 1944.
In Normandy, each Abteilung had 70 tanks, that is to say,
less than the theoretical allocation.

Panther of I. Abteilung of SS-Panzer-Regiment 9
(9.Panzer-Division "Hohenstaufen").
This division was one that had the most available tanks
at the end of the Battle of Normandy, being twenty which
counter attacked from within the Falaise pocket in order to
keep the gap clear.

Panzer V Ausf. A Panther of SS-Panzerregiment 12
(12. SS-Panzerdivision "HJ" on the Normandy front.

Panzer V Ausf. A Panther of the 2nd
company of SS-Panzer-Regiment 12
(12-SS Pz.-Div. "Hitlerjugend").
The tanks seem to have suffered
and the numbers have been
repainted without the red interior,
deemed too visible.

Panther of the 3rd company
of I. Abteilung
of SS-Panzer-Regiment 12
(12-SS-Pz.-Div. "Hitlerjugend").

Panther Ausf. A of I./Panzerregiment 6
attached to Panzerlehrregiment 130
(Pz.-lehr-Div.) as a replacement to its
still missing Panther battalion.
Note, as with the Panther 102
on the previous page, the tank's
monochrome camouflage.
This is no doubt the dark
yellow darkened with
a uniformly applied daub
of RAL 6003 olive green.

The Panther Ausf. G of the famous SS Oberscharführer Ernst Barkmann. It belonged to SS Panzerregiment 2 (2. SS-Pz.-Div. "Das Reich") during the fighting in Normandy.

Panther Ausf. G of Panzerregiment 9 (9. SS-Pz.-Div. "Hohenstaufen") in Normandy. Only the II. battalion of the regiment was equipped with tanks of this type.

Panther Ausf. G of SS -Panzerregiment 9 (9. SS-Pz.-Div. "Hohenstaufen"). This regiment was characterised by the use of tank tracks fixed to the turret. This improvisation for the replacement of armour also had its detractors.

Panther Ausf. A of the 4th company of I. Abteilung of an unknown company during the fighting in the "cauldron" of Hube, beginning of April 1944. The use of Zimmerit was not yet generalised in the vast Russian steppe as the enemy infantry was still relatively contained.

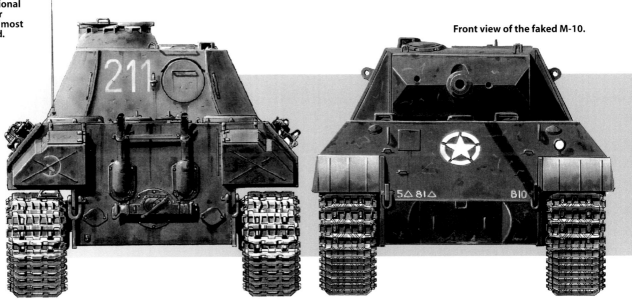

Rear view of a Panther of the 24. Panzerdivision at Arnhem, September 1944. The divisional emblem was painted either on the left or the right, but most often it was simply omitted. This tank belonged to the 2nd company of the I. Abteilung.

Front view of the faked M-10.

A Panther with modified superstructure to give it the appearance of an American M-10 Tank Destroyer during operation Greif led by Otto Skorzeny. A few Panthers were transformed in this way by the addition of plating to the turret and new paint. This solution was adopted by the Germans as they did not have enough working M-10s.

Panther Ausf. G of the 5th company of II. Abteilung of an unknown unit in 1945. The colour of the number is not confirmed, it may have been green or sand yellow outlined in white.

Panther Ausf. A of Panzerbrigade 106. This well equipped unit had a certain lack of experience that could not be compensated either by courage or the fanatical fighting of certain crews. It fought tenaciously until its utter destruction.

Panther Ausf. G of an independent brigade engaged in the fighting at Westwall in the Weissenburg, winter 1944-45. Note the effect of the geometric camouflage on the white daub.

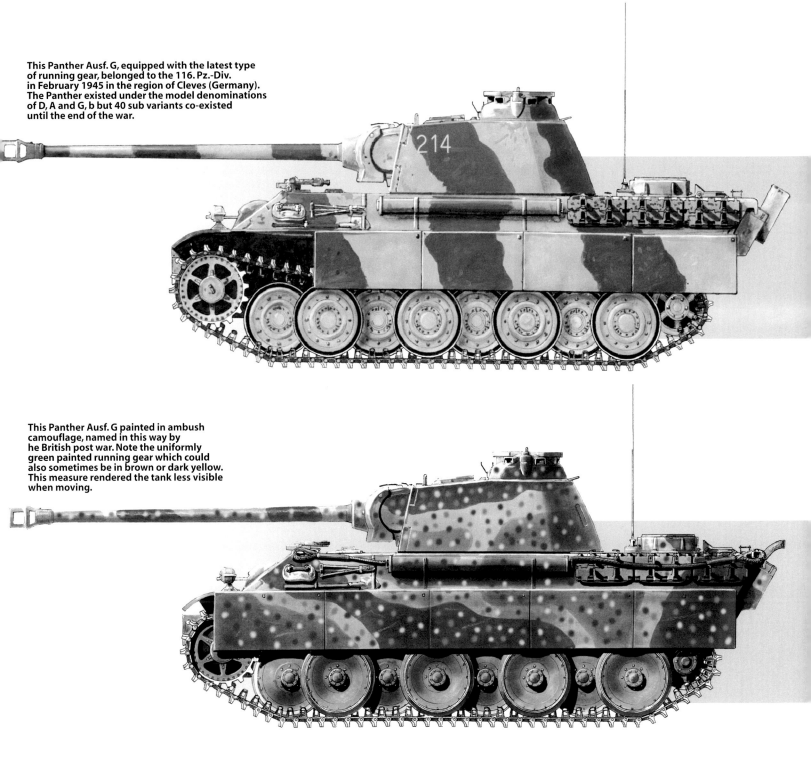

This Panther Ausf. G, equipped with the latest type of running gear, belonged to the 116. Pz.-Div. in February 1945 in the region of Cleves (Germany). The Panther existed under the model denominations of D, A and G, b but 40 sub variants co-existed until the end of the war.

This Panther Ausf. G painted in ambush camouflage, named in this way by he British post war. Note the uniformly green painted running gear which could also sometimes be in brown or dark yellow. This measure rendered the tank less visible when moving.

Panther Ausf. G. The camouflage is of the standard end of war type. Its lateral protection skirt is painted in the ambush camouflage scheme, a sign of it obviously having been recovered from a damaged tank with this type of camouflage.

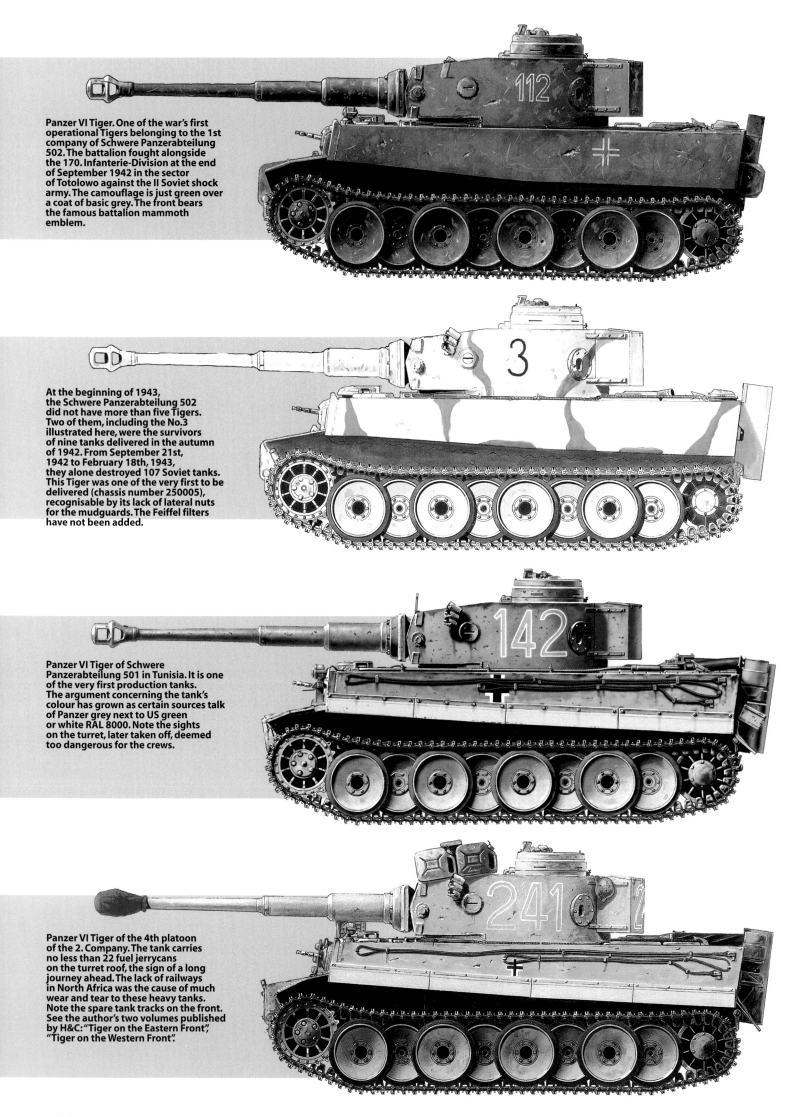

Panzer VI Tiger. One of the war's first operational Tigers belonging to the 1st company of Schwere Panzerabteilung 502. The battalion fought alongside the 170. Infanterie-Division at the end of September 1942 in the sector of Totolowo against the II Soviet shock army. The camouflage is just green over a coat of basic grey. The front bears the famous battalion mammoth emblem.

At the beginning of 1943, the Schwere Panzerabteilung 502 did not have more than five Tigers. Two of them, including the No.3 illustrated here, were the survivors of nine tanks delivered in the autumn of 1942. From September 21st, 1942 to February 18th, 1943, they alone destroyed 107 Soviet tanks. This Tiger was one of the very first to be delivered (chassis number 250005), recognisable by its lack of lateral nuts for the mudguards. The Feiffel filters have not been added.

Panzer VI Tiger of Schwere Panzerabteilung 501 in Tunisia. It is one of the very first production tanks. The argument concerning the tank's colour has grown as certain sources talk of Panzer grey next to US green or white RAL 8000. Note the sights on the turret, later taken off, deemed too dangerous for the crews.

Panzer VI Tiger of the 4th platoon of the 2. Company. The tank carries no less than 22 fuel jerrycans on the turret roof, the sign of a long journey ahead. The lack of railways in North Africa was the cause of much wear and tear to these heavy tanks. Note the spare tank tracks on the front. See the author's two volumes published by H&C: "Tiger on the Eastern Front", "Tiger on the Western Front".

56

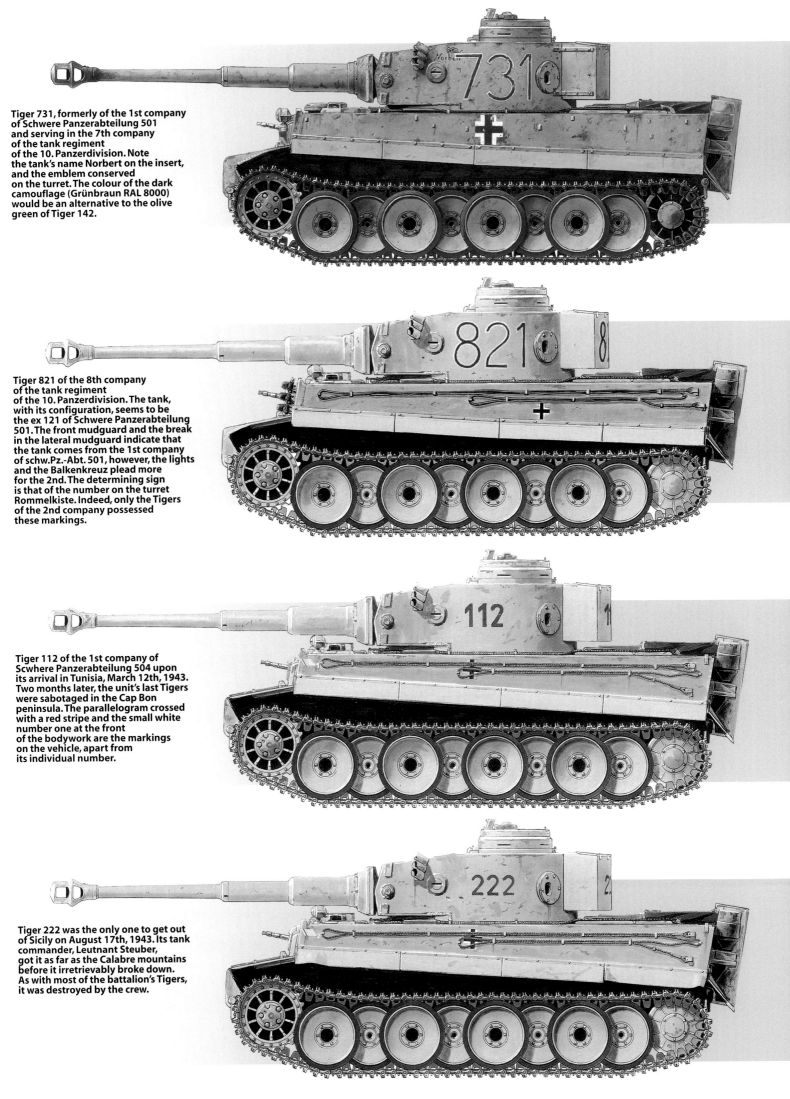

Tiger 731, formerly of the 1st company of Schwere Panzerabteilung 501 and serving in the 7th company of the tank regiment of the 10. Panzerdivision. Note the tank's name Norbert on the insert, and the emblem conserved on the turret. The colour of the dark camouflage (Grünbraun RAL 8000) would be an alternative to the olive green of Tiger 142.

Tiger 821 of the 8th company of the tank regiment of the 10. Panzerdivision. The tank, with its configuration, seems to be the ex 121 of Schwere Panzerabteilung 501. The front mudguard and the break in the lateral mudguard indicate that the tank comes from the 1st company of schw.Pz.-Abt. 501, however, the lights and the Balkenkreuz plead more for the 2nd. The determining sign is that of the number on the turret Rommelkiste. Indeed, only the Tigers of the 2nd company possessed these markings.

Tiger 112 of the 1st company of Scwhere Panzerabteilung 504 upon its arrival in Tunisia, March 12th, 1943. Two months later, the unit's last Tigers were sabotaged in the Cap Bon peninsula. The parallelogram crossed with a red stripe and the small white number one at the front of the bodywork are the markings on the vehicle, apart from its individual number.

Tiger 222 was the only one to get out of Sicily on August 17th, 1943. Its tank commander, Leutnant Steuber, got it as far as the Calabre mountains before it irretrievably broke down. As with most of the battalion's Tigers, it was destroyed by the crew.

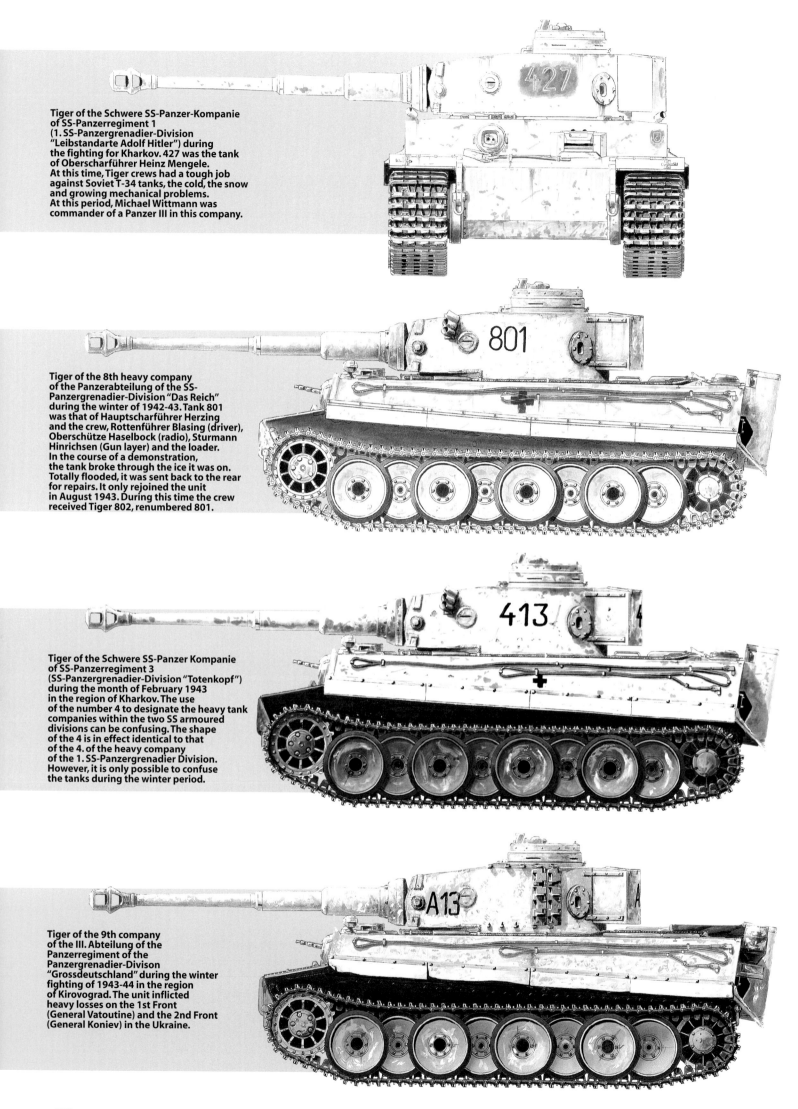

Tiger of the Schwere SS-Panzer-Kompanie of SS-Panzerregiment 1 (1. SS-Panzergrenadier-Division "Leibstandarte Adolf Hitler") during the fighting for Kharkov. 427 was the tank of Oberscharführer Heinz Mengele. At this time, Tiger crews had a tough job against Soviet T-34 tanks, the cold, the snow and growing mechanical problems. At this period, Michael Wittmann was commander of a Panzer III in this company.

Tiger of the 8th heavy company of the Panzerabteilung of the SS-Panzergrenadier-Division "Das Reich" during the winter of 1942-43. Tank 801 was that of Hauptscharführer Herzing and the crew, Rottenführer Blasing (driver), Oberschütze Haselbock (radio), Sturmann Hinrichsen (Gun layer) and the loader. In the course of a demonstration, the tank broke through the ice it was on. Totally flooded, it was sent back to the rear for repairs. It only rejoined the unit in August 1943. During this time the crew received Tiger 802, renumbered 801.

Tiger of the Schwere SS-Panzer Kompanie of SS-Panzerregiment 3 (SS-Panzergrenadier-Division "Totenkopf") during the month of February 1943 in the region of Kharkov. The use of the number 4 to designate the heavy tank companies within the two SS armoured divisions can be confusing. The shape of the 4 is in effect identical to that of the 4. of the heavy company of the 1. SS-Panzergrenadier Division. However, it is only possible to confuse the tanks during the winter period.

Tiger of the 9th company of the III. Abteilung of the Panzerregiment of the Panzergrenadier-Divison "Grossdeutschland" during the winter fighting of 1943-44 in the region of Kirovograd. The unit inflicted heavy losses on the 1st Front (General Vatoutine) and the 2nd Front (General Koniev) in the Ukraine.

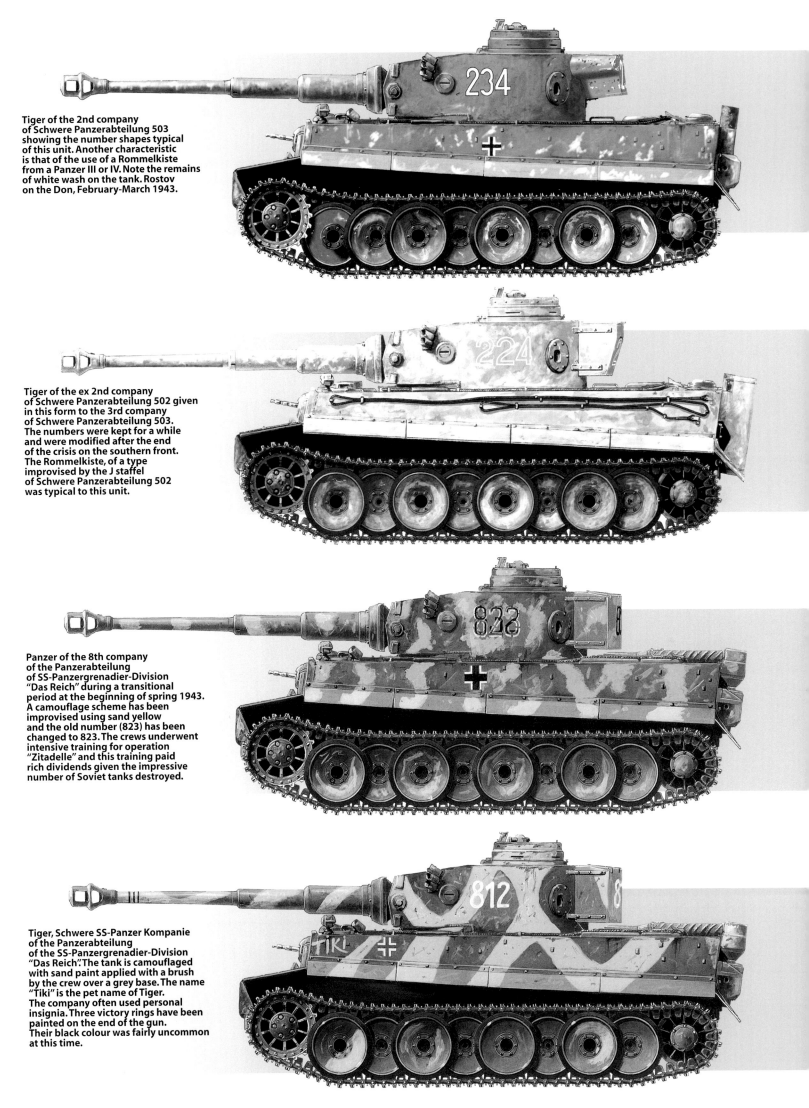

Tiger of the 2nd company
of Schwere Panzerabteilung 503
showing the number shapes typical
of this unit. Another characteristic
is that of the use of a Rommelkiste
from a Panzer III or IV. Note the remains
of white wash on the tank. Rostov
on the Don, February-March 1943.

Tiger of the ex 2nd company
of Schwere Panzerabteilung 502 given
in this form to the 3rd company
of Schwere Panzerabteilung 503.
The numbers were kept for a while
and were modified after the end
of the crisis on the southern front.
The Rommelkiste, of a type
improvised by the J staffel
of Schwere Panzerabteilung 502
was typical to this unit.

Panzer of the 8th company
of the Panzerabteilung
of SS-Panzergrenadier-Division
"Das Reich" during a transitional
period at the beginning of spring 1943.
A camouflage scheme has been
improvised using sand yellow
and the old number (823) has been
changed to 823. The crews underwent
intensive training for operation
"Zitadelle" and this training paid
rich dividends given the impressive
number of Soviet tanks destroyed.

Tiger, Schwere SS-Panzer Kompanie
of the Panzerabteilung
of the SS-Panzergrenadier-Division
"Das Reich". The tank is camouflaged
with sand paint applied with a brush
by the crew over a grey base. The name
"Tiki" is the pet name of Tiger.
The company often used personal
insignia. Three victory rings have been
painted on the end of the gun.
Their black colour was fairly uncommon
at this time.

Tiger of Scwhere SS-Panzerabteilung 101. This tank went through the whole campaign and was still there during the fighting north of Falaise.

Tiger of Schwere SS-Panzerabteilung 102 during the Normandy fighting. This tank is that of top ace Willi Fey who alone destroyed 69 Allied tanks, 22 armoured vehicles and five anti tank guns. Curiously, at the end of the Battle of Normandy, he could not get another Tiger, despite the fact that aces were in principal favoured. .

Another Tiger of the same company but belonging to the 2nd company. The 14 Tigers of this company would destroy over 220 Allied armoured vehicles during the fighting on Norman soil.

Tiger of Heeres Schwere Panzerabteilung 503. The unit was commanded by Major Scherf. It often fought for the 21. Panzerdivision on the right flank of the German front against the British. The tanks of its 3rd company were all practically destroyed by an Allied bombardment.

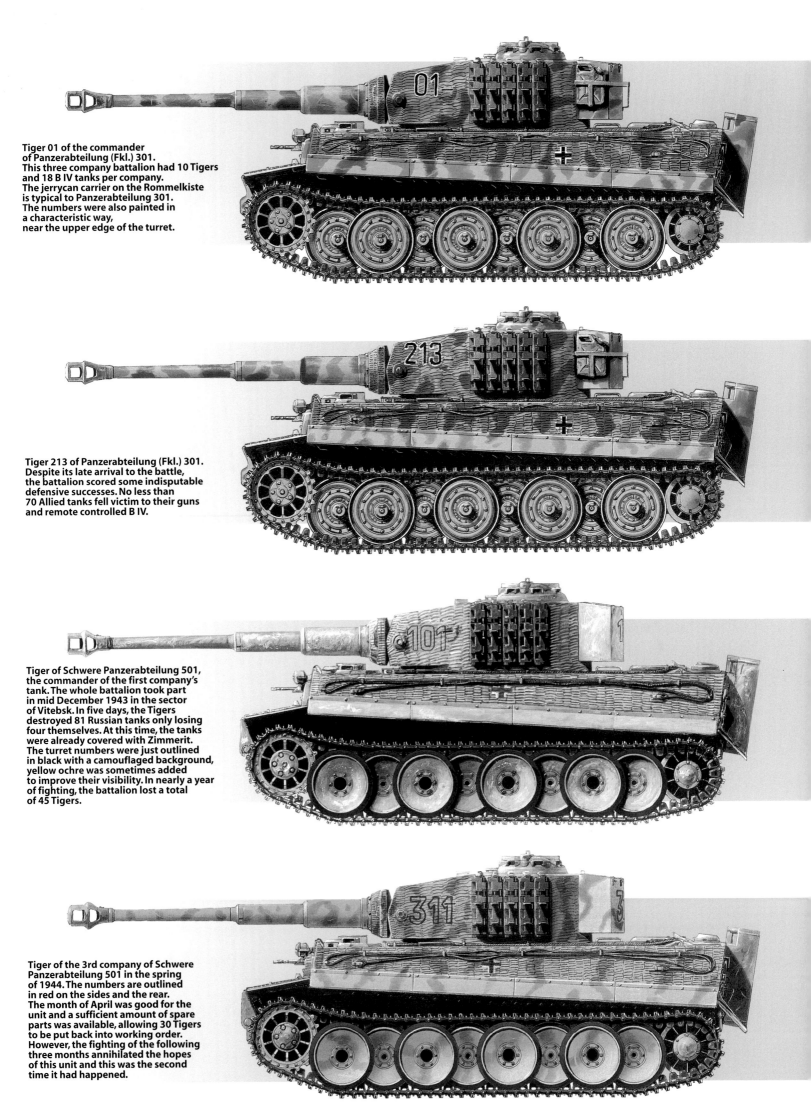

Tiger 01 of the commander of Panzerabteilung (Fkl.) 301. This three company battalion had 10 Tigers and 18 B IV tanks per company. The jerrycan carrier on the Rommelkiste is typical to Panzerabteilung 301. The numbers were also painted in a characteristic way, near the upper edge of the turret.

Tiger 213 of Panzerabteilung (Fkl.) 301. Despite its late arrival to the battle, the battalion scored some indisputable defensive successes. No less than 70 Allied tanks fell victim to their guns and remote controlled B IV.

Tiger of Schwere Panzerabteilung 501, the commander of the first company's tank. The whole battalion took part in mid December 1943 in the sector of Vitebsk. In five days, the Tigers destroyed 81 Russian tanks only losing four themselves. At this time, the tanks were already covered with Zimmerit. The turret numbers were just outlined in black with a camouflaged background, yellow ochre was sometimes added to improve their visibility. In nearly a year of fighting, the battalion lost a total of 45 Tigers.

Tiger of the 3rd company of Schwere Panzerabteilung 501 in the spring of 1944. The numbers are outlined in red on the sides and the rear. The month of April was good for the unit and a sufficient amount of spare parts was available, allowing 30 Tigers to be put back into working order. However, the fighting of the following three months annihilated the hopes of this unit and this was the second time it had happened.

Tiger of the 3rd company of Schwere Panzerabteilung 505 in the region of Nowe Kosary. The battalion's tanks have kept their bridging beams on their sides. From the autumn of 1943, the numbers were painted on the gun, initially without a coloured background (winter 1943-44) then, due to difficulties in identification, with a yellow background in the spring of 1944. The colour of the knight varied according to the paint available.

Tiger of the 2nd company of Schwere Panzerabteilung 506, second tank of the 3rd platoon. At the end of March 1944, the battalion received the new Tiger with a steel covered running gear. Of the 45 issued tanks, roughly 20 were operational. The battalion fought until the end of July 1944 with this type of tank, it then received the new Tiger II. The remaining Tigers, ten at most, were given to Panzerabteilung 503.

The Schwere Panzerabteilung 509 partly used Tigers from Schwere Panzerabteilung 503 from the summer of 1944 onwards, notably the tanks with the steel covered running gear. The one here no doubt comes from Schwere Panzerabteilung 501. The Feiffel filters were taken off just after the winter of 1943-44. The numbering system, of a Soviet style, would be abandoned in the summer of 1944. The tank belonged to the 2nd company.

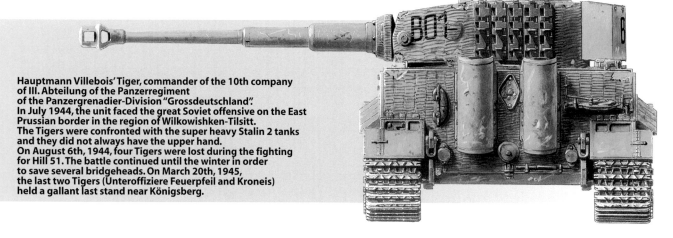

Hauptmann Villebois' Tiger, commander of the 10th company of III. Abteilung of the Panzerregiment of the Panzergrenadier-Division "Grossdeutschland".
In July 1944, the unit faced the great Soviet offensive on the East Prussian border in the region of Wilkowishken-Tilsitt.
The Tigers were confronted with the super heavy Stalin 2 tanks and they did not always have the upper hand.
On August 6th, 1944, four Tigers were lost during the fighting for Hill 51. The battle continued until the winter in order to save several bridgeheads. On March 20th, 1945, the last two Tigers (Unteroffiziere Feuerpfeil and Kroneis) held a gallant last stand near Königsberg.

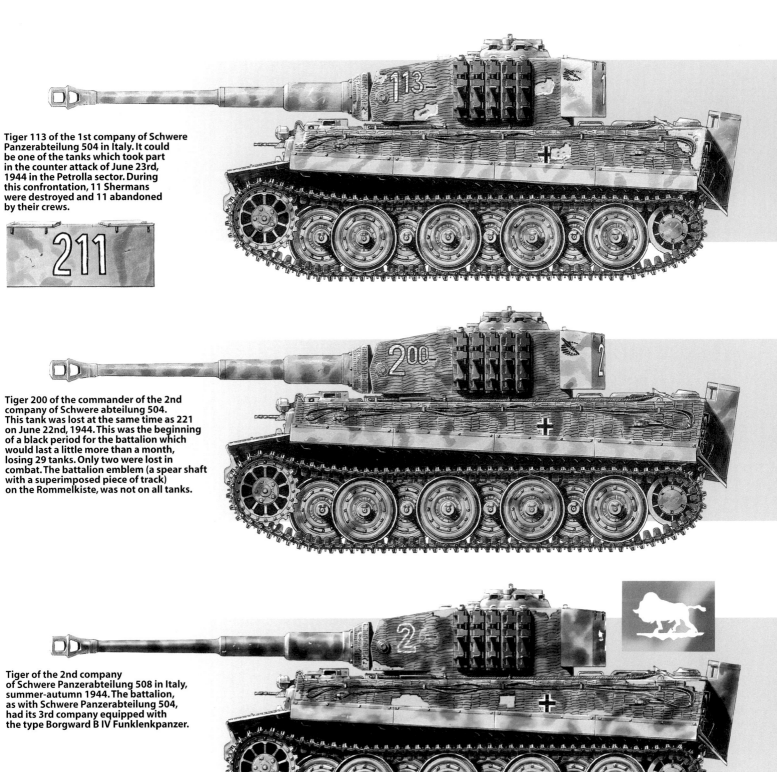

Tiger 113 of the 1st company of Schwere Panzerabteilung 504 in Italy. It could be one of the tanks which took part in the counter attack of June 23rd, 1944 in the Petrolla sector. During this confrontation, 11 Shermans were destroyed and 11 abandoned by their crews.

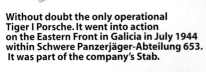

Tiger 200 of the commander of the 2nd company of Schwere abteilung 504. This tank was lost at the same time as 221 on June 22nd, 1944. This was the beginning of a black period for the battalion which would last a little more than a month, losing 29 tanks. Only two were lost in combat. The battalion emblem (a spear shaft with a superimposed piece of track) on the Rommelkiste, was not on all tanks.

Tiger of the 2nd company of Schwere Panzerabteilung 508 in Italy, summer-autumn 1944. The battalion, as with Schwere Panzerabteilung 504, had its 3rd company equipped with the type Borgward B IV Funklenkpanzer.

Without doubt the only operational Tiger I Porsche. It went into action on the Eastern Front in Galicia in July 1944 within Schwere Panzerjäger-Abteilung 653. It was part of the company's Stab.

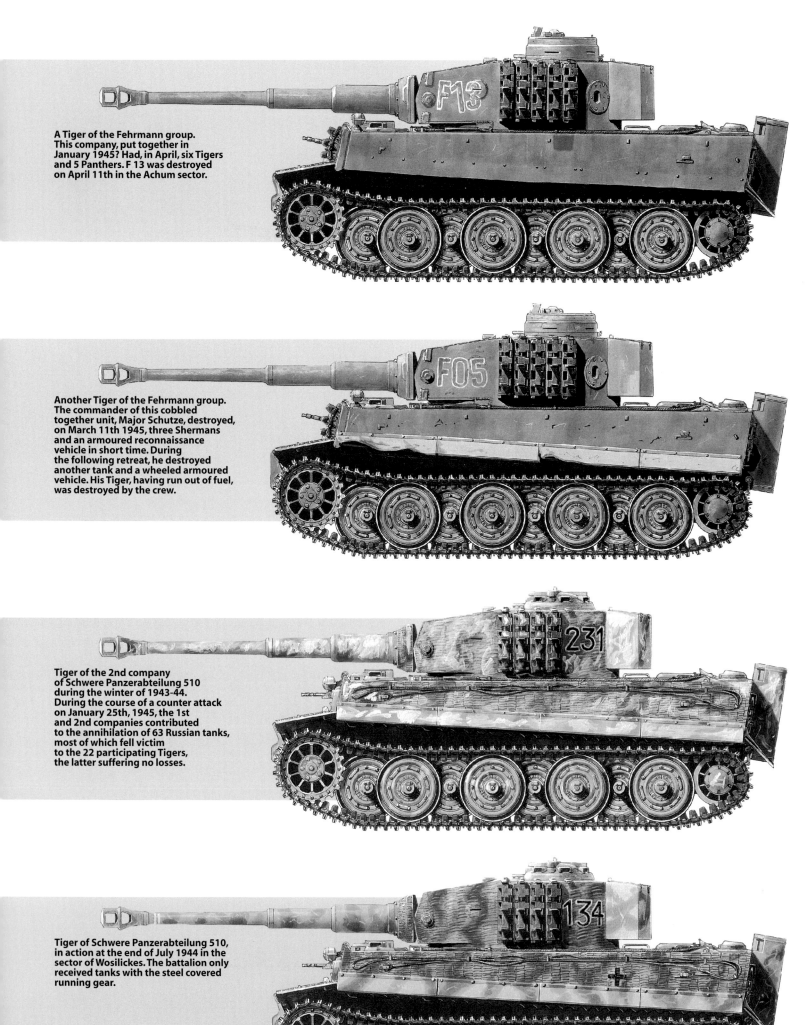

A Tiger of the Fehrmann group. This company, put together in January 1945? Had, in April, six Tigers and 5 Panthers. F 13 was destroyed on April 11th in the Achum sector.

Another Tiger of the Fehrmann group. The commander of this cobbled together unit, Major Schutze, destroyed, on March 11th 1945, three Shermans and an armoured reconnaissance vehicle in short time. During the following retreat, he destroyed another tank and a wheeled armoured vehicle. His Tiger, having run out of fuel, was destroyed by the crew.

Tiger of the 2nd company of Schwere Panzerabteilung 510 during the winter of 1943-44. During the course of a counter attack on January 25th, 1945, the 1st and 2nd companies contributed to the annihilation of 63 Russian tanks, most of which fell victim to the 22 participating Tigers, the latter suffering no losses.

Tiger of Schwere Panzerabteilung 510, in action at the end of July 1944 in the sector of Wosilickes. The battalion only received tanks with the steel covered running gear.

Tiger of the 2nd company of Schwere Panzerabteilung 509 in June 1944. After the battle of Buczacz on April 20th, 1944, where 18 Tigers shattered a Soviet attack, the battalion received 28 new tanks. Some had an unorthodox pattern of Zimmerit.

Tiger II (Ausf. B) of SS-Pz. Abt. 503. It has an ambush camouflage scheme. The one shown here is the most classic type but there were variations.

Tiger II with Porsche turret.

Tiger Ausf. B, called the Tiger II with
Porsche turret of Schwere Panzerabteilung
503. Its 1st company was almost entirely
equipped with this tank during the Battle
of Normandy.

Tiger II with Henschel turret during
the Ardennes fighting in December 1944.
It was part of the Schwere Panzerabteilung
506 which used this type of markings
for the tactical identification of the tanks.

Tiger II of Schwere Panzerabteilung
501 in the summer of 1944 during
the terrible fighting in East Prussia.
The shape of the turret number 3
was specific to this unit since its arrival
on the Eastern Front.

Tiger II of Schwere Panzerabteilung 503
during the fighting in Hungary.
In September 1944, the battalion had
a full complement of 45 Tiger II.
It still had 14 tanks in April 1945.

Tiger II of the 2nd company of Schwere
Panzerabteilung 505 during
the fighting in East Prussia.
Note the absence of lateral mudguards.

Tiger II of the 3rd company
of Schwere Panzerabteilung 505.
The colour of the chevalier is the subject
of discussion. We will continue to use
the officially used colours, green for
the Stab, white for the 1st company,
red for the 2nd and yellow for the 3rd.

Tiger II of Schwere Panzerabteilung 507
during the fighting in Germany
on the Eastern Front. The numbers
and their style of camouflage are based
on the (not always convincing)
reminiscences of veterans.

Tiger II of Schwere Panzerabteilung 509 during the fighting in Hungary. The battalion of course used the black tactical numbers placed slightly to the rear of the turret. However, the most interesting tanks are no doubt those with the turret covered in tank tracks. In January 1945, this battalion also had 45 Tiger II.

Tiger II of Schwere SS- Panzerabteilung 501 during the Battle of the Bulge.

Tiger II of Schwere SS- Panzerabteilung 501 during the Battle of the Bulge. We know, thanks to the archives, that at the beginning of February 1945, the battalion still had 30 Tiger II. We are, therefore, far from an annihilated unit. This tank, 223, was destroyed at Stavelot on December 19th, 1944. The crew managed to escape.

Tiger II of Schwere SS- Panzerabteilung 501, this tank was probably damaged by a bomb from a P-38 fighter bomber. The tank was abandoned by its crew.

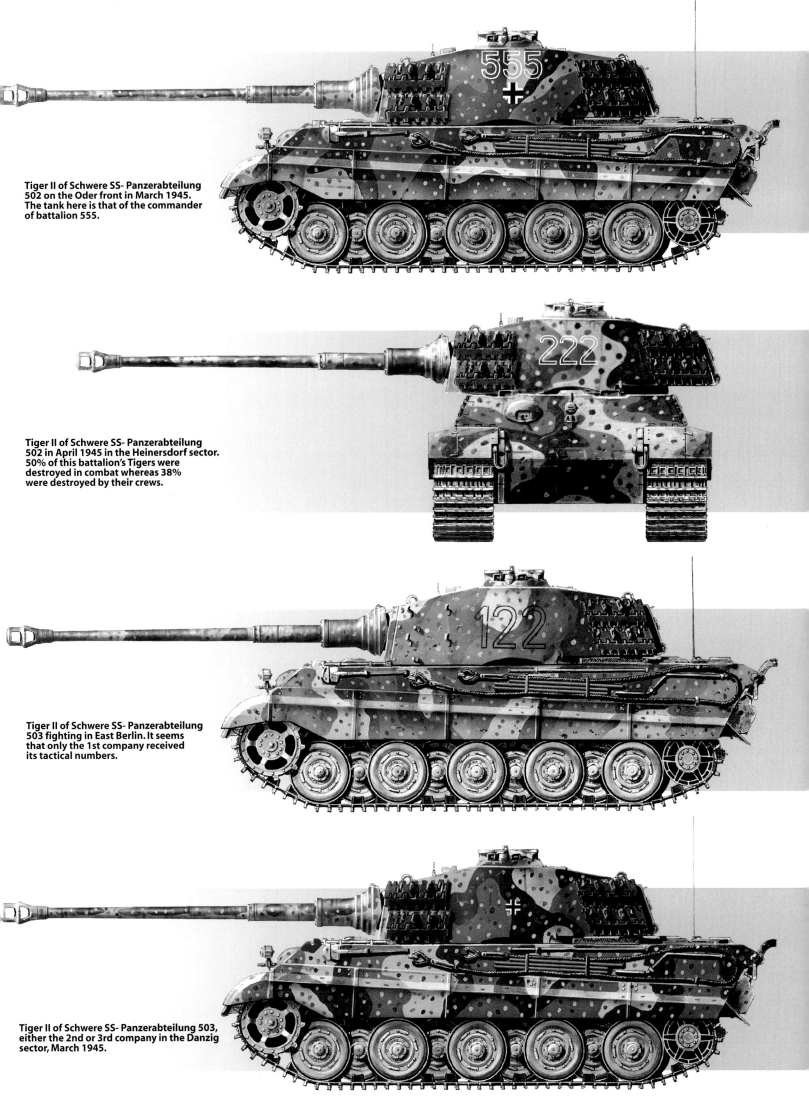

Tiger II of Schwere SS- Panzerabteilung 502 on the Oder front in March 1945. The tank here is that of the commander of battalion 555.

Tiger II of Schwere SS- Panzerabteilung 502 in April 1945 in the Heinersdorf sector. 50% of this battalion's Tigers were destroyed in combat whereas 38% were destroyed by their crews.

Tiger II of Schwere SS- Panzerabteilung 503 fighting in East Berlin. It seems that only the 1st company received its tactical numbers.

Tiger II of Schwere SS- Panzerabteilung 503, either the 2nd or 3rd company in the Danzig sector, March 1945.

69

Belgium

The Belgian army had more than 260 tanks on May 10th, 1940. The T-15, with its Carden-Loyd inspired chassis, could hardly be compared to the German Pz I (we should consider them more as tankettes). 52 of them equipped two cavalry and one light infantry division, shared out amongst nine regiments. The T-13 B1 to B3 (200 of them), had decent weaponry, a 47 mm gun that could take on the majority of German armour. Because of their bad tactical employment and dispersed deployment, they were unable to play a decisive role.

The dozen ACG 1, despite good actions, could not influence events either. Organised into an autonomous squadron, eight of the tanks were engaged.

Only four of these were destroyed in combat by 37 mm German anti tank shells, proving that this tank had solid qualities.

Integrated into the British army, the Free Belgians later fought for the liberation of their country. The mechanised units mainly used materiel of British or American origin. Tactics and organisation followed the British model.

Amongst all these units, the most famous is, without doubt, the first Belgian armoured car squadron, formed in February 1941 in Britain, and participating in the Normandy fighting from August 8th, 1944. The units attached to the Brigade Piron, although less well known and only equipped with the Bren as armoured materiel, also played a just as vital role.

The units of this brigade were independent.

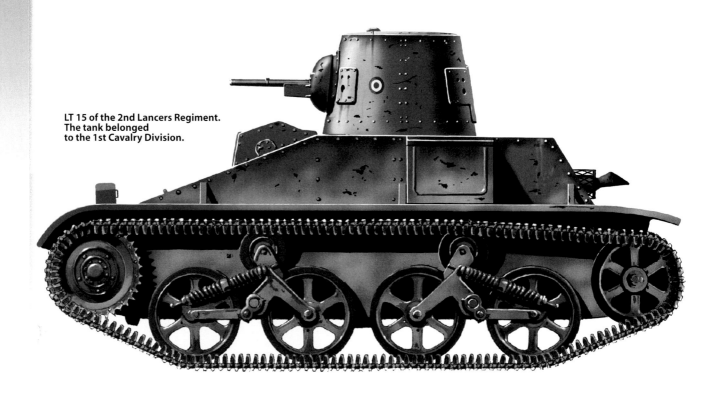

LT 15 of the 2nd Lancers Regiment.
The tank belonged
to the 1st Cavalry Division.

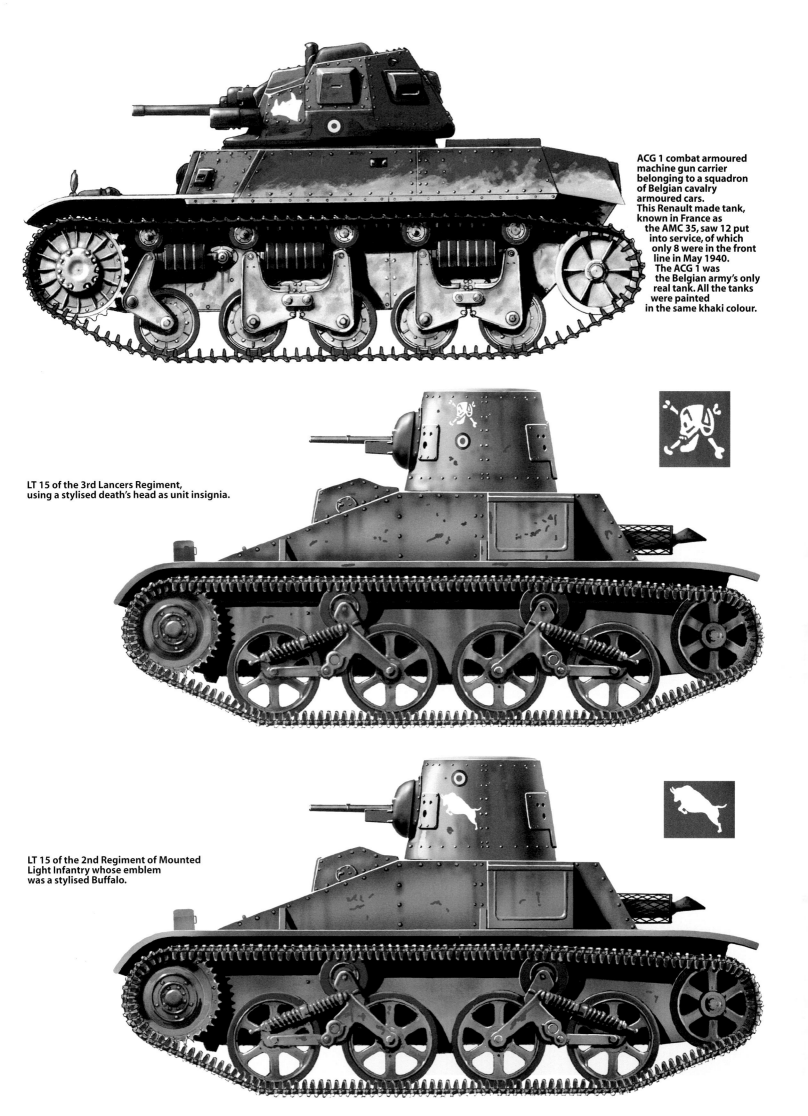

ACG 1 combat armoured machine gun carrier belonging to a squadron of Belgian cavalry armoured cars.
This Renault made tank, known in France as the AMC 35, saw 12 put into service, of which only 8 were in the front line in May 1940.
The ACG 1 was the Belgian army's only real tank. All the tanks were painted in the same khaki colour.

LT 15 of the 3rd Lancers Regiment, using a stylised death's head as unit insignia.

LT 15 of the 2nd Regiment of Mounted Light Infantry whose emblem was a stylised Buffalo.

Bulgaria

The Bulgarian armoured branch saw the light of day in 1935 with the constitution of the first tank company which became a battalion in 1939. In August 1941, it was re-designated as an armoured regiment then armoured brigade in October 1943.

In 1940-41, the battalion received 40 type R 35 tanks, complemented by 36 Skoda vz 35.

Previously, the unit had 14 CV 33 Italian tanks (dating from 1935) and eight British Vickers 6 Tons (dating from 1938).

In April 1941, Bulgarian troops, along with the armoured regiment, pushed into the Aegean Sea region with the objective of making territorial gains in Thrace and Greek Macedonia. The Bulgarians occupied territory between the Strouma and a demarcation line linking Alexandropolis and Svilengrad west of the Maritsa, as well as the islands of Thasos and Samothrace. Territory corresponding to Yugoslavian Macedonia was also occupied by the Bulgarians.

By 1943, the armour had become completely obsolete and the Germans delivered 25 Stug IIIG assault guns (55 according to some sources), named the Maybach T IV by the Bulgarians. In the summer of 1944, the Bulgarian army only had a total of 121 tanks.

After the mysterious — and very well timed — death of King Boris in August 1943 and a period of regency, a new communist led government, the Patriotic Front, took power with the approach of Soviet troops on September 9th, 1944 and lost no time in declaring war on Germany.

The Bulgarian armoured units participated in the fighting of the liberation, changing their distinctive markings, the black cross (or X) of the 1st Division tanks, to a coat of arms in the national colours of white, green and red. The last fighting took place in Hungary, with the survivors of the 1st Armoured Division, alongside the Soviet army.

40 R-35 were delivered to the Bulgarians by the Germans between 1940 and 1941. It is difficult to know whether the markings were like those seen here. However, they are cited by several sources.

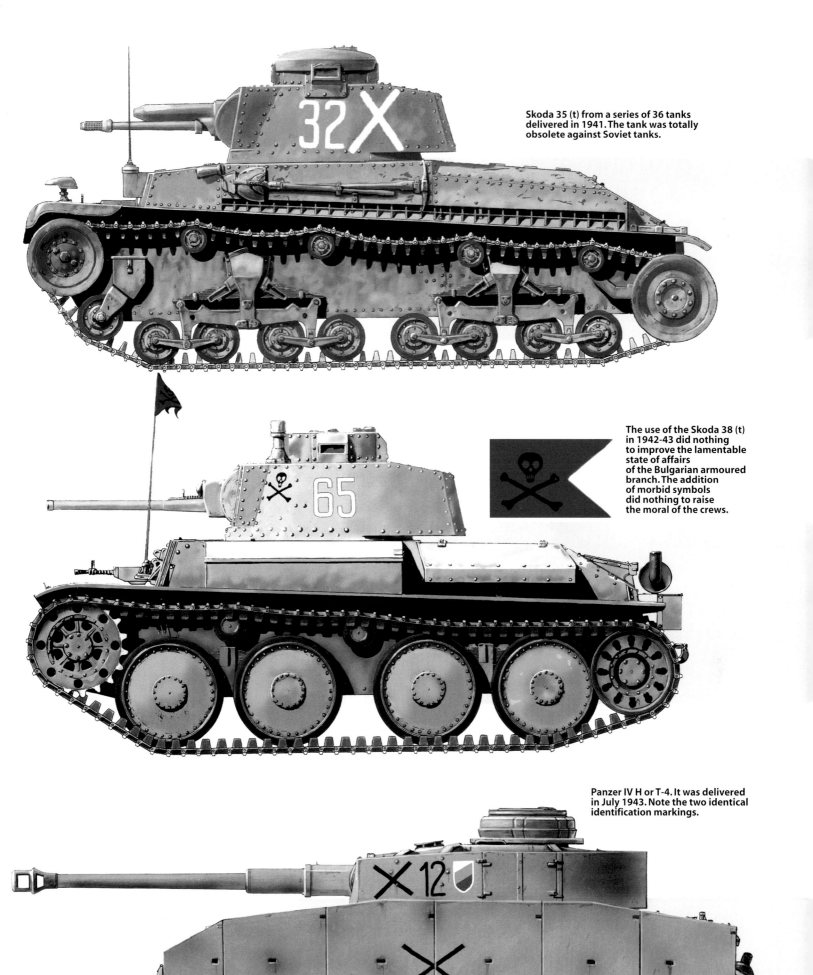

Skoda 35 (t) from a series of 36 tanks delivered in 1941. The tank was totally obsolete against Soviet tanks.

The use of the Skoda 38 (t) in 1942-43 did nothing to improve the lamentable state of affairs of the Bulgarian armoured branch. The addition of morbid symbols did nothing to raise the moral of the crews.

Panzer IV H or T-4. It was delivered in July 1943. Note the two identical identification markings.

China

FT-17 could be found next to the Carden-Loyd M31 and M36, Vickers 6 Ton, British Bren Carrier, Soviet T-26, Italian CV 33 or the German Pz I… and that is only the tracked vehicles. German deliveries ceased as the relationship with the Japanese became closer. Each type of tank was issued in small numbers (20 Vickers 6 Ton tanks, 10 PzI…) Only 88 T-26 had a semblance of a reasonably coherent armoured branch were it not for the scale of the country. It is obvious that in such conditions, with such a varied amount of tanks, it was impossible to obtain homogenous units. As the war evolved, the situation of the armoured branch improved. This was initially within the framework of Lend Lease, with American materiel being delivered between 1943 and 1945 (48 Stuarts and 35 M5 Shermans which were superior to whatever the Japanese could confront them with). Later, the Soviets would also deliver materiel, the exact numbers of which are not precisely known.

The disparity of the materiel used by the Chinese is certainly the main characteristic of their armoured units. The various types came from almost every country, complemented by locally manufactured, poor quality tanks. The old French

The FT 17 was certainly part of the first deliveries made to China.

British Carden Loyd or Vickers Mk I Light, painted in a very British green.

One of the 10 Panzer I delivered to China by Germany. The original paintwork remained unchanged.

6 ton Model E type A Vickers
in its original camouflage.

T-26 of Soviet origin, used
by the Chinese. It seems obvious
that the Chinese, allied with
the Americans, also received
great quantities of materiel
from Uncle Sam.
Details are not yet known.

One of the 35 Shermans received
by the Chinese. These were characterised
by a very "animalist" decoration which
would be used by the Americans
in Korea 10 years later.

Croatia

On April 6th, 1941, the day of the German-Italian-Hungarian attack, Yugoslavia could field only 118 tanks, these often being obsolete: 56 FT-17 and M-28, 54 Renault R35, eight light tanks and a few tankettes.

With ten axis tanks for every Yugoslavian one, they were dispersed and most of them were destroyed.

With the invasion in full swing, the province of Croatia broke away and proclaimed its independence on April 10th. The new state was immediately recognised by the Reich and its allies.

The progress of this province, with ethnic German origins, towards independence, should have, in the pre-war context, been obtained peacefully. However, the steps to obtain this were definitively rejected in 1934. Those seeking independence, or Ustashis, therefore resorted to terrorist methods that were almost a tradition in Yugoslavia. When the Germans invaded in April 1941 they were greeted with open arms by the people of Croatia. As early as April 11th, 1941, a defence army was formed by Pavelic, initially made up of 6 divisions (later 16). Although the Croats played an important role as Germany's allies in the air force, where some pilots scored an impressive number of kills, and to a lesser degree by supplying three infantry divisions to the German army (369, 373, 392 ID) and two for the Waffen-SS, the same could not be said for the armoured forces which remained embryonic (15 Panzer III N and Panzer IV). Its role was practically nil. However, Croatia remained loyal to the Reich until the end of the war and even beyond as the last 200,000 defenders fought until May 1945. Some units preferred to surrender to the British, fearing the awful conditions of Communist camps. The last units lay down their weapons on May 16th-17th, 1945. The toughness and cruelty of the Ustashi fighters was only equalled by Tito's partisans.

One of the few French R-35 tanks used by the Yugoslav army during the campaign in the Balkans, April 1941.

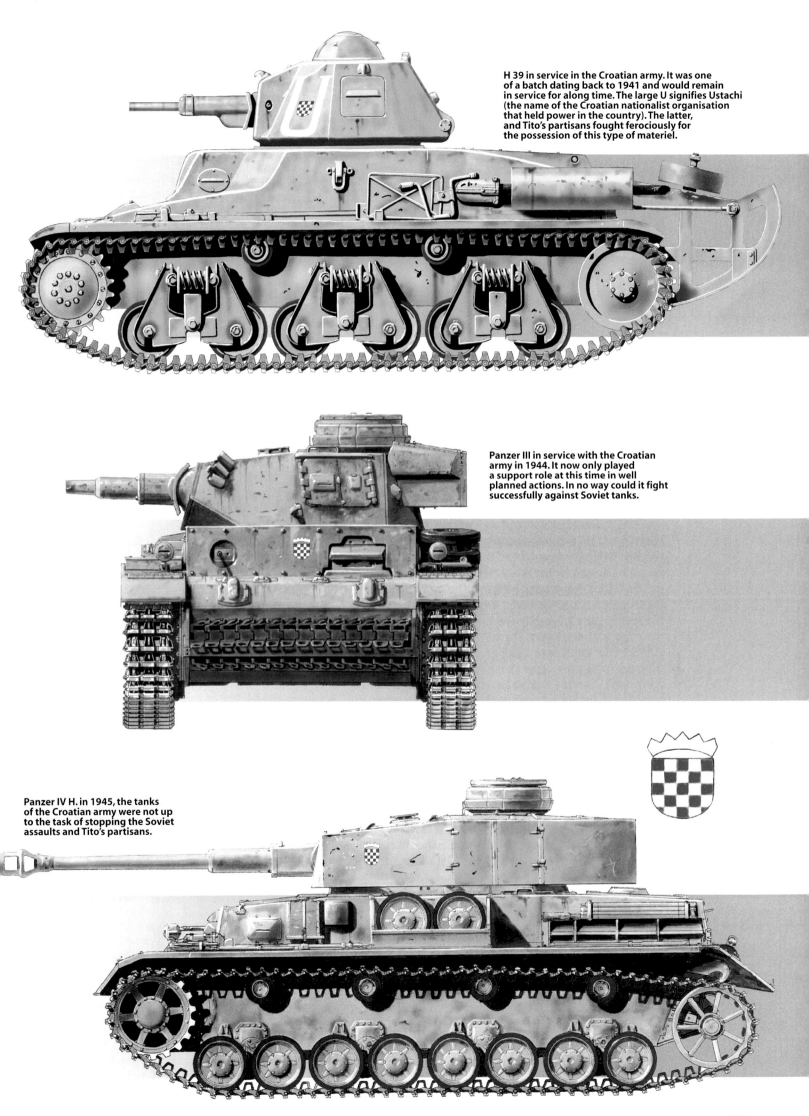

H 39 in service in the Croatian army. It was one of a batch dating back to 1941 and would remain in service for along time. The large U signifies Ustachi (the name of the Croatian nationalist organisation that held power in the country). The latter, and Tito's partisans fought ferociously for the possession of this type of materiel.

Panzer III in service with the Croatian army in 1944. It now only played a support role at this time in well planned actions. In no way could it fight successfully against Soviet tanks.

Panzer IV H. in 1945, the tanks of the Croatian army were not up to the task of stopping the Soviet assaults and Tito's partisans.

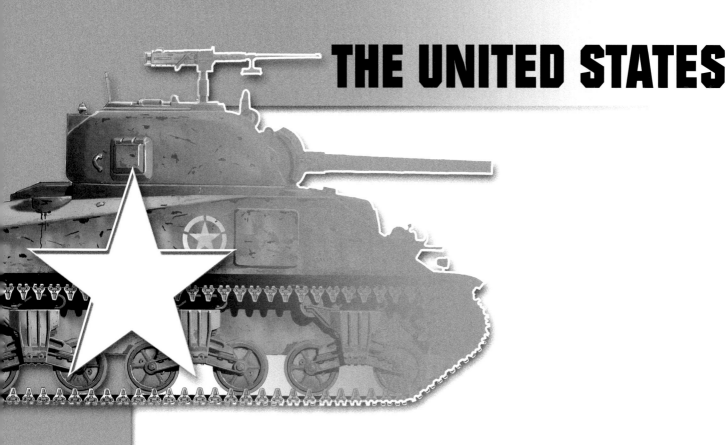

Far from being a peaceful nation, as it is all too often described (it had just finished a 'punitive' expedition Mexico, commanded by General Pershing in 1916-17), the United States, with the appearance of the tank in 1916, were not, apart from rare exceptions, conscious of the future role of this revolutionary weapon and the tactical advantages of such a technique for the many military operations (150 to this day) that they would instigate. During the course of these multiple interventions, the use of Caterpillar type tracked tractors for supply, was still not enough persuade the country to use tanks. The state of the terrain and the weight of the tanks were major handicaps at this time. This is no doubt why they later chose the small FT-17 that was more manoeuvrable than its large British counterpart, the Mark I or II. America therefore adopted this tank within its armoured units. Widely used in the latter part of the Great War, the American army acquired great experience in using these tanks. After the war, this tank remained the model of the genre and was built under licence. At the beginning of the 1930's, it was given a new more powerful Franklin engine, increasing its speed by nearly 15 kph. The American army with its strong cavalry spirit, due to the vastness of the country, needed a rapid tank and a faster running gear. The first firm to design a simple and efficient running gear, which could also be used on the road without tracks, was Christie. The Christie T4 Combat Car was born and, like its older brother, the FT-17, would profoundly influence the evolution of future tanks. The M 1931 Medium tank should have followed but it was not accepted by the US Army due to its high price and performance which fell short of the specifications. Paradoxically, it was not in the United States that these tanks with their surprising performances, were mass produced, but by their future direct rival, the Soviets with their BT tanks then the T-34.

In the United Kingdom, this type of running gear influenced the series of Cruiser, Crusader and Cromwell. In return, the United States developed another type of running gear which would be found on the majority of American tanks

beginning at the end of the thirties, the mass produced T2 and precursor of the M2 and above all the M3 Stuart. This type of running gear meant the creation of a new type of tank track, made up of several parts and using rubber bearings. This type of track has, in the meantime, become the NATO type and is used by almost all the member countries. Another type of running gear was also developed, using the Panzer III system. It resulted in the M 24 Chaffee which entered service in April 1944 and used by most of the western countries after the Second World War. Badly used, its weaponry and armour revealed themselves inferior against German tanks but also the T-34/85 during the Korean war.

With the T2 came the T5 in 1938, a medium tank which would lead to the M3 Lee and Grant that was almost obsolete when it entered service in the summer of 1941. The problem only lasted a few months as the Americans had, from February 1942, the first Shermans, a tank that would become legendary. With over 44,000 examples made and many variants, the Sherman was the second most highly manufactured tank in the world. The Pershing, equipped with a 90 mm gun and based on the T 20 running gear, was the last of the American tanks to be sent to Europe in January 1945. It would be the precursor of the future M47 Patton.

The United States, like Germany with the Maus, Great Britain and the Conqueror and Tortoise, France and its ARL 44 and AMX 50, also succumbed to the call for gigantic tanks by developing the T 28. Five of these 95 tonne monsters were made, equipped with a gun capable of firing 15 kilometres. The project was abandoned before hostilities ended as it had obvious drawbacks. The T 29, a sort of super Pershing, should have replaced the latter (already weighing 45 tonnes) considered as insufficient against the Tiger II. The war ended before the production of this series.

1. Only a few companies realised the importance of this weapon. In 1917, some of them, including the Oakland Motor Company (today's Pontiac) put pressure on President Wilson to break his election promise not to enter under any circumstance, the European war. We know what followed, as President Roosevelt made the same promise to his electorate.

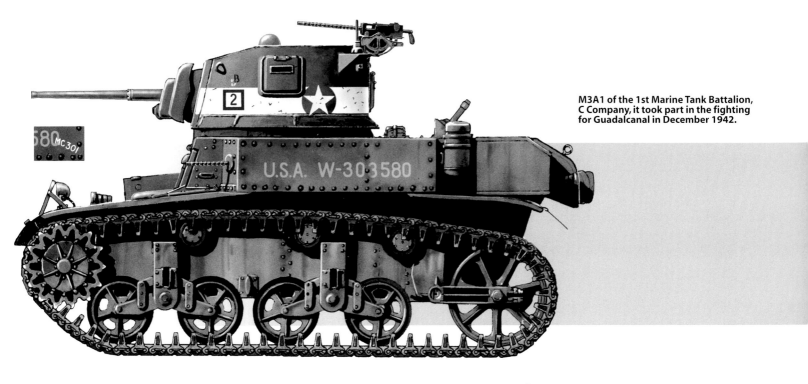

M3A1 of the 1st Marine Tank Battalion, C Company, it took part in the fighting for Guadalcanal in December 1942.

M3A1 of the 1st Armoured Division, 1st Battalion, 3rd Company, during the fighting in Tunisia in December 1942. Note the presence of the 48 star American flag and the rivets on the bodywork.

M3A1 of the same unit. The absence of a flag is possibly because it was deemed as too visible. The tank was destroyed in the December fighting, as were the other two tanks seen here.

M3A1 of the 1st Armored
Division, 1st Battalion,
C Company. The flag is still
present on the bodywork
which presumably places
it before December 1942.

Light tank M5AI of one
of the Armored Regiments
of the 3rd Armored Division.
The tank was photographed a short time
after landing on Norman soil.
The crew has removed the mudguards
and kept the lower part
of the engine's seal housing.

M5 Stuart light tank
of the 601st TD Battalion.
The tactical insignia
is uncommon.
It later disappeared.

M5AI Light Lank of an unknown American unit. The large white 16 seems to have been added at the last minute before being loaded onto the LCT. The American crews, as with the British crews, had no hesitation in covering the turret and front with tank tracks or spare sprockets, in an attempt to add to the very thin armour of this small reconnaissance tank.

M5A1 Light Tank of an unknown American unit. Launched onto the roads of Normandy as scouts for their regiment, the crew of this Stuart have not forgotten to lay the orange identification sheet across the rear of the tank in order to avoid being attacked by Allied aircraft.

M5A1 Stuart of the 704th Tank Battalion, destroyed on December 17th, 1944 at Heinerscheid. In this sector, D Company lost 11 tanks in ten minutes.

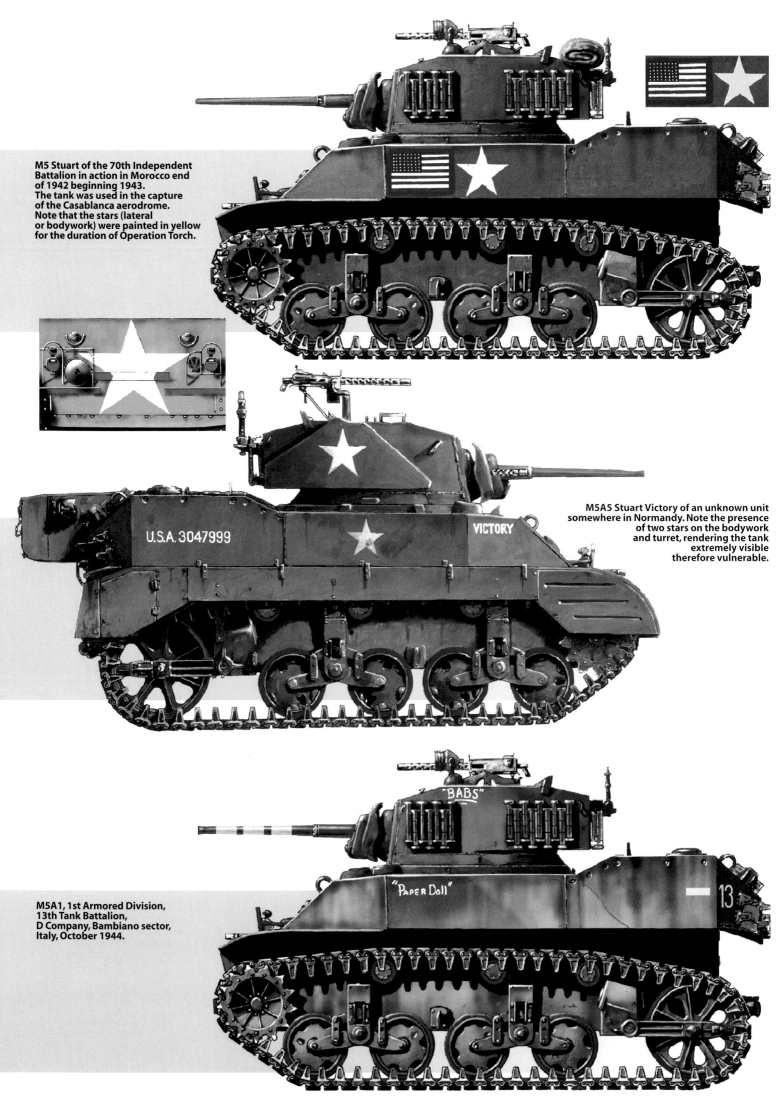

M5 Stuart of the 70th Independent Battalion in action in Morocco end of 1942 beginning 1943.
The tank was used in the capture of the Casablanca aerodrome.
Note that the stars (lateral or bodywork) were painted in yellow for the duration of Operation Torch.

U.S.A. 3047999

VICTORY

M5A5 Stuart Victory of an unknown unit somewhere in Normandy. Note the presence of two stars on the bodywork and turret, rendering the tank extremely visible therefore vulnerable.

"BABS"

"Paper Doll"

13

M5A1, 1st Armored Division, 13th Tank Battalion, D Company, Bambiano sector, Italy, October 1944.

M3 Lee, 1st Armored Division,
2nd Battalion, E Company, 3rd Platoon,
Morocco-Tunisia at the end of 1942.
These tanks were obsolete
at the end of the African campaign.

U.S.A. W-309072

M3 Lee, 1st Armored Division,
2nd Battalion, D Company.
Most of these tanks were destroyed
in combat. The survivors were used
as infantry support.

U.S.A. W-209073

M3 Lee.
Front view
of a M3 Lee
of the 1st Armored
Division,
2nd Battalion,
D Company.

M3 Lee
of the 165th Tank
Regiment Combat
Team at Tarawa.

319

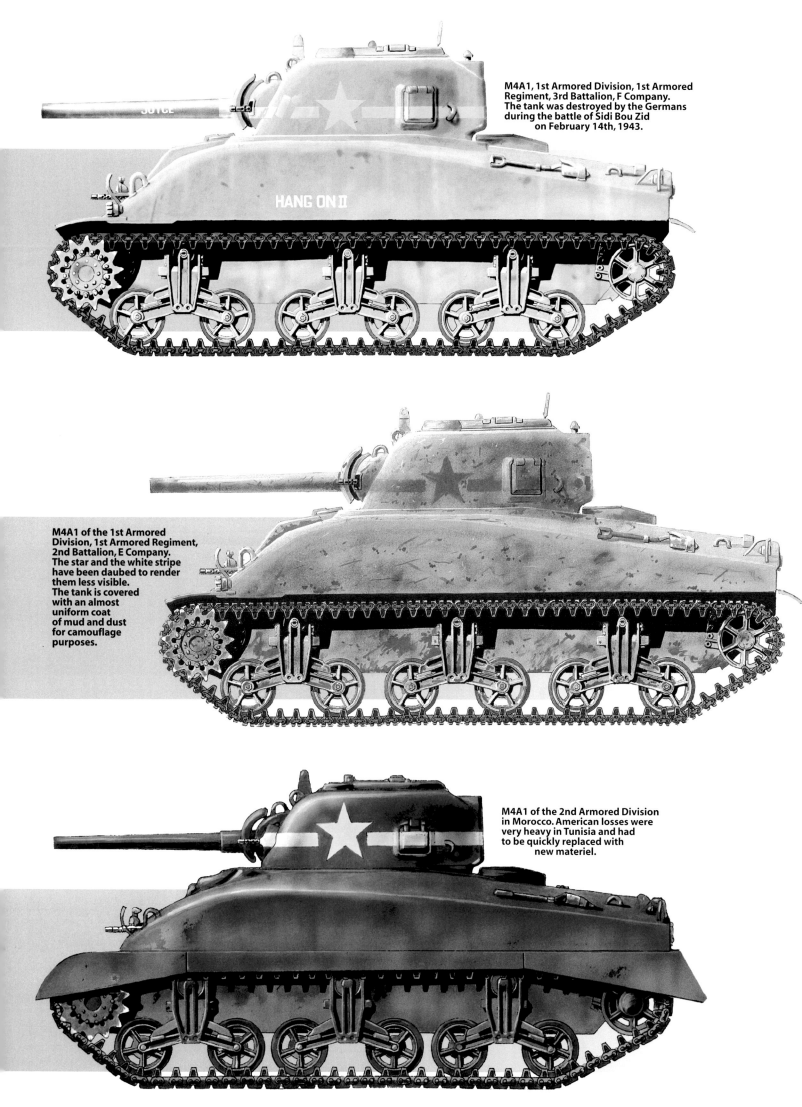

M4A1, 1st Armored Division, 1st Armored Regiment, 3rd Battalion, F Company. The tank was destroyed by the Germans during the battle of Sidi Bou Zid on February 14th, 1943.

M4A1 of the 1st Armored Division, 1st Armored Regiment, 2nd Battalion, E Company. The star and the white stripe have been daubed to render them less visible. The tank is covered with an almost uniform coat of mud and dust for camouflage purposes.

M4A1 of the 2nd Armored Division in Morocco. American losses were very heavy in Tunisia and had to be quickly replaced with new materiel.

Sherman M4 of the 1st Armored Division, the battalion is not known. It was destroyed in North Africa at Sidi Bou Zid (Tunisia). Because of the theatre of operations, the tank has been completely painted in sand yellow, the original Olive Drab paint shows through in places.

M4 of the 1st Armored Division. It too has received the same sort of camouflage as the tank seen above.

M4 A1 of the 1st Armored Division destroyed during the battle of Sidi Bou Zid. The tank still has its lateral skirting.

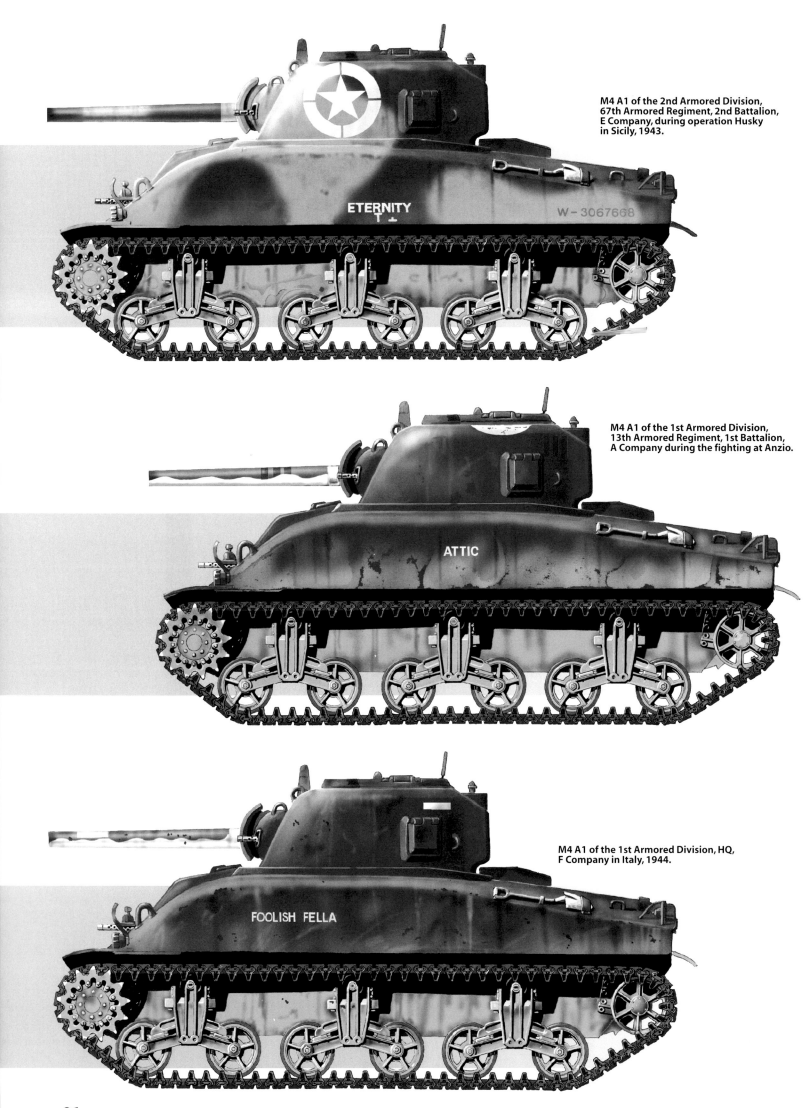

M4 A1 of the 2nd Armored Division, 67th Armored Regiment, 2nd Battalion, E Company, during operation Husky in Sicily, 1943.

ETERNITY
T

W – 3067668

M4 A1 of the 1st Armored Division, 13th Armored Regiment, 1st Battalion, A Company during the fighting at Anzio.

ATTIC

M4 A1 of the 1st Armored Division, HQ, F Company in Italy, 1944.

FOOLISH FELLA

M4 A1 of 1st Marine Amphibious
Tank Battalion, C Company.

CONDOR

Bachelor Boys is a M3 American
Sherman of an unidentified unit.
For the big day, the latter has kept
the very visible turret markings
from the beginning of the war.

BACHELOR BOYS

U.S.A.30·····

M4 A3 Sherman of an unidentified American
unit in Normandy during the month
of July 1944. The OD paint seems quite worn.
Many Shermans of the 2nd Armored Division
saw their regimental workshops apply more
and more frequently, irregular darker brown
or green stripes as a camouflage measure.

U.S.A.3022636

Sherman M4 of the 5th Armored Division. This unit played a vital role in the creation of the Falaise pocket, then in the advance on Paris.

Sherman M4 of the 755th Tank Battalion.

This Sherman M4A3 belonged to an unidentified American Tank Battalion. An extra plate of armour has been welded on the left flank during the course of the campaign, covering the American star. It is probable that the lateral mudguard plates will soon disappear. Lost or just abandoned on the road side.

M4A2 of the 4th Armored Division
during operation Cobra,
Normandy 1944.

FURY

U.S.A. 036197

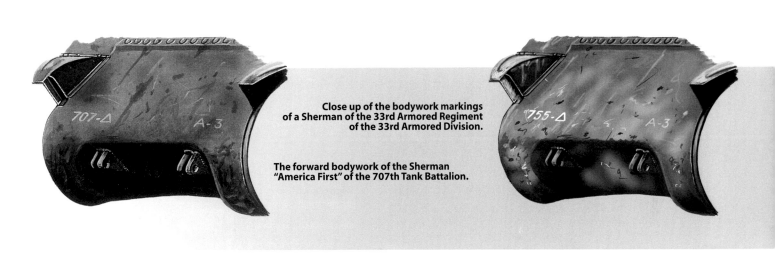

Close up of the bodywork markings
of a Sherman of the 33rd Armored Regiment
of the 33rd Armored Division.

The forward bodywork of the Sherman
"America First" of the 707th Tank Battalion.

707-Δ   A-3

755-Δ   A-3

Sherman of the 707th Tank Battalion,
A Company. The white star has been
smothered in mud as it was too visible.

AMERICA FIRST

USA 3120016

M4A3 of the 1st Armored Division, 4th Tank Battalion, in the Santa Lucia sector, Italy, October 1944. The tank belonged to the 2nd Platoon as indicated by the two stripes on the gun. The red colour indicates that is part of the 1st Company.

M4A3 of the 4th Armored Division, 37th Tank Battalion during the fighting for Bastogne. The tank is that of Major Creighton Abrams, the American tank ace.

M4A3 of the 14th Armored Division, 25th Tank Battalion, B Company in the sector of Gemerscheim in March 1945.

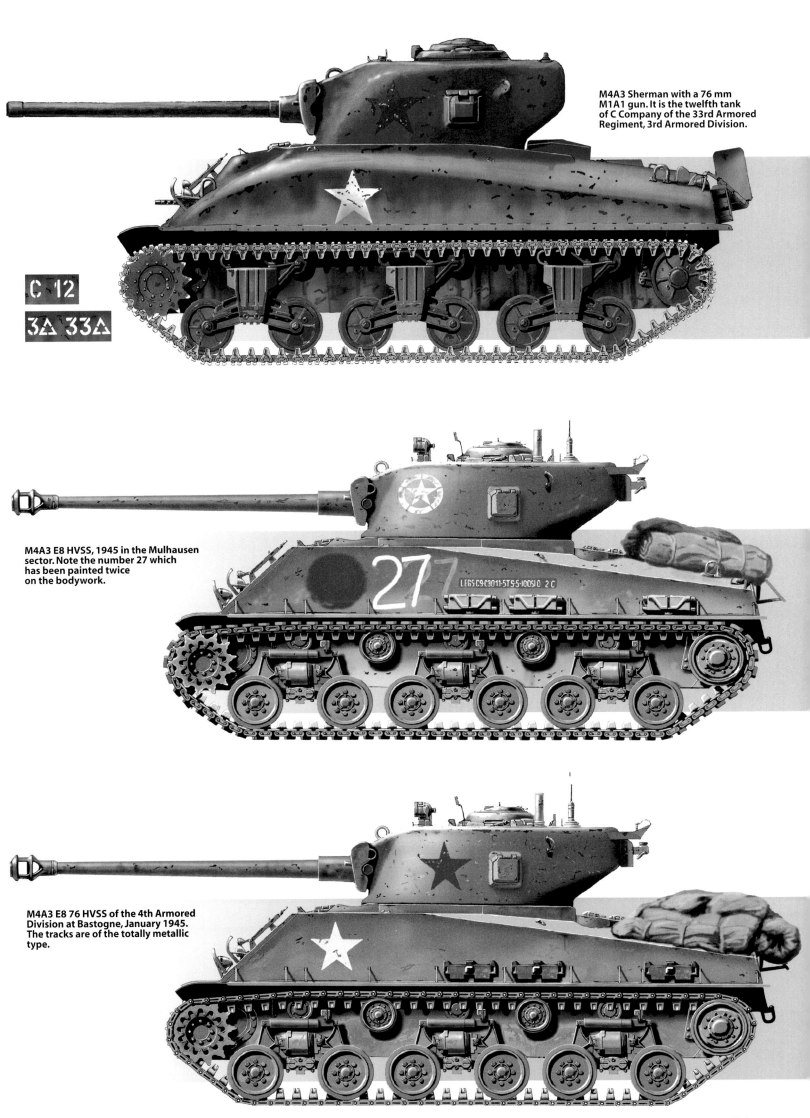

M4A3 Sherman with a 76 mm M1A1 gun. It is the twelfth tank of C Company of the 33rd Armored Regiment, 3rd Armored Division.

C 12

3△ 33△

M4A3 E8 HVSS, 1945 in the Mulhausen sector. Note the number 27 which has been painted twice on the bodywork.

27 27

LEGS·C9·C3011·5T·S·5·100510 2 C

M4A3 E8 76 HVSS of the 4th Armored Division at Bastogne, January 1945. The tracks are of the totally metallic type.

M24 Shaffee. The arrival
of the M-24 was a relief for the crews
of light tanks who would at last benefit
from a tank equipped a good gun
(75 mm) in place of the Stuart's 37 mm
already obsolete when the tank
came out in 1941.

M24 Chaffee during
the fighting
on the Belgian border
in November 1944.

ALLY OOP III

USA
30177514

1△-13△   D 2

M24 Chaffee
of the 1st Armored Division,
13th Armored Battalion,
D Company, plain of Pô,
Italy, April 1945.

The M24 Chaffee seen from this angle has a particularly "racée" silhouette.

M26 Pershing of the 9th Armored Division, 14th Armored Battalion, A Company, Germany 1945.

M26 Pershing of the 7th Armored Division, 23rd Armored Battalion, C Company, Nordhausen sector at the beginning of April 1945.

Finland

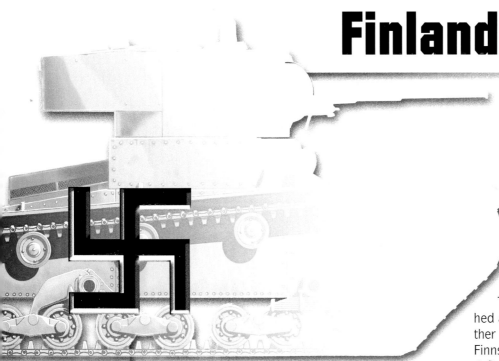

The history of Finland's armoured forces is without doubt the most surprising of all. At the beginning of the Second World War, it only had 26 Vickers tanks (similar to the Soviet T-26 and armed with the same 45 mm Soviet gun), as well as various other tanks, types T-26, T-37, T-38. This gave a total strength of forty tanks.

Attacked by the Soviet Union in the winter of 1941, the Finns, although greatly outnumbered, fought bravely and inflicted a crushing defeat on the invaders. When the fighting ceased, they recovered all that the Soviet tide had left behind it. This was to be found in great quantities; the materiel, however, was obsolete. The spoils consisted mainly of the T-28 and T-26 that the Finns were able to re-use within units or as spare parts for the most damaged. It was only from February 1942, that the Finns introduced a brigade system with two, three company battalions. At this time, they had over sixty tanks, mainly the type T-26 or similar to it, and as many Komsomolets armoured tractors. It was only in June 1942 that they had a first armoured division. From June 26th, 1941, Finland took part in the attack against the Soviet Union. Very quickly, the materiel sho-

wed itself to be inadequate and was retired from service. Finland then received 30 StuG III from its German ally.

The great Soviet offensive in the summer of 1944 brushed aside the Finnish defences. The latter received another 29 StuG III and fifteen Panzer IV. In the meantime, the Finns had recovered all the Soviet armour left on the battlefield. It was the same for the aircraft which had the same disparity as the armoured forces. Crushed by the Soviet steam roller and despite acts of superhuman bravery, Finland signed its capitulation on September 4th, 1944, nearly five years to the day since the beginning of the World War. Fighting continued however, but against German troops retreating into Lapland.

Note that the Finnish "HAKARISTI" ("Hakenkreuz" in German), the blue swastika, the traditional symbol of Finland, placed on tanks and aircraft, has no political signification. Count Von Rosen, of Swedish origin, introduced into Finland's air force on March 6th, 1918, fighting with the "Whites" for Finland's independence against the Russian Bolsheviks. It was the family symbol and not from India as is sometimes said, painted on his Morane-Saulnier L (Parasol) fighter. This symbol was kept in his honour until 1944. It is the symbol of happiness and is used with the same meaning by Hindus, Buddhists and… Nazis. The opposite negative signification of this cross is, therefore, completely ridiculous and without foundation. Note also that the symbol that is, for some, of "hyperborean" origin, can be found in the frieze later known as Greek.

Vickers 6 Ton Mod, B version, transformed for the Finns. Initially, the FT 17 35 mm gun was mounted on the tank, then after the long Bofors 37 mm gun. During the fighting of the winter of 1941, the two guns turned out to be too weak.

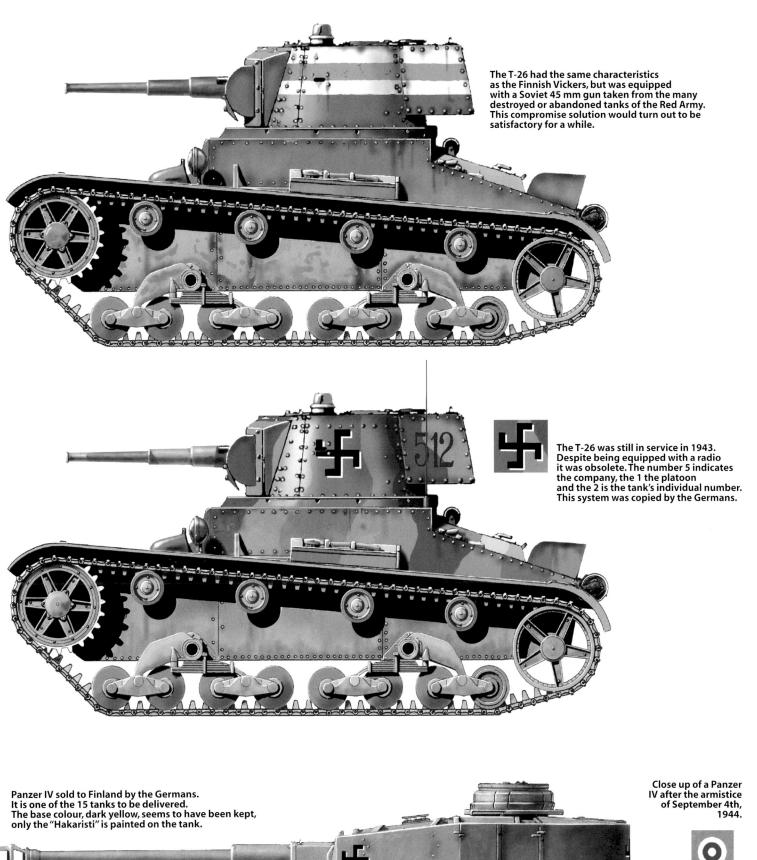

The T-26 had the same characteristics as the Finnish Vickers, but was equipped with a Soviet 45 mm gun taken from the many destroyed or abandoned tanks of the Red Army. This compromise solution would turn out to be satisfactory for a while.

The T-26 was still in service in 1943. Despite being equipped with a radio it was obsolete. The number 5 indicates the company, the 1 the platoon and the 2 is the tank's individual number. This system was copied by the Germans.

Panzer IV sold to Finland by the Germans. It is one of the 15 tanks to be delivered. The base colour, dark yellow, seems to have been kept, only the "Hakaristi" is painted on the tank.

Close up of a Panzer IV after the armistice of September 4th, 1944.

France

France, like Great Britain, understood the vital role that armour would play, thanks to the far-sighted General Estienne. At the end of 1917, a revolutionary tank made its appearance at the Front after the medium Schneider CA 1 tank and its rival, the Saint Chaumond. This was the two man Renault FT. Besides this, 1916 saw the development of a breakthrough tank which resulted, in 1919, with the FCM 2C (10 were made), 70 metric ton tank which was totally obsolete in 1940. At the end of the First World War, with the well organised manufacturing of the Renault Ft, 4,000 tanks left the production lines, 3,500 still remained twenty five years later.

After the Great War, initial development of the FT led to the NC tank of 1922-27 which remained at the development stage in France but which was exported, mainly to Japan. Then, with improved armour and an extra crew member — radio operator —, this light new model Renault tank became the D 1 (160 were made) armed with a turret mounted 47, reaching the end of its evolution in the form of the twenty metric ton D 2 (100 were made) with 40 mm armour. Thus, the FT variants became, imperceptibly, powerful tanks, even rivals to the Char B battle tank, wanted by General Estienne, and which would impose itself, too late, as the main combat tank.

The Char B, designed in 1921, seeing the light of day in the form of several different prototypes in 1924, and finding its definitive outer appearance 10 years later, with a twin armament of a body mounted 75 mm gun and a turret mounted 47 mm anti tank gun. Exceeding 31 metric tons and with 60 mm armour, the Char B 1 bis (369 were made plus 31 lesser armoured B 1), was the most powerful combat vehicle in the West in 1940. This tank constituted the framework of the Divisions Cuirassées (1re, 2e, 3e and 4e DCr) formed between January and May 1940.

As for the light tanks, the real successors to the FT in its category (two men) were the result of a 1933 programme. Three models were adopted and mass produced, the Renault R 35 (approximately 1,680 were made, including the R 40 version), the Hotchkiss H 35 (400 were made)

then the H 39 (approximately 800 were made) and the FCM 36 (100 were made), the latter, being equipped with a diesel engine. The R 35 was also exported to Poland, Rumania, Turkey and Yugoslavia.

At the same time, the French cavalry, totally distinct from the Chars de Combat (these were part of the infantry), became mechanised and, from these 1931-32 programmes, were born several families of armoured vehicle. Those that belonged to the tanks (that is to say armoured vehicles with integrated tracks and a turret) were the small reconnaissance machine gun carriers, the AMR 33 and Renault 35, similar to the PzKpfW I, and above all, the combat machine gun carriers, the three man AMC 34 and Renault 35 which were in fact veritable fast tanks.

The AMC programme finally resulted in the remarkable "char de cavalerie", the 20 metric ton Somua S 35 (approximately 430 were made), the flagship of the French mechanised cavalry. On May 10th, 1940, the cavalry had three mechanised light divisions (1re, 2e and 3e DLM), which were, despite their name, of a composition that was very close to that of the German Panzerdivisions. Besides, they preceded the Germans, as the idea of the DLM dated from 1933. With numbers equivalent to those of the Germans in May 1940, and with superior armour and often a more powerful armament also, the French tanks suffered from a variety of problems; deployment in conditions that were not forecast (scattered, including divisional tanks that were "requisitioned" by higher authorities ignorant of their use), unworkable radios or none at all, fighting whilst retreating where tanks that had simply run out of petrol could not be saved.

Despite the heroism and the countless brilliant actions of the crews, French tanks faded into the campaign of May-June 1940, not without undertaking a certain number of massed engagements, like at Hannut (2e and 3e DLM against the 3. and 4. PzD.) which was the first great tank battle of the Second World War.

After 1940, the French army reorganised overseas, initially using a mixed materiel of French origin for the troops that remained in the Empire, or British for the Free French forces. Later, all these elements joined together and completely re-equipped with new American materiel (Stuart, Sherman, M 10). Three large French armoured units took part in the liberation, the 1er, 2e and 5e DB (divisions blindées/Armoured Divisions).

During this time, work resumed in the research department, to such an extent that the prototype of the transitional tank, ARL 44 (drawn up in November 1944), a curious mix of a Char B with a Tiger II turret, came out only a few months after the end of the Second World War.

Gun equipped tank No. 68097 belonging to the 343ᵉ CACC (ex-2ᵉ Compagnie of the 11ᵉ BCC Alpin), attached to the 2ᵉ Division légère de chasseurs in April 1940, destined to operate in Norway. The wide white stripe around the turret is characteristic of the 11ᵉ BCC. On the other hand, the turret ace symbol (a club here for the 1st platoon) was that of the 343ᵉ CACC.

FT tank of an unidentified French unit. This one is machine gun tank. A very great number of these totally obsolete tanks were in existence and still made up, notably, eight battalions of the army in May 1940. However, the Hotchkiss 8 mm machine gun version now only existed with certain tanks of territorial units. In the BCC, this machine gun had been replaced by the 7.5 mm MAC 31.

Renault FT tank "Le Champagne" No. 73160 of a protection platoon guarding Port-Lyautey airport (Casablanca, Morocco) Photographed just after November 8th by the Americans. It came from one of the FT combat tank battalions in North Africa in 1939-40:
62ᵉ (one company), 64ᵉ or 66ᵉ.

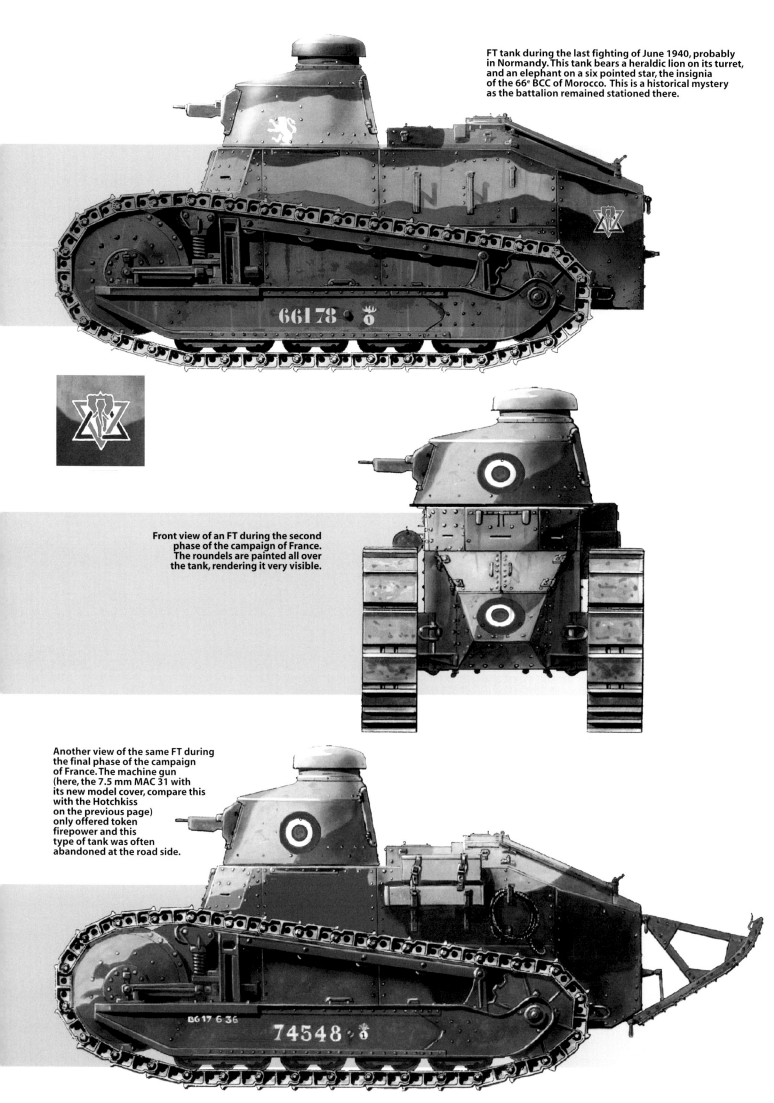

FT tank during the last fighting of June 1940, probably in Normandy. This tank bears a heraldic lion on its turret, and an elephant on a six pointed star, the insignia of the 66ᵉ BCC of Morocco. This is a historical mystery as the battalion remained stationed there.

66178

Front view of an FT during the second phase of the campaign of France. The roundels are painted all over the tank, rendering it very visible.

Another view of the same FT during the final phase of the campaign of France. The machine gun (here, the 7.5 mm MAC 31 with its new model cover, compare this with the Hotchkiss on the previous page) only offered token firepower and this type of tank was often abandoned at the road side.

BG 17 6 36   74548

Profile of the
super heavy
FCM 2C tank "Picardie"
in the 1920s, whilst in service
with the 3ᵉ battalion of the 551ᵉ RCC.
At this period, its lateral identification was just a large number 2
at the front of the armour. During the 1930s, the numbers used,
1 to 10, were replaced by the same units preceded
by the number nine (except the 10, which became 90).

No. 90 "Poitou", the tank
of Lieutenant Voillaum
(1ʳᵉ compagnie of the 51ᵉ BCC)
bore for a brief period during
the winter of 1939-40, this as sinister
as it is spectacular emblem, n
ormally used by those
"on the other side".
General Bruneau, who at this time
commanded the tanks
of the IIIᵉ Armée, saw this emblem
during an inspection and ordered
it to be removed.

FCM 2C No. 99 "Champagne", repainted in a three tone
camouflage in 1940 along with all the other tanks of this type of the 51ᵉ BCC.
On the other hand, the somewhat strange scheme used, seems specific
to this tank. Out of the six tanks taken by the Germans on the railway near
the village of Meuse, No. 99 was the only one whose exterior was intact.
It was transported to Germany then captured by the Russians,
what happened to it afterwards is unknown.

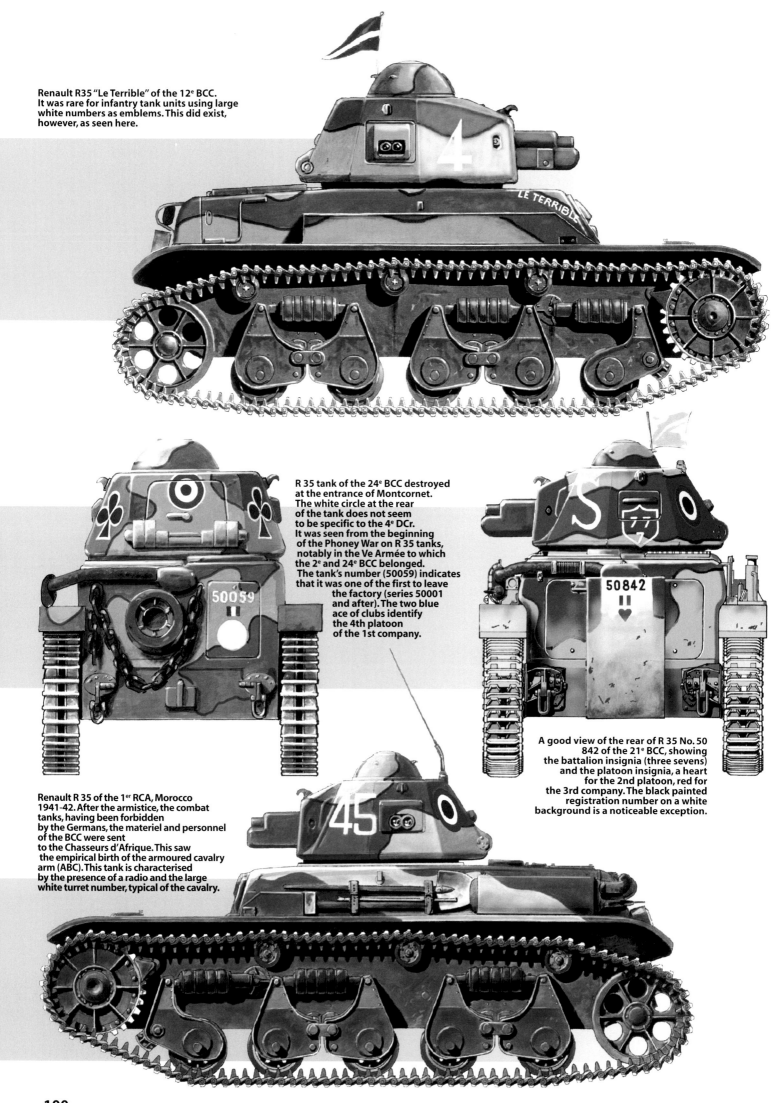

Renault R35 "Le Terrible" of the 12ᵉ BCC. It was rare for infantry tank units using large white numbers as emblems. This did exist, however, as seen here.

R 35 tank of the 24ᵉ BCC destroyed at the entrance of Montcornet. The white circle at the rear of the tank does not seem to be specific to the 4ᵉ DCr. It was seen from the beginning of the Phoney War on R 35 tanks, notably in the Ve Armée to which the 2ᵉ and 24ᵉ BCC belonged. The tank's number (50059) indicates that it was one of the first to leave the factory (series 50001 and after). The two blue ace of clubs identify the 4th platoon of the 1st company.

A good view of the rear of R 35 No. 50 842 of the 21ᵉ BCC, showing the battalion insignia (three sevens) and the platoon insignia, a heart for the 2nd platoon, red for the 3rd company. The black painted registration number on a white background is a noticeable exception.

Renault R 35 of the 1ᵉʳ RCA, Morocco 1941-42. After the armistice, the combat tanks, having been forbidden by the Germans, the materiel and personnel of the BCC were sent to the Chasseurs d'Afrique. This saw the empirical birth of the armoured cavalry arm (ABC). This tank is characterised by the presence of a radio and the large white turret number, typical of the cavalry.

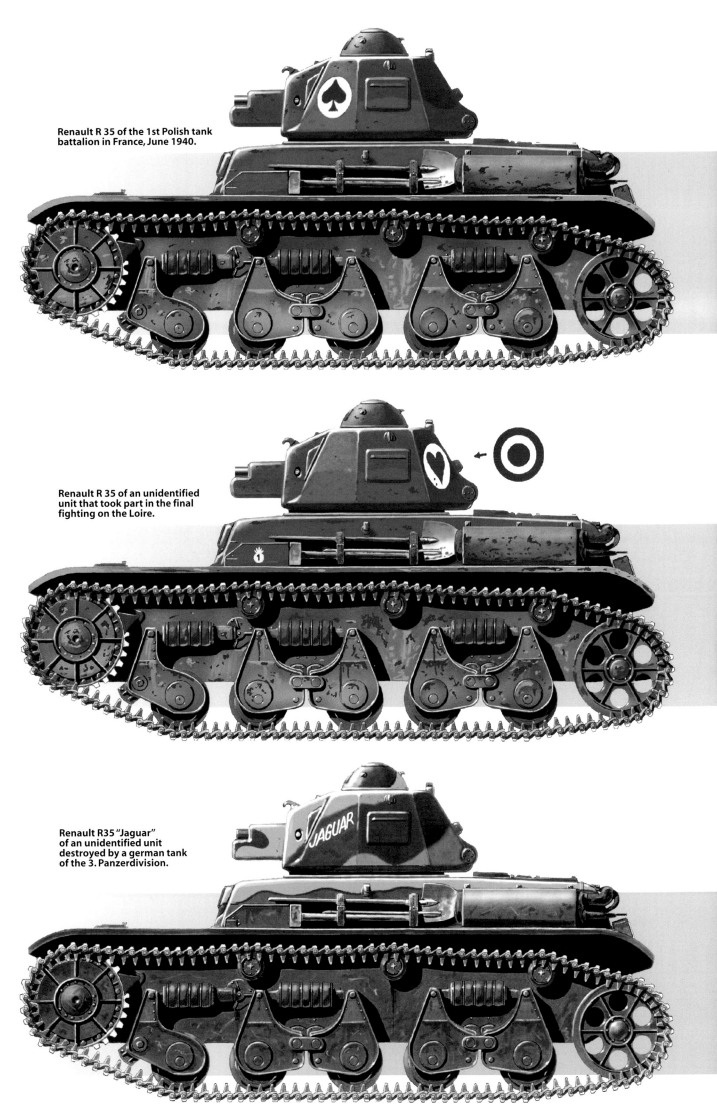

Renault R 35 of the 1st Polish tank battalion in France, June 1940.

Renault R 35 of an unidentified unit that took part in the final fighting on the Loire.

Renault R35 "Jaguar" of an unidentified unit destroyed by a german tank of the 3. Panzerdivision.

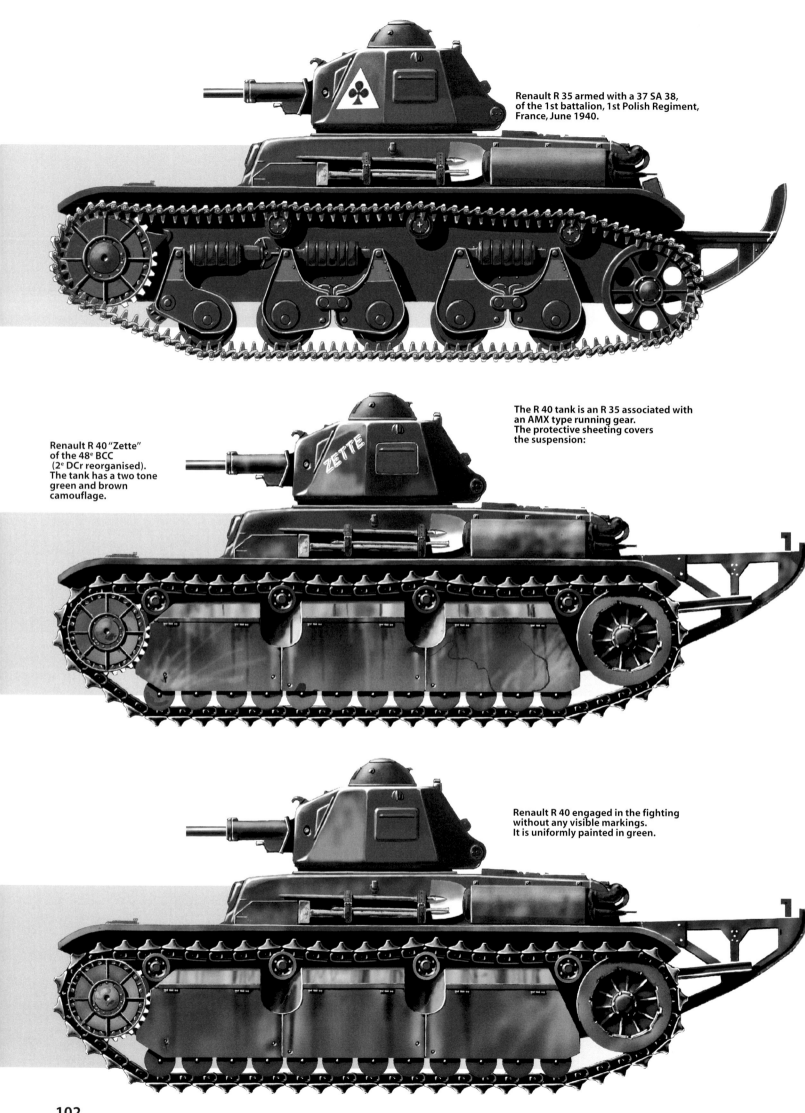

Renault R 35 armed with a 37 SA 38,
of the 1st battalion, 1st Polish Regiment,
France, June 1940.

The R 40 tank is an R 35 associated with
an AMX type running gear.
The protective sheeting covers
the suspension:

Renault R 40 "Zette"
of the 48ᵉ BCC
(2ᵉ DCr reorganised).
The tank has a two tone
green and brown
camouflage.

Renault R 40 engaged in the fighting
without any visible markings.
It is uniformly painted in green.

Hotchkiss H 35 No. 40 067 of the 4ᵉ Cuirassiers, a unit which is easily identified thanks to its coat of arms representing Joan of Arc. This tank, with its radio, is that of the platoon commander.

Number "5" (No. 40 009) is the 5th tank of the 1st platoon.

Hotchkiss H 35 of the 4ᵉ Cuirassiers (1ʳᵉ DLM). Each tank bears a different number, issued later. The 4 is therefore the 4th tank of the 1st platoon.

H 35 of the 2ᵉ escadron of the 29ᵉ Dragons (2ᵉ DLM). The tanks in this division had a dual system of identification: a large white cavalry number and the platoon ace (platoon aces were created for the "chars de combat").

The Hotchkiss H 35 immediately differentiates itself from its successor, the H 39, by its steeply sloping engine hood at the rear. This houses a small 75 horsepower engine, making it the lowest powered "modern" French tank. The cavalry received 292 tanks of the 400 H 35s that were made.

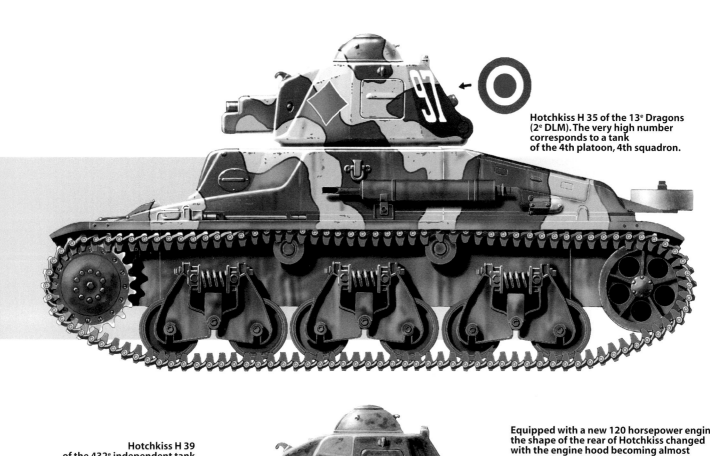

Hotchkiss H 35 of the 13e Dragons (2e DLM). The very high number corresponds to a tank of the 4th platoon, 4th squadron.

Hotchkiss H 39 of the 432e independent tank company. Loaded onto ships at Brest, this company fought at Narvik. Later shipped to Great Britain, the tanks and crews joined the Free French.

Equipped with a new 120 horsepower engine, the shape of the rear of Hotchkiss changed with the engine hood becoming almost square. The tank, now a "H 39", was now capable of 36 kph. It was almost as fast as the Somua, but less powerful.

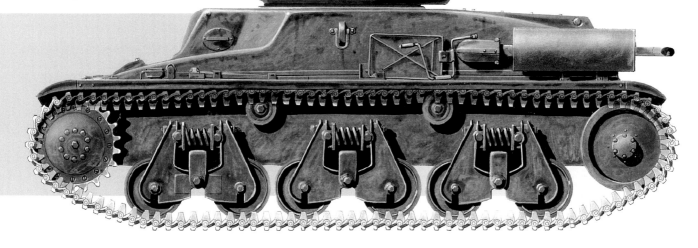

The "Doryphore" is a Hotchkiss H 39 from an unidentified cavalry squadron. It has the new trench crossing tail but has not received the 37 SA 38 gun.

I 40797

Hotchkiss H 39 No. 40 797, named "La Louvière", belonging to the 1er Cuirassiers (3e DLM).

I 40692

Hotchkiss H 39 No. 40 692 with a large white turret "20".

This Hotchkiss H 39 light tank was photographed in the Dunkirk region. This type of turret insignia, where the four aces designate the captain commanding the company, was definitely seen in the 14e BCC (2e DCr), but other light battalions cannot be excluded (1re to 2e DCr). The presumed blue colour is that of the 2nd company.

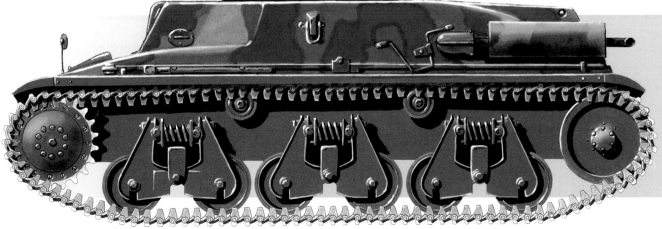

This Hotchkiss H 39 of the 7ᵉ Cuirassiers, de Langle de Cary group (large white 61, number 40 914), was knocked out south of the Somme on June 6th, 1940. The tanks of this unit bore large white numbers on the turret, but were not always of the same shape, being sometimes rounded, sometimes squared.

Hotchkiss H 39 number "62" of the 7ᵉ Cuirassiers, de Langle de Cary group. This combat regiment was due to, along with its namesake, the 3ᵉ Cuirassiers (combat), the 10ᵉ Cuirassiers (reconnaissance) and the 7ᵉ Régiment de Dragons Portés (mechanised), to form the future 4ᵉ DLM, events, however, meant that they would be divided up, the last three joined the 4ᵉ DCr of Colonel de Gaulle.

This Hotchkiss H 39 also belonged to the 3rd squadron of the 7ᵉ Cuirassiers. It was probably one of the five tanks of the 3rd platoon. The factory camouflage is standard to Hotchkiss, made up of two tones of very merged olive green and brown. Of all the tanks lost by the 3/7ᵉ Cuirassiers, 64 was the most photographed. In front of it, the Germans had made a temporary grave marked with a cross and five helmets.

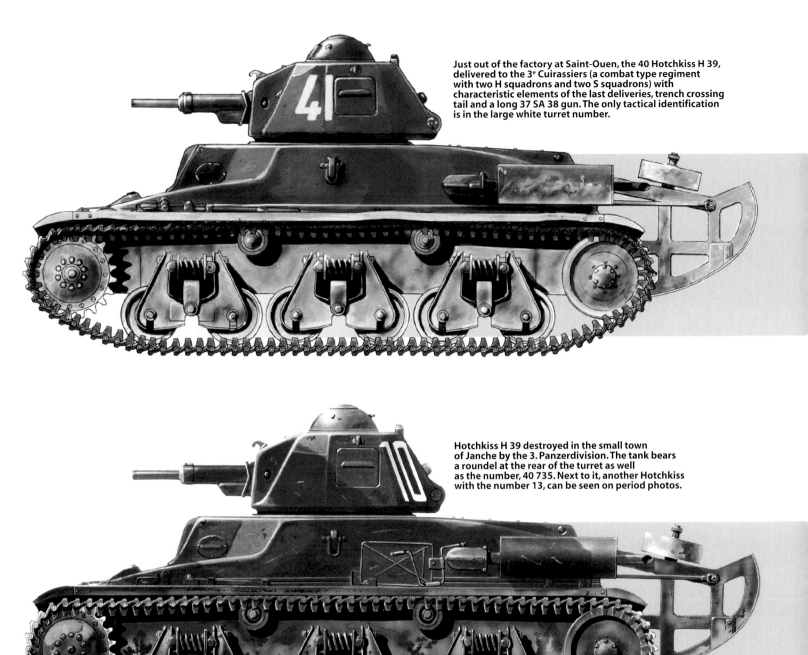

Just out of the factory at Saint-Ouen, the 40 Hotchkiss H 39, delivered to the 3ᵉ Cuirassiers (a combat type regiment with two H squadrons and two S squadrons) with characteristic elements of the last deliveries, trench crossing tail and a long 37 SA 38 gun. The only tactical identification is in the large white turret number.

Hotchkiss H 39 destroyed in the small town of Janche by the 3. Panzerdivision. The tank bears a roundel at the rear of the turret as well as the number, 40 735. Next to it, another Hotchkiss with the number 13, can be seen on period photos.

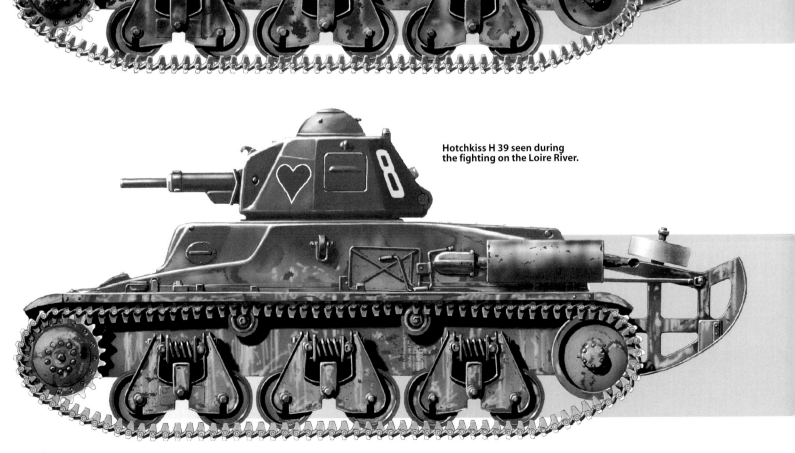

Hotchkiss H 39 seen during the fighting on the Loire River.

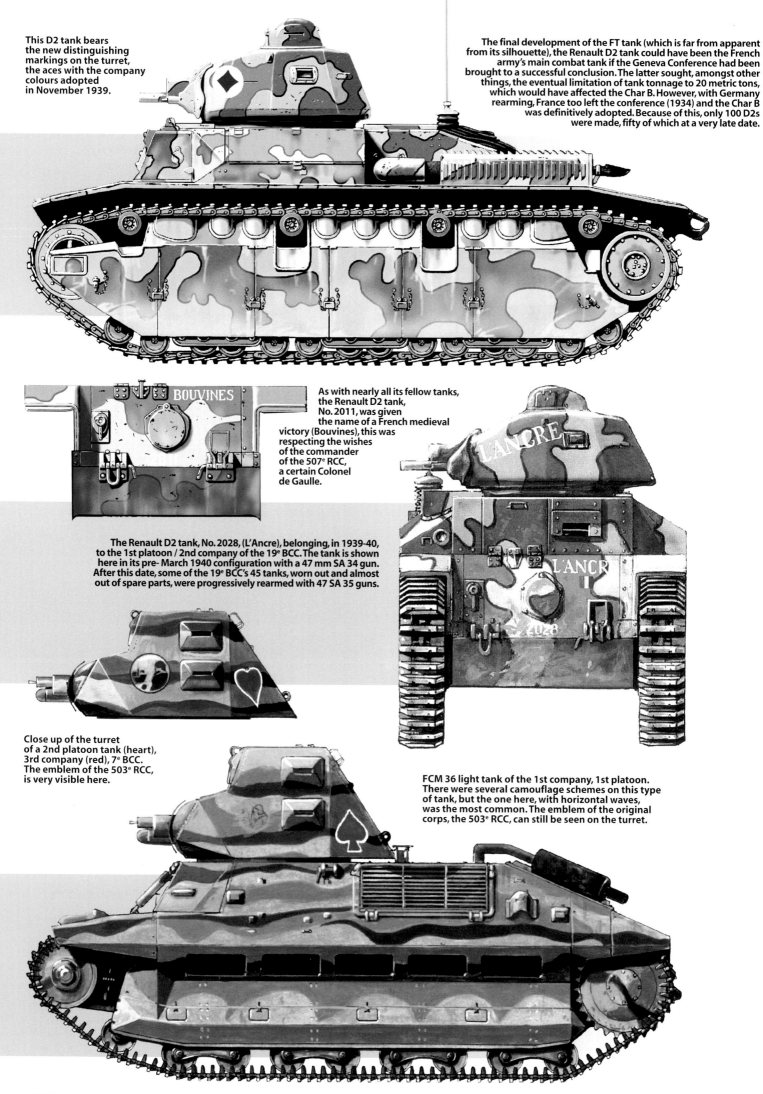

This D2 tank bears the new distinguishing markings on the turret, the aces with the company colours adopted in November 1939.

The final development of the FT tank (which is far from apparent from its silhouette), the Renault D2 tank could have been the French army's main combat tank if the Geneva Conference had been brought to a successful conclusion. The latter sought, amongst other things, the eventual limitation of tank tonnage to 20 metric tons, which would have affected the Char B. However, with Germany rearming, France too left the conference (1934) and the Char B was definitively adopted. Because of this, only 100 D2s were made, fifty of which at a very late date.

As with nearly all its fellow tanks, the Renault D2 tank, No. 2011, was given the name of a French medieval victory (Bouvines), this was respecting the wishes of the commander of the 507e RCC, a certain Colonel de Gaulle.

The Renault D2 tank, No. 2028, (L'Ancre), belonging, in 1939-40, to the 1st platoon / 2nd company of the 19e BCC. The tank is shown here in its pre- March 1940 configuration with a 47 mm SA 34 gun. After this date, some of the 19e BCC's 45 tanks, worn out and almost out of spare parts, were progressively rearmed with 47 SA 35 guns.

Close up of the turret of a 2nd platoon tank (heart), 3rd company (red), 7e BCC. The emblem of the 503e RCC, is very visible here.

FCM 36 light tank of the 1st company, 1st platoon. There were several camouflage schemes on this type of tank, but the one here, with horizontal waves, was the most common. The emblem of the original corps, the 503e RCC, can still be seen on the turret.

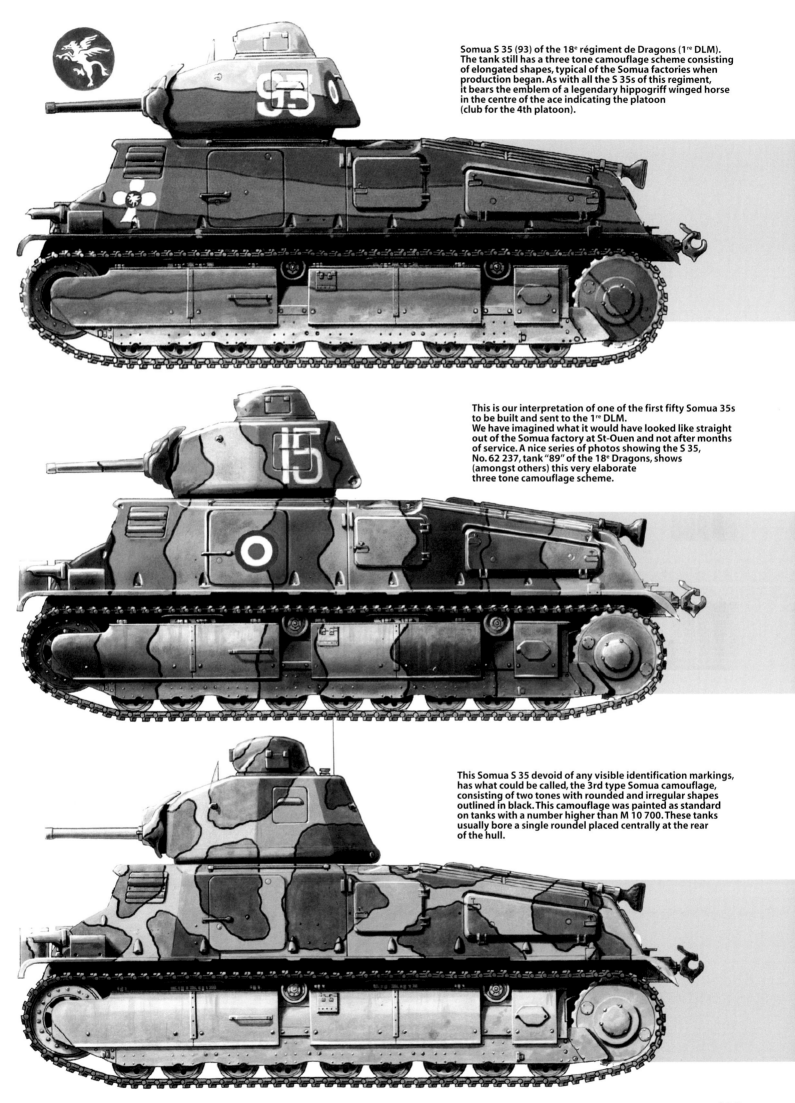

Somua S 35 (93) of the 18ᵉ régiment de Dragons (1ʳᵉ DLM).
The tank still has a three tone camouflage scheme consisting of elongated shapes, typical of the Somua factories when production began. As with all the S 35s of this regiment, it bears the emblem of a legendary hippogriff winged horse in the centre of the ace indicating the platoon (club for the 4th platoon).

This is our interpretation of one of the first fifty Somua 35s to be built and sent to the 1ʳᵉ DLM.
We have imagined what it would have looked like straight out of the Somua factory at St-Ouen and not after months of service. A nice series of photos showing the S 35, No. 62 237, tank "89" of the 18ᵉ Dragons, shows (amongst others) this very elaborate three tone camouflage scheme.

This Somua S 35 devoid of any visible identification markings, has what could be called, the 3rd type Somua camouflage, consisting of two tones with rounded and irregular shapes outlined in black. This camouflage was painted as standard on tanks with a number higher than M 10 700. These tanks usually bore a single roundel placed centrally at the rear of the hull.

B1 No. 105 "Strasburg", 1940. The B1 is different from the B1 bis in a certain number of details not shown here. The most obvious is the 47 SA 34 gun.

B1 No. 132 "Poitou", 1940. This tank was one of the 15 machines of this type that, after having left the 37ᵉ BCC (this unit having received new B1 bis tanks), went on campaign within various "unités de marche". The "Poitou" was the personal tank of Lieutenant Gaudet who, at Rethel, gathered together enough tanks to form a large company in order to fight within General de Lattre de Tassigny's 14ᵉ DI. The "Poitou" has the "longitudinal" camouflage typical of tanks assembled by the FCMs of La Seyne-sur-Mer.

B1 bis No. 217 "Cantal" of the 15ᵉ BCC (2ᵉ DCr). This tank belonged to the battalion's 2nd compnay, the only one of the three to have large white numbers on its 10 tanks. The 2nd company is also recognisable by the large white square on the side of the tank. As for the platoon, identified by its large ace of diamonds, it comprised tanks 5, 7 and 8.

B1 bis No. 252 "Flamberge" of the 1st platoon, 2nd company of the 15ᵉ BCC (2ᵉ DCr), 1940. On the right, the tank's number is painted on the side door. This tank was sent to a variety of units part of the 8ᵉ BCC, and was sent to the 15ᵉ on April 18th, 1940. It later found itself at Rethel in Gaudet's company from May 18th. The roundel appeared on the Char B in the second half of the campaign.

B1 bis No. 289 "Brazzaville" of the 1st platoon, 3rd company, 28e BCC (1re DCr), May 1940. In this battalion, apart from the ace, a large turret number (radio code) identifies each platoon. The dot, placed in front of or behind the letter, indicates the two subordinate tanks (the platoon leader's tank has no dot). This rather complex system was used again by the battalion when it reformed with new tanks at the end of May.

B1 bis No. 330 "Cher" of the 1st platoon, 1st company, 37e BCC (1re DCr), 1940. One particularity of this battalion was that it bore the tank's name on both sides of the turret, a reminder of the B1 period. Furthermore, the codes and markings of the 37e BCC are complete, the large outlined square identifies the 1st company, also shown by the blue ace, being here a spade (1st platoon). The radio code, M, also indicates this platoon because with the 1re DCr, the 37e BCC after the 28e which used the first letters of the alphabet.

B1 bis No. 339 "Aisne" of the 1st platoon, 2nd company, 4e BCC (3e DCr), May 1940. In this battalion, the companies are identified by a long wavy blue stripe along the turret and the two symbols on either side of the rear of the turret, in a white outlined quadrilateral.

B1 bis "Chanzy" of the 3rd platoon, 2nd company, 28e BCC, reconstituted (1reDCr), June 1940. The presence of the name on the side is a rarity confirmed by a photograph. On the other hand, the right door is pure supposition based on other known examples.

"Valmy", M3A3 No. 420406
of the 1st platoon,
4th company, 501ᵉ RCC.

M5A1, commander
of the 1st platoon, 1st squadron,
2ᵉ Cuirassiers 1ʳᵉ Division Blindée
(1st armoured Division).

M3A3 light tank of the 3rd platoon,
1st squadron RICM, during the fighting
in Toulon, August 1944. The tanks bears
all the markings in use at this time,
registration number 420710,
code TQM MES 41221 in green,
olive green and fawn squadron stripes,
national flag and identification star.

M4 Sherman of the 3rd squadron, 12e Cuirassiers. This tank bears the name of a 1918 battle.

M4 Sherman of the 3rd company, 501e combat tank regiment (RCC). Notre-Dame-de-Lorette is the name of a famous battle in 1914-15.

M4 Sherman, 3rd platoon, 12e Régiment de Chasseurs d'Afrique (African Light Cavalry).

Commonwealth

The British were the first to introduce the notion of Tank into everyday vocabulary.

This name became the very symbol of this weapon, the rhombus, used tactically by the Germans.

The first massive use of tanks by the British saw them achieve a great breakthrough and came as an unpleasant surprise to the Germans. The attack could have resulted in a disaster for the German Army, were it not for the artillery, some of whose guns fired over open sights on the tanks ; the discipline and tenacity of the German soldier and, above all, the fact that the British infantry did not manage to follow the tanks and mop up, due to isolated areas of resistance. Admittedly, even if most of the ground taken was later retaken, a new era, that the German High Command had not seen coming, had begun. This British innovation saw its development slow down a little after the Great War. Partly following the example of the FT-17, the British developed suspension systems and tanks with turrets that were lighter than the Mark I-IV or Whippet. However, even if prototypes of huge tanks were made in the inter war period, one can only note a certain stagnation in the research department-led development programmes. Two models were, however, successfully exported, the Carette, a small tank mounted on a Carden-Loyd system and of course, the Vickers 6 Ton, the licence of which was sold to many countries including China, Finland, the Soviet Union, Poland and so on. The "tank market" was flooded with this model, along with the machine gun of the same name. But it would seem that Britain rested on its laurels, as apart from the Matilda, and at a push, the Valentine, nothing of much interest appeared at this time.

After war was declared on Germany on September 3rd, 1939, Britain, sure of its geographical position of strength, did not feel that it needed to make a serious effort in the development of tanks. Isolated from the continent and with its colonies very far from Germany, only aircraft and ships were really successfully developed, as was later seen.

In May 1940, the British realised the seriousness of the situation. The B.E.F. suffered a terrible defeat in the campaign of France, incapable, with its 200,000 men, of stopping the Germans in its sector. It was only a miracle that allowed some of the B.E.F. to escape from France ; the result was, however, that they left all their heavy materiel behind.

Against the Italians in the African deserts, the Matilda was known as the 'Queen of the desert', but this was due to its excellent armour and the weakness of the Italians and in no way because of its ballistic capability, and even less in its tactical deployment. The other A 9 or A 10 tanks revealed themselves to be barely superior to those of the Italians apart from the awful M 39). Matilda's flattering nickname disappeared with the arrival of the Panzers. The latter, although less numerous, were better employed. The 88 mm guns fired over open sights took a great toll on British tanks.

It was only with the massive arrival of American materiel, initially with the Stuart and Grant, then the Sherman, that the British armoured forces began to regain their strength, even taking up the offensive against an enemy that did not have much heavy materiel. However, the first tanks to be delivered were far from satisfactory, as the Grant, for example, did not have any anti tank shells for its 75 mm gun and had to use captured German shells that were modified to their needs. Luckily, this situation did not last long and the situation was rectified. At the same time, the British developed a new heavy tank, the Churchill, a tank that first went into action at Dieppe in the summer of 1942, an operation that ended in fiasco. This operation revealed to the Germans the secrets of this latest British tank and they were not very impressed with what they saw. The North African campaign ended with a German defeat at the hands of the Allies in May 1943. At this time, the 8th Army was a solid and powerful force, even if the majority of its materiel was American. The British continued to develop their own tanks, such as the Cromwell, mounted on a Christie type chassis that had proved itself with the Cruiser and Crusader, tanks that had thin armour and a weak armament. The Cromwell had the same disadvantages as the Tiger I with its straight-sided armoured plating, but with armour that was no comparison and a gun that lacked firepower.

The improved version, the Comet, was the forerunner of the legendary Centurion. The latter could not be completed before the end of the war. But one should not forget British ingenuity, with the improvisation and creation of the formidable Firefly, built on a Sherman chassis. This tank was armed with the powerful 17-pounder gun that was more or less equivalent to the German 88 mm, firing, amongst others, the APDS shell.

The other Commonwealth nations, such as Canada with the RAM and Kangaroo tanks, or Australia with the Sentinel, could not really provide support in the domain of the tank even though they created their own types. On the other hand, their support was decisive to production.

Light Tank Mk VI of the 10th Hussars (the white number on a red square identifies this unit). This regiment belonged to the 2nd Armoured Brigade, part of the 1st Armoured Division. This last version of the Mk VI was armed with two Besa machine guns, one 7.92 mm and the other a 15 mm.

"Wallaby" is an Australian Mark VIb tanks. At the beginning of the war in the Pacific, the Allies only had very weak forces at their disposal to defend New Guinea and even Australia. The latter, had, on paper, an armoured division, but according to the official history, did not have any tanks. Perhaps the Vickers was not considered to be a tank? Their use as reconnaissance vehicles or as a training tank perhaps explains this official claim.

Light Tank Mk VIB of an unidentified unit on the Malta air base. The majority of the vehicles of the island's defence forces were painted in this characteristic way. This tank, T5878, would be later painted in an even more graphic manner.

South African Vickers II still used in North Africa 1940.

Light Tank Mk II B of the 6th Australian Cavalry Division on the Egypt-Libya border, 1940. The tactical value of this tank was very low and its 10 mm armour virtually non existent. The British camouflage, complicated to analyse, was constantly undergoing changes. The base colour is sand yellow, partially covered by strips of a great variety of colours, brown and sky blue were, however, the most commonly used in the western desert.

A Matilda of the 7th RTR.

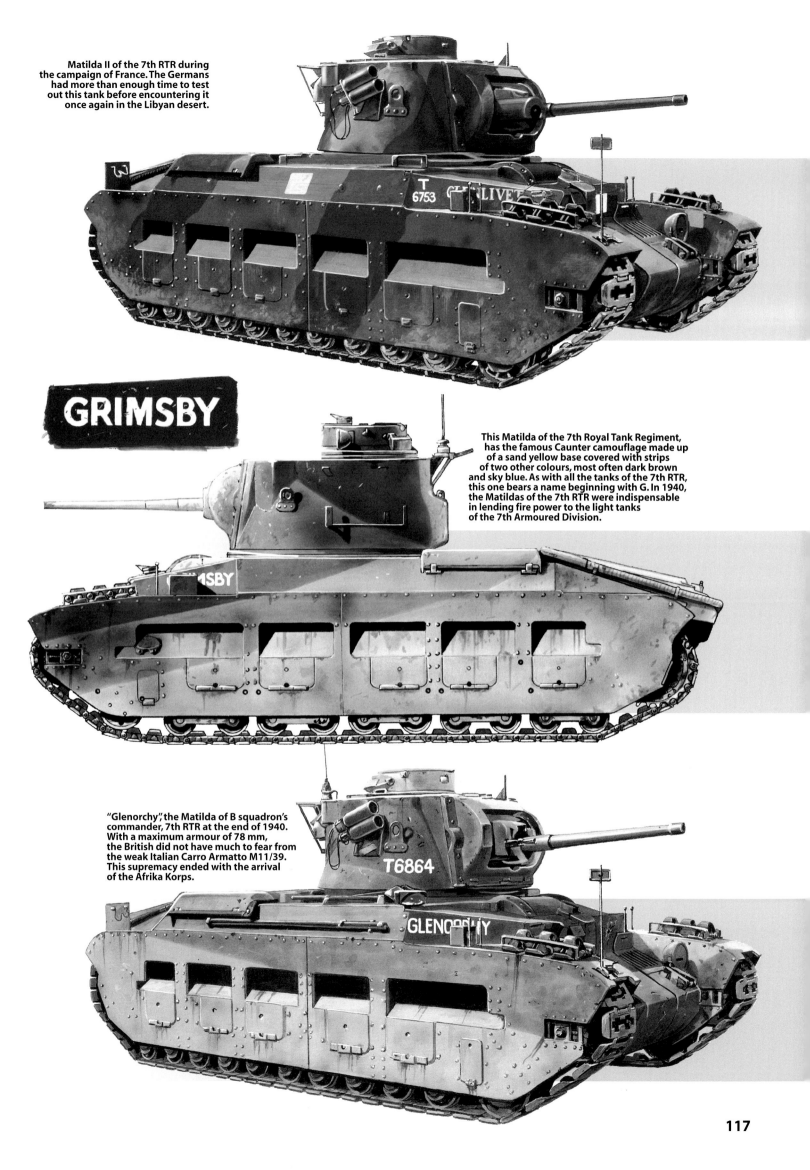

Matilda II of the 7th RTR during the campaign of France. The Germans had more than enough time to test out this tank before encountering it once again in the Libyan desert.

GRIMSBY

This Matilda of the 7th Royal Tank Regiment, has the famous Caunter camouflage made up of a sand yellow base covered with strips of two other colours, most often dark brown and sky blue. As with all the tanks of the 7th RTR, this one bears a name beginning with G. In 1940, the Matildas of the 7th RTR were indispensable in lending fire power to the light tanks of the 7th Armoured Division.

"Glenorchy", the Matilda of B squadron's commander, 7th RTR at the end of 1940. With a maximum armour of 78 mm, the British did not have much to fear from the weak Italian Carro Armatto M11/39. This supremacy ended with the arrival of the Afrika Korps.

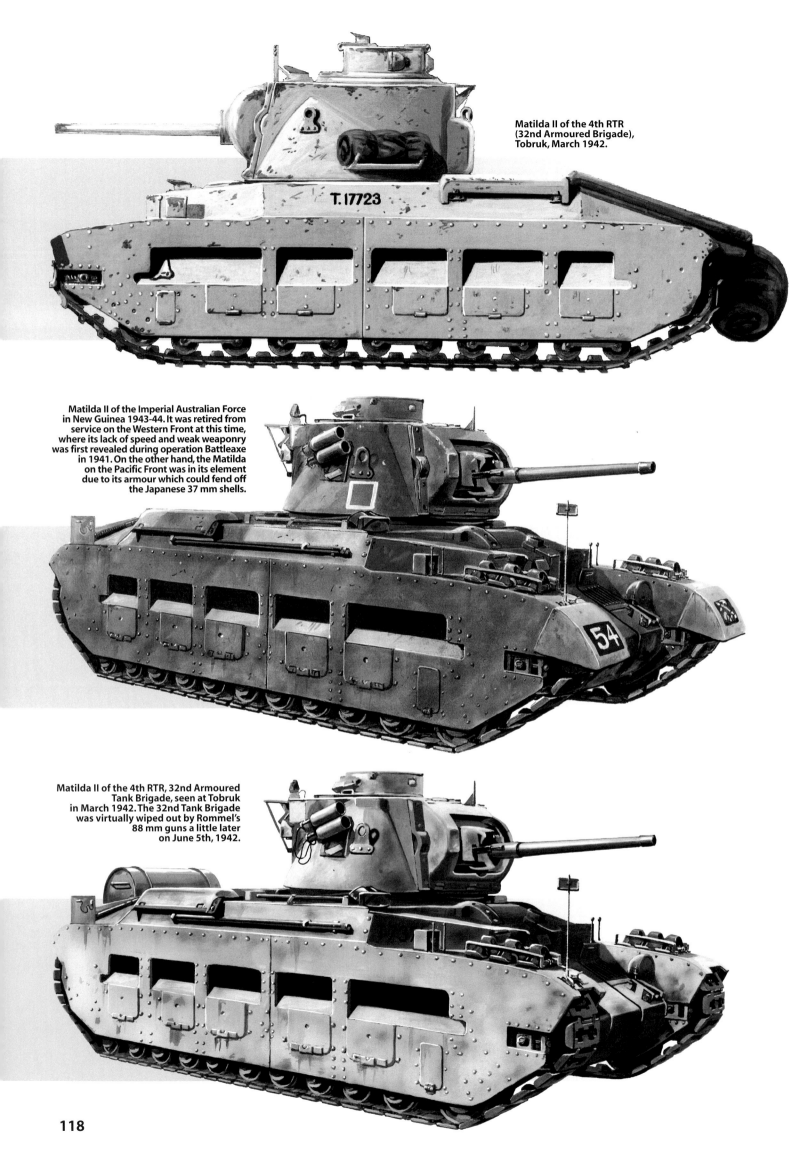

Matilda II of the 4th RTR
(32nd Armoured Brigade),
Tobruk, March 1942.

T.17723

Matilda II of the Imperial Australian Force
in New Guinea 1943-44. It was retired from
service on the Western Front at this time,
where its lack of speed and weak weaponry
was first revealed during operation Battleaxe
in 1941. On the other hand, the Matilda
on the Pacific Front was in its element
due to its armour which could fend off
the Japanese 37 mm shells.

54

Matilda II of the 4th RTR, 32nd Armoured
Tank Brigade, seen at Tobruk
in March 1942. The 32nd Tank Brigade
was virtually wiped out by Rommel's
88 mm guns a little later
on June 5th, 1942.

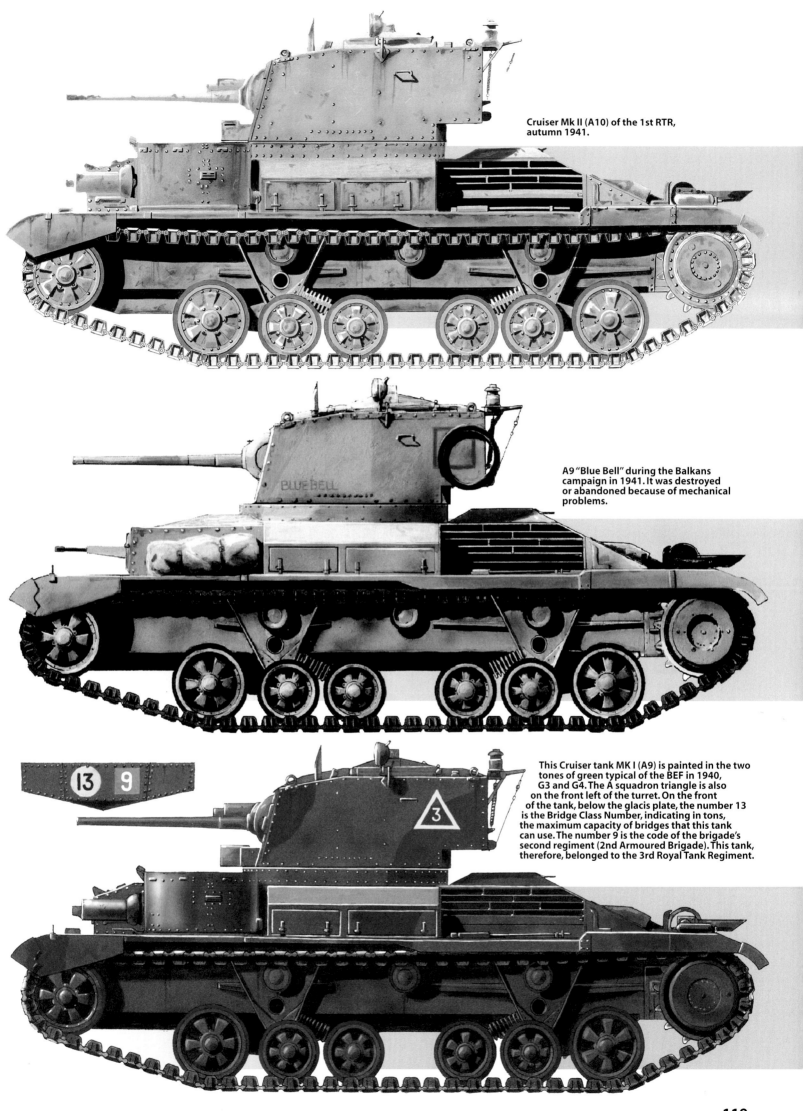

Cruiser Mk II (A10) of the 1st RTR, autumn 1941.

A9 "Blue Bell" during the Balkans campaign in 1941. It was destroyed or abandoned because of mechanical problems.

This Cruiser tank MK I (A9) is painted in the two tones of green typical of the BEF in 1940, G3 and G4. The A squadron triangle is also on the front left of the turret. On the front of the tank, below the glacis plate, the number 13 is the Bridge Class Number, indicating in tons, the maximum capacity of bridges that this tank can use. The number 9 is the code of the brigade's second regiment (2nd Armoured Brigade). This tank, therefore, belonged to the 3rd Royal Tank Regiment.

Cruiser Mk II (A10) of the 2nd Armoured Brigade, 1st Armoured Division. Abbeville sector, France 1940.

14 9

Cruiser Mk II (A10) 7th Armoured Division, 7th Armoured Brigade, 2nd RTR, Libya 1942. The tank was so obsolete at this time that even the Germans did not re-use it.

Cruiser tank Mk IV A (A 13 Mk II) of a B company of a 1st Division RTR. The Mk IV was the most armoured of the Mk III, its thickness going from 14-30 mm at its thickest points. The essential difference between the two types is in the turret's shape, here with V shaped sections.

T 9158

Cruiser Mk IV A (A13)
of the 1st Armoured Division,
1st Armoured Brigade,
near Abbeville in France.

Front view of a Cruiser Mk IV A (A13)
of the 2nd Royal Tank Regiment.

Cruiser Mk IV A (A 13) of the 2nd Royal
Tank Regiment at the end
of November 1941. The old light blue
camouflage can be seen under the coat
of desert yellow paint.

121

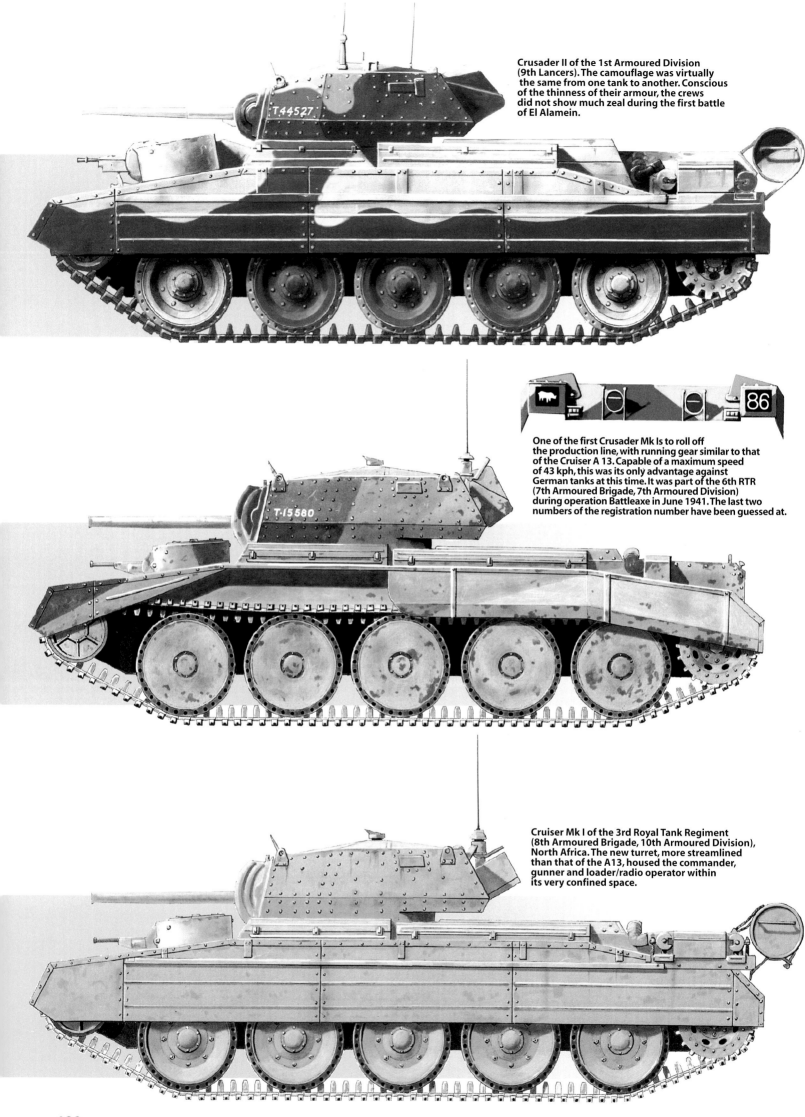

Crusader II of the 1st Armoured Division (9th Lancers). The camouflage was virtually the same from one tank to another. Conscious of the thinness of their armour, the crews did not show much zeal during the first battle of El Alamein.

One of the first Crusader Mk Is to roll off the production line, with running gear similar to that of the Cruiser A 13. Capable of a maximum speed of 43 kph, this was its only advantage against German tanks at this time. It was part of the 6th RTR (7th Armoured Brigade, 7th Armoured Division) during operation Battleaxe in June 1941. The last two numbers of the registration number have been guessed at.

Cruiser Mk I of the 3rd Royal Tank Regiment (8th Armoured Brigade, 10th Armoured Division), North Africa. The new turret, more streamlined than that of the A13, housed the commander, gunner and loader/radio operator within its very confined space.

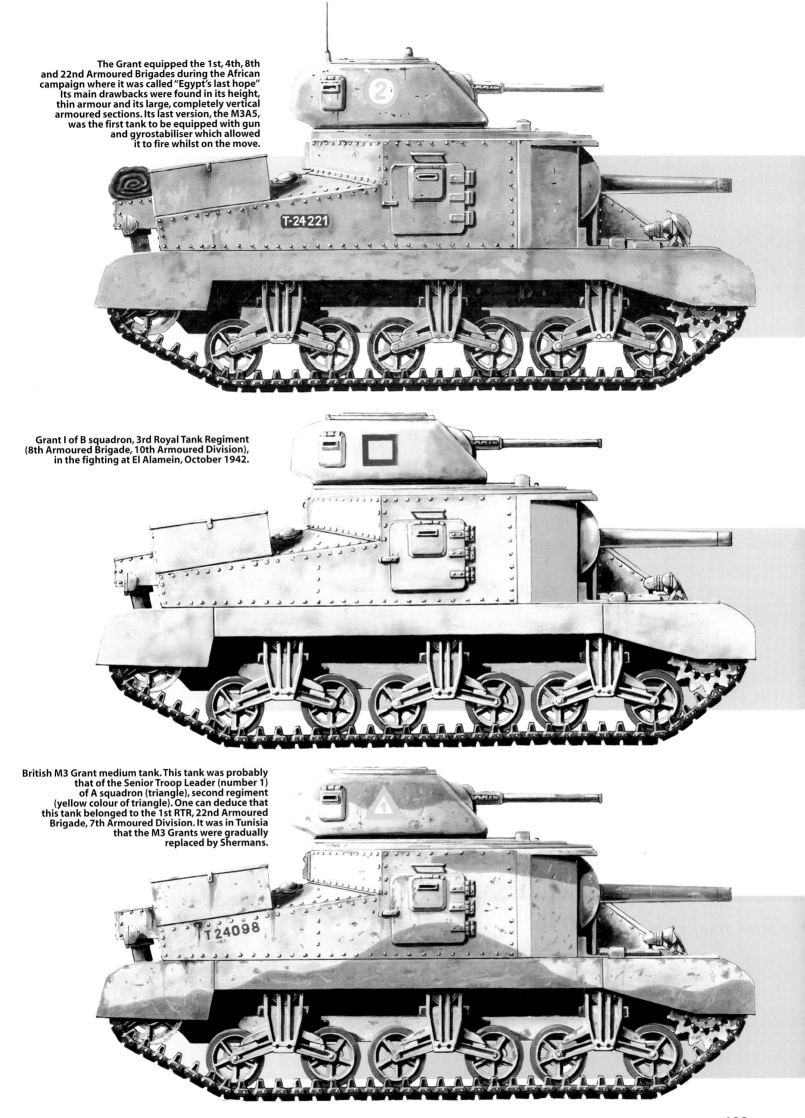

The Grant equipped the 1st, 4th, 8th and 22nd Armoured Brigades during the African campaign where it was called "Egypt's last hope" Its main drawbacks were found in its height, thin armour and its large, completely vertical armoured sections. Its last version, the M3A5, was the first tank to be equipped with gun and gyrostabiliser which allowed it to fire whilst on the move.

Grant I of B squadron, 3rd Royal Tank Regiment (8th Armoured Brigade, 10th Armoured Division), in the fighting at El Alamein, October 1942.

British M3 Grant medium tank. This tank was probably that of the Senior Troop Leader (number 1) of A squadron (triangle), second regiment (yellow colour of triangle). One can deduce that this tank belonged to the 1st RTR, 22nd Armoured Brigade, 7th Armoured Division. It was in Tunisia that the M3 Grants were gradually replaced by Shermans.

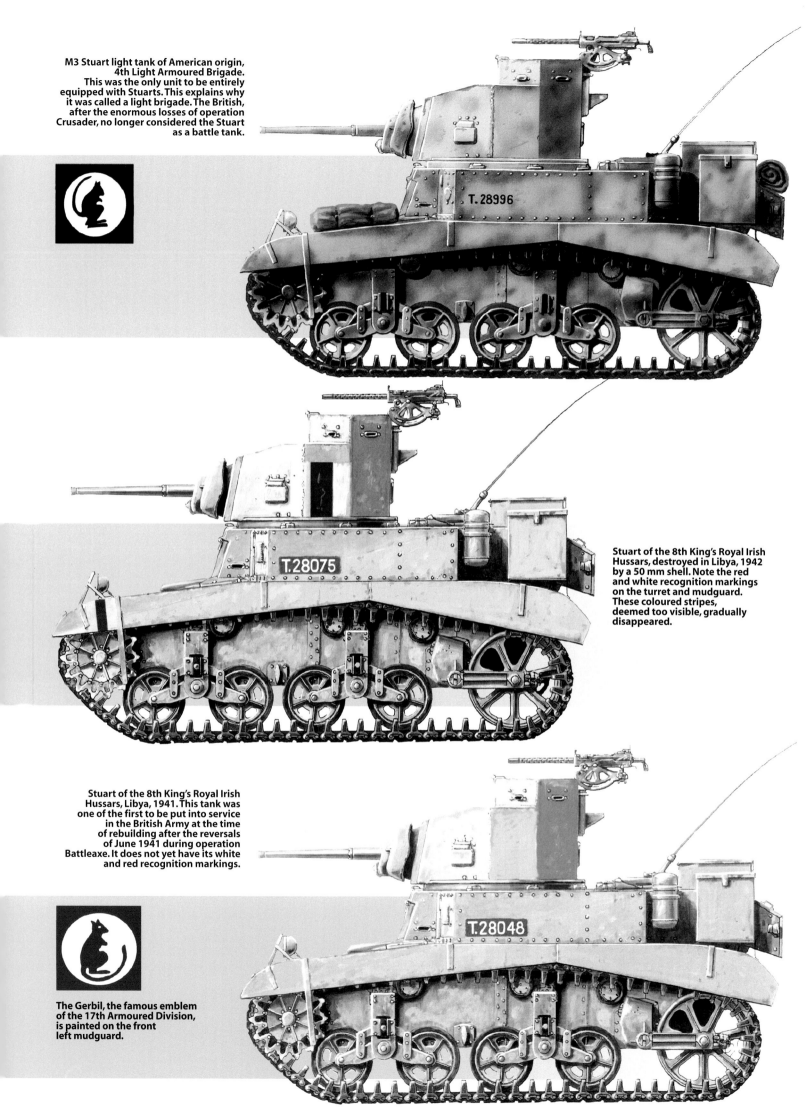

M3 Stuart light tank of American origin, 4th Light Armoured Brigade. This was the only unit to be entirely equipped with Stuarts. This explains why it was called a light brigade. The British, after the enormous losses of operation Crusader, no longer considered the Stuart as a battle tank.

T. 28996

Stuart of the 8th King's Royal Irish Hussars, destroyed in Libya, 1942 by a 50 mm shell. Note the red and white recognition markings on the turret and mudguard. These coloured stripes, deemed too visible, gradually disappeared.

T.28075

Stuart of the 8th King's Royal Irish Hussars, Libya, 1941. This tank was one of the first to be put into service in the British Army at the time of rebuilding after the reversals of June 1941 during operation Battleaxe. It does not yet have its white and red recognition markings.

The Gerbil, the famous emblem of the 17th Armoured Division, is painted on the front left mudguard.

T.28048

124

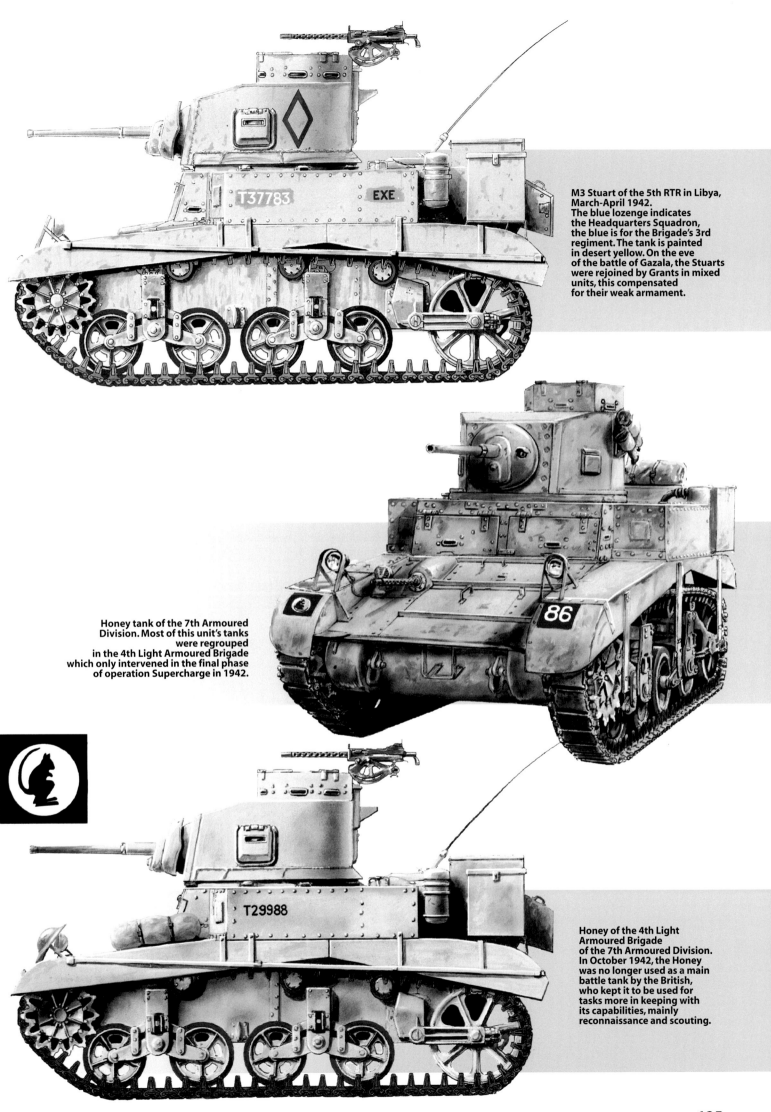

M3 Stuart of the 5th RTR in Libya, March-April 1942.
The blue lozenge indicates the Headquarters Squadron, the blue is for the Brigade's 3rd regiment. The tank is painted in desert yellow. On the eve of the battle of Gazala, the Stuarts were rejoined by Grants in mixed units, this compensated for their weak armament.

Honey tank of the 7th Armoured Division. Most of this unit's tanks were regrouped in the 4th Light Armoured Brigade which only intervened in the final phase of operation Supercharge in 1942.

Honey of the 4th Light Armoured Brigade of the 7th Armoured Division. In October 1942, the Honey was no longer used as a main battle tank by the British, who kept it to be used for tasks more in keeping with its capabilities, mainly reconnaissance and scouting.

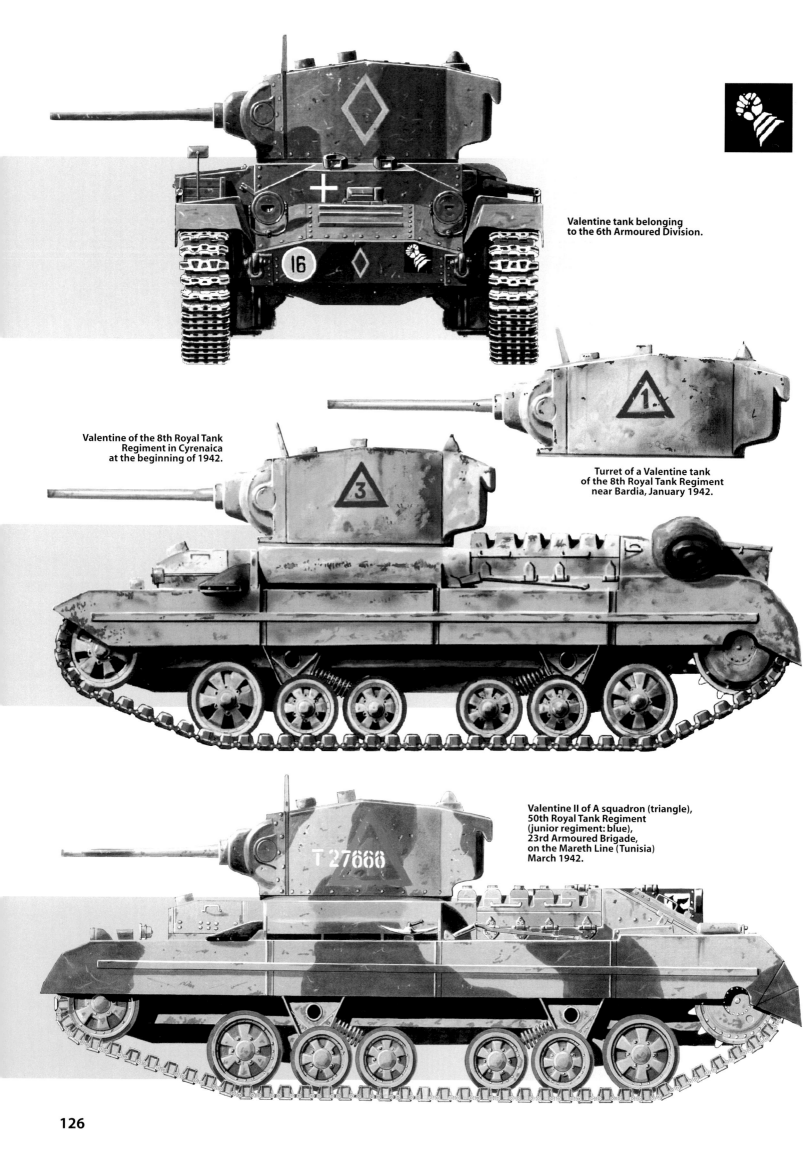

Valentine tank belonging
to the 6th Armoured Division.

Valentine of the 8th Royal Tank
Regiment in Cyrenaica
at the beginning of 1942.

Turret of a Valentine tank
of the 8th Royal Tank Regiment
near Bardia, January 1942.

Valentine II of A squadron (triangle),
50th Royal Tank Regiment
(junior regiment: blue),
23rd Armoured Brigade,
on the Mareth Line (Tunisia)
March 1942.

Valentine Mk VI made
by Canadian Pacific in Montreal.

Valentine II of the 1st Army Tank
Brigade. The Brigade was destroyed
by a German 88 mm shell during
operation Crusader.

Valentine of the 4th RTR, 32nd Armoured
Tank Brigade. The Brigade was completely
wiped out on July 22nd at the battle
of Rouweisat.

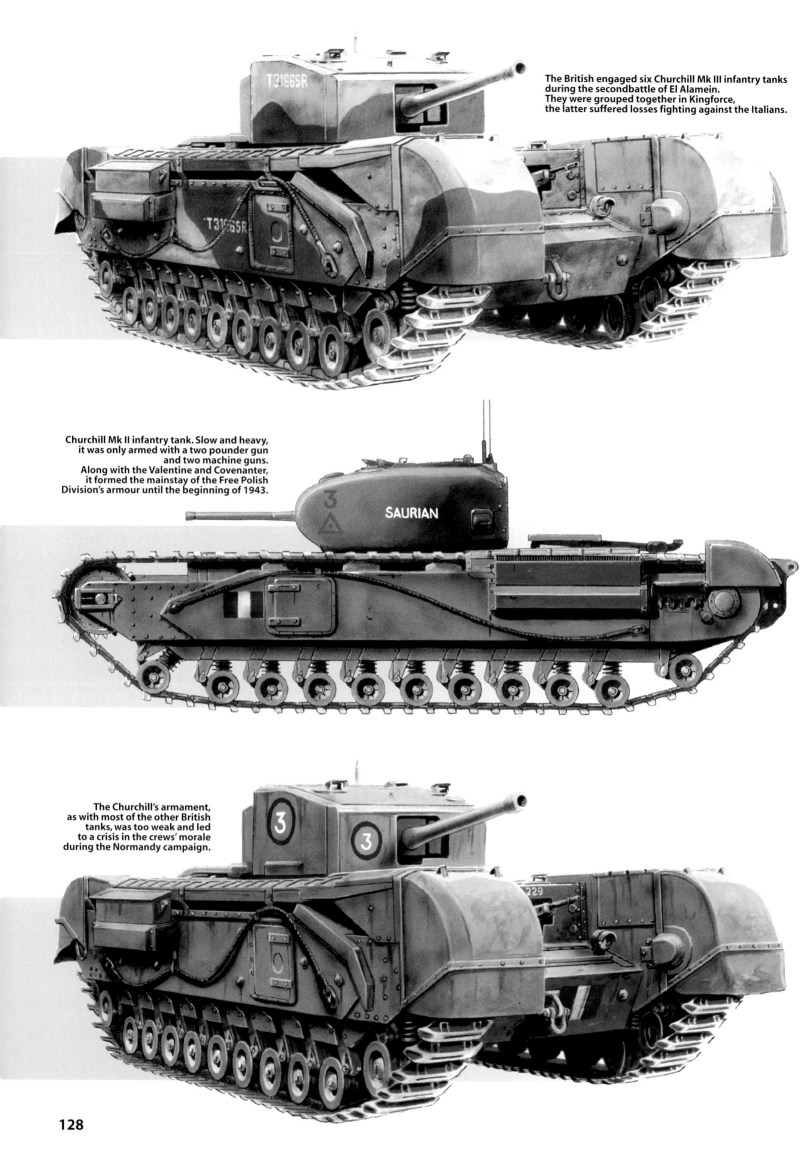

The British engaged six Churchill Mk III infantry tanks
during the secondbattle of El Alamein.
They were grouped together in Kingforce,
the latter suffered losses fighting against the Italians.

Churchill Mk II infantry tank. Slow and heavy,
it was only armed with a two pounder gun
and two machine guns.
Along with the Valentine and Covenanter,
it formed the mainstay of the Free Polish
Division's armour until the beginning of 1943.

SAURIAN

The Churchill's armament,
as with most of the other British
tanks, was too weak and led
to a crisis in the crews' morale
during the Normandy campaign.

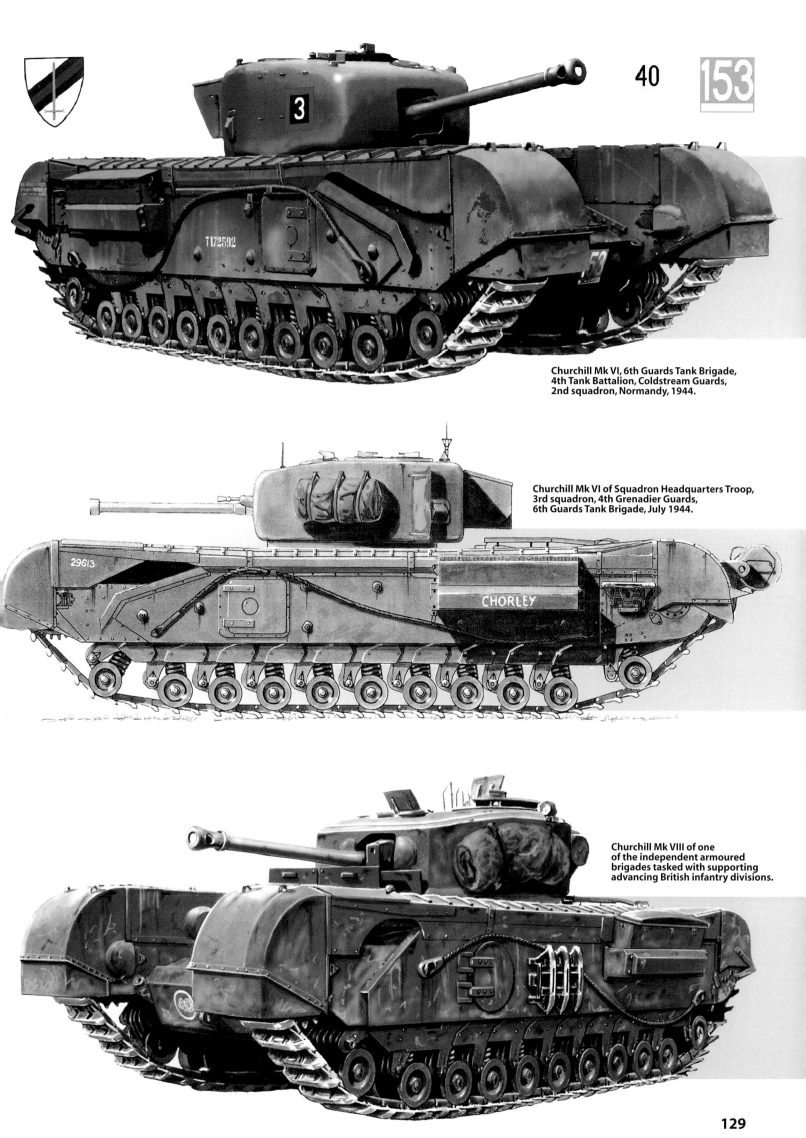

Churchill Mk VI, 6th Guards Tank Brigade,
4th Tank Battalion, Coldstream Guards,
2nd squadron, Normandy, 1944.

Churchill Mk VI of Squadron Headquarters Troop,
3rd squadron, 4th Grenadier Guards,
6th Guards Tank Brigade, July 1944.

Churchill Mk VIII of one
of the independent armoured
brigades tasked with supporting
advancing British infantry divisions.

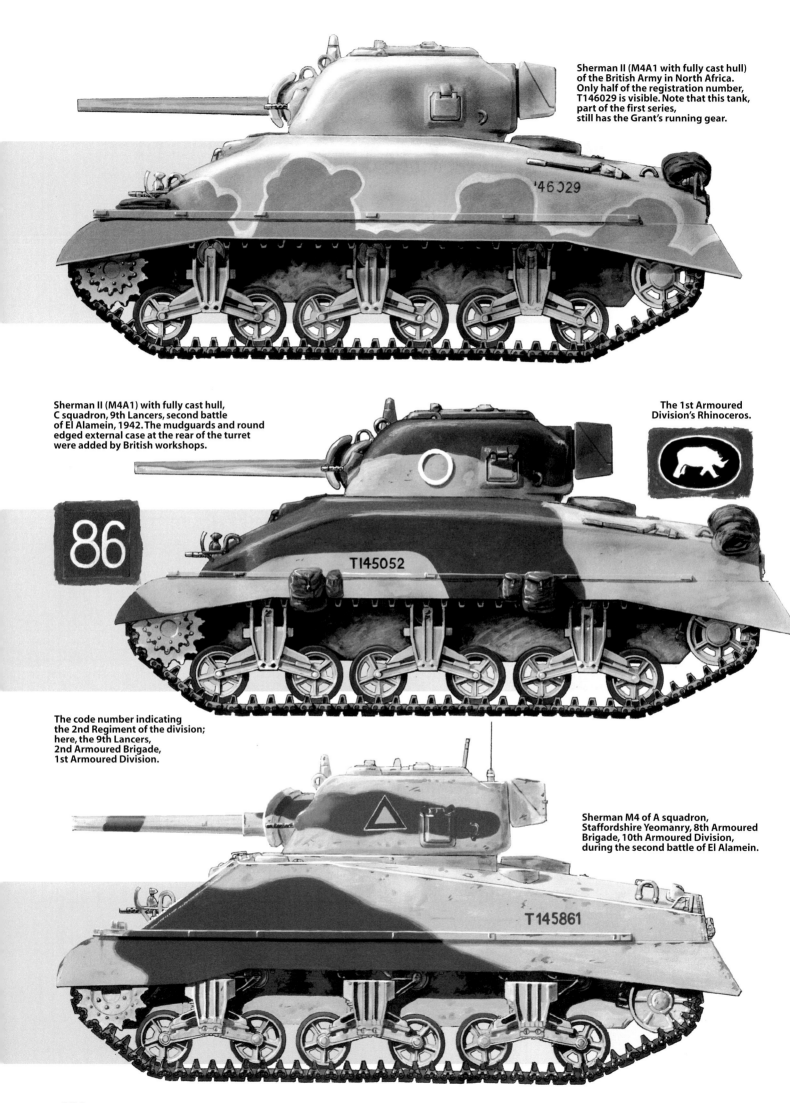

Sherman II (M4A1 with fully cast hull)
of the British Army in North Africa.
Only half of the registration number,
T146029 is visible. Note that this tank,
part of the first series,
still has the Grant's running gear.

Sherman II (M4A1) with fully cast hull,
C squadron, 9th Lancers, second battle
of El Alamein, 1942. The mudguards and round
edged external case at the rear of the turret
were added by British workshops.

The 1st Armoured
Division's Rhinoceros.

The code number indicating
the 2nd Regiment of the division;
here, the 9th Lancers,
2nd Armoured Brigade,
1st Armoured Division.

Sherman M4 of A squadron,
Staffordshire Yeomanry, 8th Armoured
Brigade, 10th Armoured Division,
during the second battle of El Alamein.

130

In terms of performance, the Sherman was more or less on a par with the Panzer IV and STuG III and IV assault guns which suffered from a lack of mobility and mechanical unreliability.

BULLET

A well known British Sherman with the 'Saint' emblem, taken from the famous detective novels. It was destroyed by a Tiger on the Italian Front in the spring of 1944.

SR 11523G
4-G-1031   LINK IOF 3   T 224560

Sherman M4A4 "Arrant" belonging to the 12th Canadian Armoured Regiment, the Three Rivers Regiment.

ST16/34
ARRANT
174
16

T-146552

ARRANT

View of the glacis plate and turret flank on the Sherman seen at left.

"Alla" is a Sherman M4A4 of the 12th Canadian Armoured Regiment (The Three Rivers Regiment), a unit which served with the 8th Army in Italy then in north east Europe in March 1945.

Sherman M4A1 of the 44th RTR, 4th Armoured Brigade whose emblem was a black gerbil, a reminder of its fighting in Egypt, Libya and Tunisia.

Sherman M4A2 of the 24th Lancers (number 995), 8th Armoured Brigade. This regiment was replaced by the 13/18th Hussars on July 29th, 1944. The 24th Hussars, as well as all the other regiments of the brigade, were equipped with Duplex Drive Shermans on D-Day. The skirts of course disappeared during the course of the campaign.

A Sherman Firefly
on a M4 A4 chassis
of the 11th Armoured
Division during operation
Plunder at the beginning
of April 1945.

T·262871

A Sherman Firefly on a M4 A4 chassis "Hybrid"
which is the 17 pounder version of the famous
American medium tank, 7th Armoured
Division. This tank belongs to the 1st RTR
(Royal Tank Regiment), white code number 51
on a red square.

T260030

Sherman Firefly VC (M4 A4)
of one of the regiments to land in the first
days of Normandy. The large numbers
painted on the turret could designate
one of the Shermans armed with
the very efficient
17th pounder,
perhaps a tank
of the 13/18th Hussars
for example.

71

CAROLE

1126/LCT4/212

789

A Sherman Firefly of the 4th Armoured Brigade. It was part of the 3rd County of London Yeomanry which is indicated by the tactical 123 sign. The Brigade went into action at a late point in the battle for Hill 112 and then only in a limited way, its commander, Lord Carver, refusing to throw the Shermans into the teeth of the Tigers.

T-212716

This Sherman Vc belonged to one of the two armoured divisions that played a proper role in the attack of July 18th. The number 52 designates the second regiment of an Armoured Brigade. It there fore belongs to either, the 3rd Royal Tank, or the 1st Armoured Battalion. The blue square shows that it belongs B squadron.

T-21268C
BELVEDERE
E

Sherman M4A1 (76 mm) with a T 23 turret, of a New Zealand armoured unit. The 76 mm gun, although superior to the standard 75 of the other Shermans, remained inferior to the British 17 pounder.

NELSON II
T-262836

A Cromwell of the 8th King's Royal Irish Hussars, Reconnaissance Regiment of the 7th Armoured Division "Desert Rats". It is equipped with the hedge cutters, useless on the plains of Caen, but of great help in the "bocage" of the Falaise sector.

Two views of a Cromwell belonging to the 2nd Northamptonshire Yeomanry of the 11th Armoured Division, 1944. With this tank, the firing of the 75 mm gun and coaxial Besa machine gun, was pedal operated.

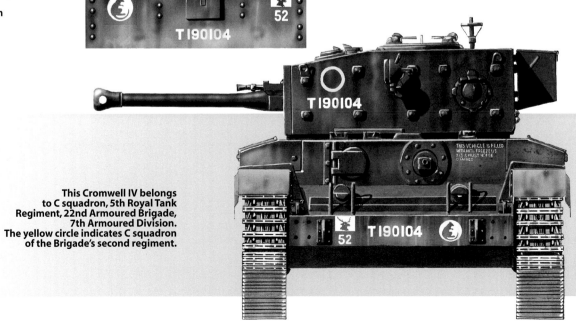

This Cromwell IV belongs to C squadron, 5th Royal Tank Regiment, 22nd Armoured Brigade, 7th Armoured Division. The yellow circle indicates C squadron of the Brigade's second regiment.

135

Cromwell of the 2nd Armoured Reconnaissance Battalion, Welsh Guards. This unit was the reconnaissance regiment of the Royal Armoured Corps (white code number 45 on a blue and green square) a battalion not part of a brigade (white) for the squadron identification square of the Guards Armoured Division (white eye emblem on a blue shield). Normandy, end of June 1944.

Cromwell of the 7th Armoured Division "Shufti Cush".

Cromwell of the Guards Armoured Division, 2nd Battalion Welsh Guards, the Division's reconnaissance regiment. In the last weeks of the war, these tanks were mostly replaced by their far superior successor, the Comet within the 11th Armoured Division but not in the ranks of the Guards Armoured Division which kept its Cromwells. The front of the hull bears the Division's 'All seeing eye' symbol.

This Comet bears a very visible insignia that was not used on the front line; it is typical of units training in Great Britain. This view shows perfectly that the Comet was the direct descendent of the Cromwell. The hull and running gear are notably very similar.

Comet of the 11th Armoured Division in the closing weeks of the war. The Comet was an optimised version of the Cromwell with a short 17 pounder gun. The first Comets arrived in the Ardennes theatre of operations in December 1944. A more substantial number arrived, always in the 11th Armoured Division, in the course of 1945.

This Comet bears a very visible registration number, it is probably one of the first Comets to be made. The Comet's gun is a 17 pounder, modified by Vickers-Armstrong to make it less voluminous. This barrel was at first called the Vickers HV 75 mm, then 77 mm.

Hungary

were made). Note that the latter, although equipped with a short 75 mm gun, could not stop their Soviet enemies at a reasonable distance, due to the weak capabilities of their projectiles. The Division's first action was in the Carpathians in 1944 ; the Hungarian tanks were obviously unable to put up much of a fight against the new Soviet tanks. Aware of the situation, the Germans supplied a few Marder III tank hunters, Panthers and three Tigers, but nothing could stop the Soviet steamroller.

By October 5th, 1944, the 1st Armoured Division only had six Hungarian made tanks compared to 64 for the 2nd Armoured Division ! Added to the low number of tanks was the problem of training the drivers. Whereas until January 1943 tank crews were highly trained (tank drivers on average covered 3,500 kilometres !), the wear and tear on materiel destined for the front lines (the low output of Hungarian industry did not allow for the manufacture of specific training tanks), meant that the time allocated to training was reduced to 1,000 hours in order to avoid too much wear and tear.

The result of this was that, in 1944, the rate of inexperienced new drivers arriving on the front line could reach 80% in some companies. Maintenance problems did nothing to improve the situation either.

At the beginning of the Second World War, Hungary did not have much experience in the production of armoured vehicles as this had only begun in 1938 and they only had a few armoured units mainly destined for reconnaissance. These units mostly used Toldi type tanks, a version of the Swedish L-60 made under licence, and the tankette of Italian origin, the Ansaldo CV 33. The Hungarian army took part in the Yugoslavian campaign alongside its German ally, then in the "Crusade against Bolshevism" in June 1941 as a motorised army corps. At this time, the Hungarian army deployed 95 Toldi tanks and 65 CV 33 tankettes.

It was only in 1942 and during the terrible fighting against the Soviet Union, that it formed its first armoured brigade which later became a division) mostly with the Skoda 38 (t) (102 in total) and 22 Panzer IV D. The other tanks were the obsolete (Pz I). A second division would be formed later, exclusively equipped with Hungarian made materiel such as the Turan I tank (285 were made between the beginning of 1942 and the spring of 1943) and the Turan II (139

H 351

A Toldi I tank. A reinforced armour variant, the Toldi II, appeared in 1942. The armament was identical for both versions: a 36M model 20-mm cannon and a 34/37 model 8-mm machinegun.

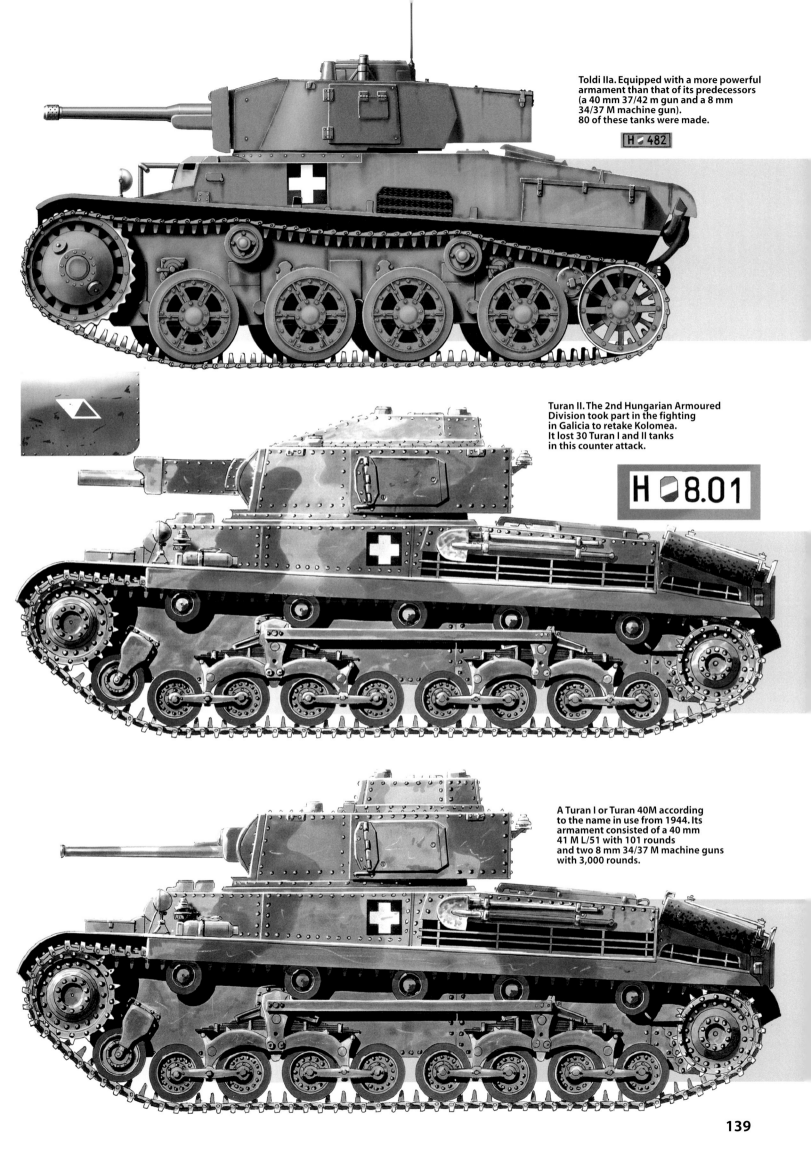

Toldi IIa. Equipped with a more powerful armament than that of its predecessors (a 40 mm 37/42 m gun and a 8 mm 34/37 M machine gun).
80 of these tanks were made.

H 482

Turan II. The 2nd Hungarian Armoured Division took part in the fighting in Galicia to retake Kolomea.
It lost 30 Turan I and II tanks in this counter attack.

H 8.01

A Turan I or Turan 40M according to the name in use from 1944. Its armament consisted of a 40 mm 41 M L/51 with 101 rounds and two 8 mm 34/37 M machine guns with 3,000 rounds.

Italy

Italy was interested in tanks from the very beginning. With typical Roman realism, they opted for a version of the FT-17 after having tested the Schneider tank. They also developed their own heavy tank, the Fiat 2000 which was armed with a turret mounted 65 mm gun and seven hull mounted machine guns. This streamlined tank was ahead of its time but only two were made (six according to some sources). Fiat also transformed the FT-17 which was built under licence, into the Fiat 3000 (100 were made). Around 1929, the acquisition of a Carden Loyd would influence future Italian tank production with the appearance of the Carro Veloce CV 33-35. The war between Italy and Ethiopia showed the necessity of using heavier materiel. The Carro Armato M 11/39 was thus developed (100 were made) and was already obsolete when it entered into service in 1939. It was followed by the Carro Armato Fiat M 13/40 (799 were made), equipped with an excellent 47 mm gun, capable of destroying any British tank.

1939 saw the formation of the first three armoured divisions, "Centauro, Ariete and Littorio". In June 1940, when Italy attacked France, 326 light tanks (CV 33 tankettes and L 3 tanks) had been made. The Centauro Division's first actions in Albania were disastrous and the unit went through a long period of crisis before showing what it was capable of in the Tunisian campaign of 1943. The Ariete Division, fought bravely on the African battlefields, to such an extent that three Gold Medals for Bravery were awarded ; as for the Littorio Division, it was sent into action in the battle of the Alps in 1940 and suffered serious defeats. It later took part in the Yugoslavian campaign where it advanced very quickly, not coming up against any resistance. Its destiny awaited it in Africa ; after having lost all of its tanks at El Ghazala, it was re-equipped and disappeared in the final actions at El Alamein.

110 tanks and 15 Semovente self-propelled guns fought in the Soviet Union as part of the CSIR. They were mostly used in a support role for infantry and alpine units.

They are often neglected by many model kit enthusiasts for whom Italian tanks seem to have played no role in the war. This is a serious mistake. The weakness of the Italian armoured force was more in its staff than in the crews and materiel used. Another fault was undeniably in the quality of Italian steel ; this was brittle and fixed by rivets, which if hit by a shell could end up killing the crew.

Despite Mussolini's wish, expressed in 1942, to develop the Ariete, Centauro and Littorio armoured divisions, in order to provide them with a firepower that was on a par with that of their enemies, such a reconstruction could not be carried out. Paradoxically, it was another unit, the M armoured division, formed by the MSVN, the fascist militia and not by the Army, that was the best equipped of all the divisions, despite its late formation on June 25th, 1943. Supposed to be the elite unit of the armoured forces, it was 'cleansed' and renamed after the Mussolini government's downfall.

In cooperation with the Germans, the Italians showed courage and tenacity in combat, despite the poor quality of their armour and the risks that they knew they faced. The M 13/40 chassis led to several models of Semovente 75-18, then the M 42-32 used as a very efficient tank hunter by the Italians first, then by the Germans. The M 14/41 (1,103 were made) was an improved M 13/40 adapted for desert warfare and with a greater range. Some were also sent to the Russian Front. The M 15 (82 were made) was the last improvement made to this type of tank, with a longer gun which increased its velocity, a lengthened chassis without a side hatch, a better engine and thicker armour. It served mostly with the Germans, after the fighting of Rome on September 8th - 10th, 1943, in the hands of elements of the Ariete Division. Some could be found in the anti partisan units fighting in Yugoslavia. The Carro Armato P 40 (80 were made), considered as being a medium tank, used a 420 hp diesel engine, similar to that of the T-34, which gave it an excellent power to weight ratio. Its 75 mm gun was also a real improvement and was on a par with those of the Allies. The chassis would be used in the construction of the excellent Semovente M-42 assault gun, equipped with a 75 mm gun, or M 42 -L (105 mm gun). This tank was also successively used by the Germans as a tank hunter. Note also that French tanks, captured by the Germans in 1940, were found within Italian armoured units, mainly the R 35 but also the Somua S 35 (in Sardinia). The surviving tanks were recovered by the Germans after September 1943.

After the Armistice of September 1943 and the fighting for Rome, the Allies forbade Italy from fighting alongside them with armoured units.

Carro Armato L6/40.
The Italians were the first to use sandbags to reinforce their tanks' frontal armour.

Carro Armato L6/40. 19 of this type of tank were sent to the Soviet Union as part of the CSIR, the Italian Expeditionary Corps in Russia.

The twenty four M11/39 of the Raggrupamento Carri Speciale M, it was the best tank that the Italians had in June 1940, allowing them to carry out operations against neighbouring British colonies. However, once the British Cruisers and Matildas arrived, this Italian tank was definitively outclassed.

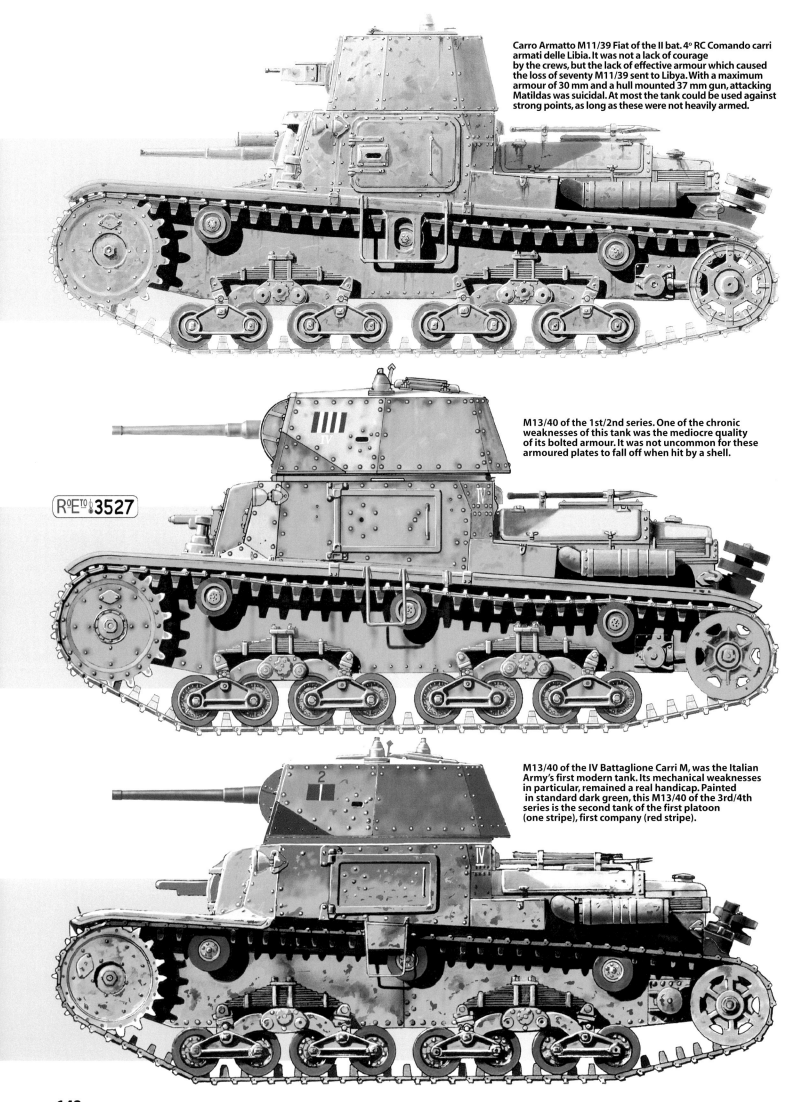

Carro Armatto M11/39 Fiat of the II bat. 4° RC Comando carri armati delle Libia. It was not a lack of courage by the crews, but the lack of effective armour which caused the loss of seventy M11/39 sent to Libya. With a maximum armour of 30 mm and a hull mounted 37 mm gun, attacking Matildas was suicidal. At most the tank could be used against strong points, as long as these were not heavily armed.

M13/40 of the 1st/2nd series. One of the chronic weaknesses of this tank was the mediocre quality of its bolted armour. It was not uncommon for these armoured plates to fall off when hit by a shell.

RºETº 3527

M13/40 of the IV Battaglione Carri M, was the Italian Army's first modern tank. Its mechanical weaknesses in particular, remained a real handicap. Painted in standard dark green, this M13/40 of the 3rd/4th series is the second tank of the first platoon (one stripe), first company (red stripe).

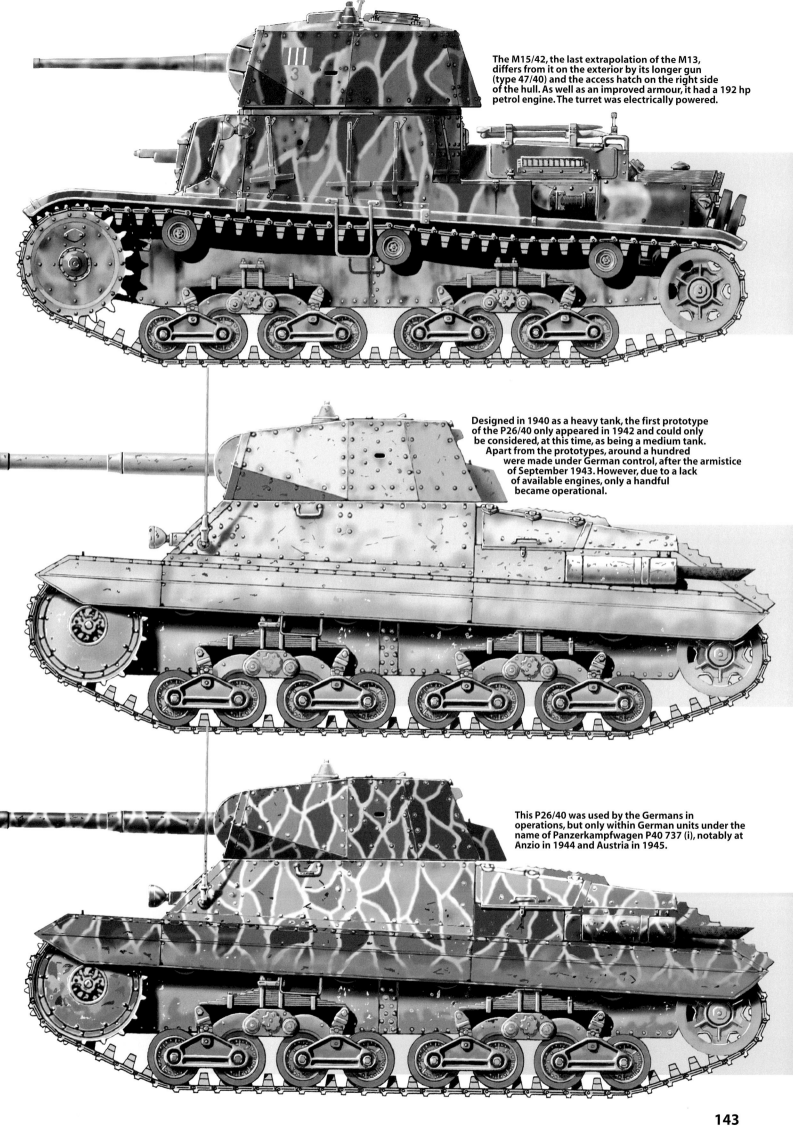

The M15/42, the last extrapolation of the M13, differs from it on the exterior by its longer gun (type 47/40) and the access hatch on the right side of the hull. As well as an improved armour, it had a 192 hp petrol engine. The turret was electrically powered.

Designed in 1940 as a heavy tank, the first prototype of the P26/40 only appeared in 1942 and could only be considered, at this time, as being a medium tank. Apart from the prototypes, around a hundred were made under German control, after the armistice of September 1943. However, due to a lack of available engines, only a handful became operational.

This P26/40 was used by the Germans in operations, but only within German units under the name of Panzerkampfwagen P40 737 (i), notably at Anzio in 1944 and Austria in 1945.

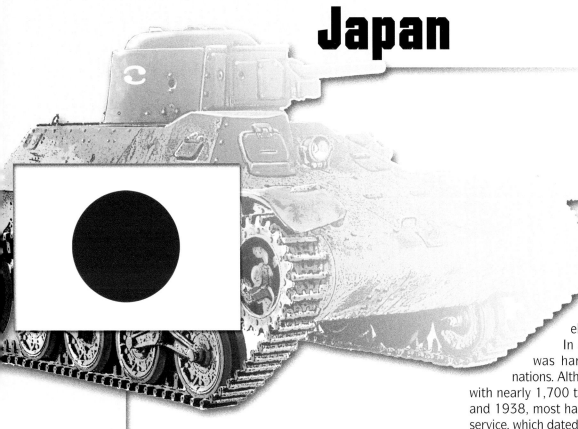

Japan

As is the case with Italy, one might smile at the idea of studying the history of Japan's armoured forces. This would, however, be unjustified. Japan, did not have at its disposal countryside that lent itself to the massed used of armour. Only China represented an area where the Japanese could employ their tanks and show their ability to carry out large pincer movements. Japan also knew how to use its offensive capacity, strategically as well as tactically, in the first part of the conflict. The other battlefields, such as Malaysia, Burma and the Philippines, were not good tank country. The big mistake made by the Japanese was that they saw the tank only in an infantry support role. They thus deprived themselves of the possibility of launching sudden attacks that could destabilize and cut off the enemy's line of communication. This inability to grasp opportunities was fatal to them in Manchuria, but also elsewhere later on.

In addition to this, the quality of tanks was hardly comparable to those of other nations. Although production was fairly impressive, with nearly 1,700 tanks of all types built between 1931 and 1938, most had not evolved since they had entered service, which dated to the middle of the nineteen thirties. Production problems, due to Japan's geography (more than 500 islands) also added to the list of handicaps.

The inspection of captured equipment and help from Germany, led to a slight evolution in Japanese armoured materiel, which was, as it happens, equipped with excellent guns. At the end of the war, they had types of tank and tank hunters that were capable of fighting Allied armour on equal terms , but not in sufficient numbers to pose a real threat (Types 3 Chi-Nu, Chi-Hy a,d Chi-Ri).

This evolution had, however, come too late to influence the outcome of the war.

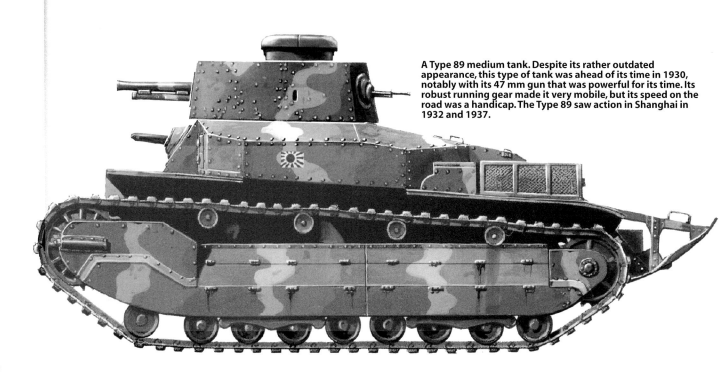

A Type 89 medium tank. Despite its rather outdated appearance, this type of tank was ahead of its time in 1930, notably with its 47 mm gun that was powerful for its time. Its robust running gear made it very mobile, but its speed on the road was a handicap. The Type 89 saw action in Shanghai in 1932 and 1937.

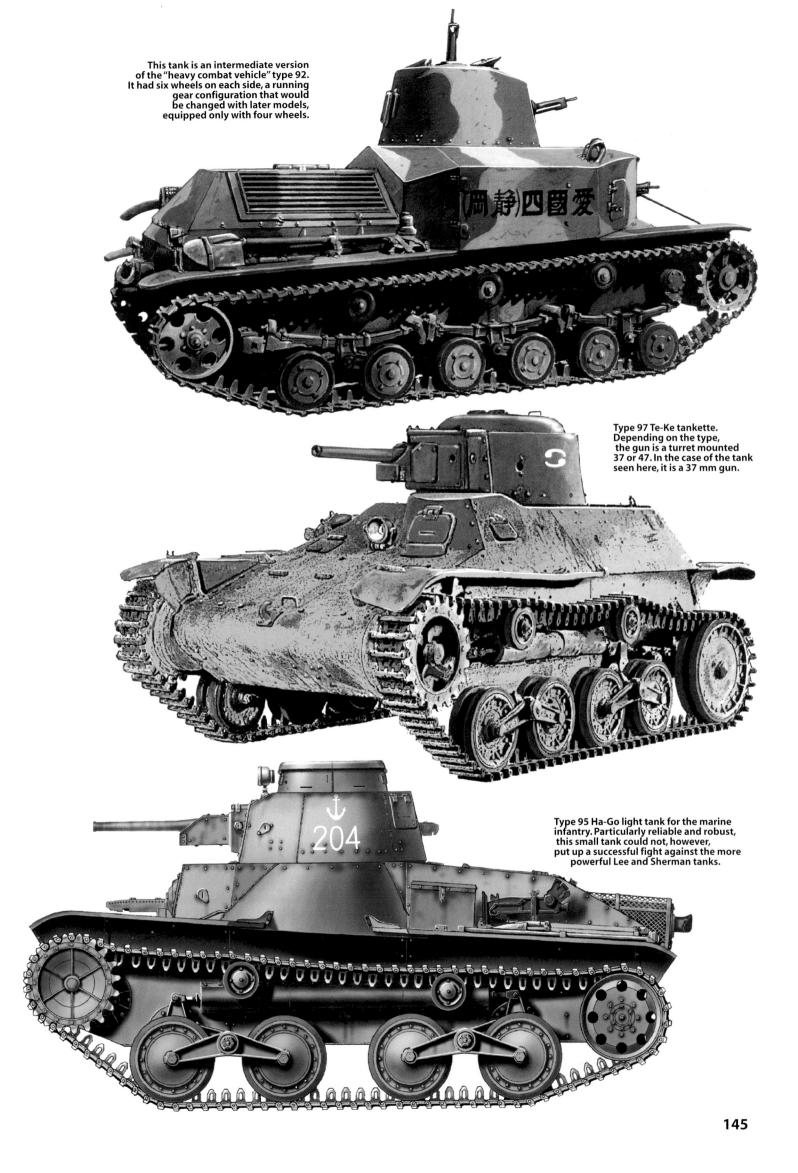

This tank is an intermediate version of the "heavy combat vehicle" type 92. It had six wheels on each side, a running gear configuration that would be changed with later models, equipped only with four wheels.

愛國四（静岡）

Type 97 Te-Ke tankette. Depending on the type, the gun is a turret mounted 37 or 47. In the case of the tank seen here, it is a 37 mm gun.

Type 95 Ha-Go light tank for the marine infantry. Particularly reliable and robust, this small tank could not, however, put up a successful fight against the more powerful Lee and Sherman tanks.

204

The Chi-Ha, or type 97 medium tank, in its first version, equipped with aerial and armed with a short 57 mm gun. The running gear was much improved compared to the type 89, allowing it to achieve 38 kph.

The Chi-Ha had a four man crew. The thickness of its armour varied from 9 to 33 mm. It had a range of 248 kilometres.

The last version of the Chi-Ha appeared after the terrible defeat suffered by the Japanese against Joukov in 1939. It had a large turret capable of housing a long high velocity 47 mm gun.

146

Poland

Partly founded on territory annexed from Germany, Austria and Russia after the First World War, it was inevitable that Poland would have problems at its borders. The Dantzig affair would complicate matters even further. The new Polish armoured army based its training on the French model and saw action, from 1919, in the conflict against the Soviet Union, mainly using the FT-17 tank. It was, therefore, this tank that would equip the army. It was transformed, improved and its speed increased by 13 kph. In 1930, it was obsolete compared to the Soviet tanks already in service. Poland bought fifty Vickers 6 Ton tanks with double or single machine gun equipped turrets. It was from these that the new 7TP was taken, weighing now 9 metric tonnes for Polish requirements. This tank was an innovation, as it was, in 1934, the world's first tank to use a diesel engine (the Swiss Saurer 6 cylinder engine, VBLDb). However, the transformations did not stop there. The armour was increased, going from 18 mm to 40 mm and it was planned to build a tank equipped with a gun turret. In 1937, the first 7TP tanks (169 were made) left the production lines, equipped with the excellent 37 mm Bofors gun and a 7.92 mm coaxial machine gun. The difficulties encountered in getting the turrets delivered from Sweden slightly held up production.

The 7TP soon revealed itself to be an excellent transformation, superior to the Vickers 6 Ton in every domain and capable of taking on the Red Army's T-26 and their efficient 45 mm gun as well as the Panzer III and its 37 mm gun, both of which were less well armoured.

But, the Polish also proved themselves to be innovative with their TK tankettes (TK3 = approximately 300 made). Small, fairly easy to handle and capable of receiving a variety of specific weaponry, this materiel would be used several decades later, via the Wiesel, in part designed by Porsche and used in German parachute units. The concept, like the period, was simple and, above all cheap, and what is more, worked well. It was versatile, and capable, at the time, of taking a machine gun, a 20 mm gun and /or later, four pro-totypes of a 37 mm or 47 mm gun, without undergoing major transformations. It would seem that the prototypes took part in the final fighting for Warsaw.

The beginning of hostilities did not come as a surprise for Poland. It had partially mobilised its troops since March 1939, and announced general mobilisation on August 29th. On August 26th, the German Army was ready to launch the attack whilst Hitler waited in vain for a final plenipotentiary the 30th and 31st September. Sure of receiving help from its French and British allies, the Polish made no effort to find a diplomatic solution. Like Gamelin, they thought that Germany would not be able to continue with its attack on Poland. According to Gamelin, Hitler would be overthrown by his people in the case of war, provoking such chaos that the German Army would have to give up its offensive and march back to Berlin to restore order. Unfortunately, Gamelin and Warsaw were wrong.

It was the Polish Army that collapsed, despite putting up a heroic fight. They fought so tenaciously that Ribbentrop, on September 8th, urged Molotov to launch a Soviet attack along the Russian-Polish border. It was only when Stalin realised that Polish resistance was crumbling and that Warsaw would soon fall, that he decided to take part in the proceedings. On the morning of the 17th, Soviet troops entered Poland.

A better tactical and strategic use of Polish tanks, mainly the TP7 type, but also the R35 type, could have eventually brought about a different result against the more numerous, but inferior, Pz I and II tanks.

Many Polish soldiers managed to get to France, then Britain. Two armoured units were created, one fought in North Africa against the Afrika Korps then later in Italy, where it became the 2nd Armoured Division. The second, and the best known, was the 1st Armoured Division which fought in Normandy, northeast France, Belgium and Germany. All of these units were equipped with British and American materiel (Cromwells for the 1st,Shermans, Fireflys, M 10s etc.) and were under Allied command.

1943 saw the formation and rapid engagement, in the Soviet Union, of a Polish liberation army that was independent of the Soviet command. It was called the "Ludowe Wojsko Polskie" or "Polish People's Army". It was organised in the same way as the Soviets. During the course of the war, it became the 1st Armoured Corps (1. Korpus Pancery) and put into the field two independent armoured brigades (1st and 16th), two heavy armoured regiments (4th and 5th). It suffered grievous losses in the final battles in the East.

Poland was the biggest buyer amongst the many countries that bought the Vickers 6-ton, acquiring 38, sixteen of which had two machine gun turrets as seen here. In 1939, they equipped the two mechanised cavalry brigades, each one having 16 Vickers per company.

7 TP tank with double turret, each armed with a light machine gun. This tank, therefore, suffered greatly from a lack of firepower. With its puny armour, it was incapable of efficiently fighting against the Panzer Divisionen.

7 TP2 tank, certainly part of the 3rd Polish Armoured Battalion. Based on the British Vickers E, the 7TP was already obsolete in 1939. Its armament was on a par with the Panzer III, and even its 17 mm armour was equivalent to that of the Ausf. A, B and C. However, the armour of the Panzer III D was almost twice as thick.

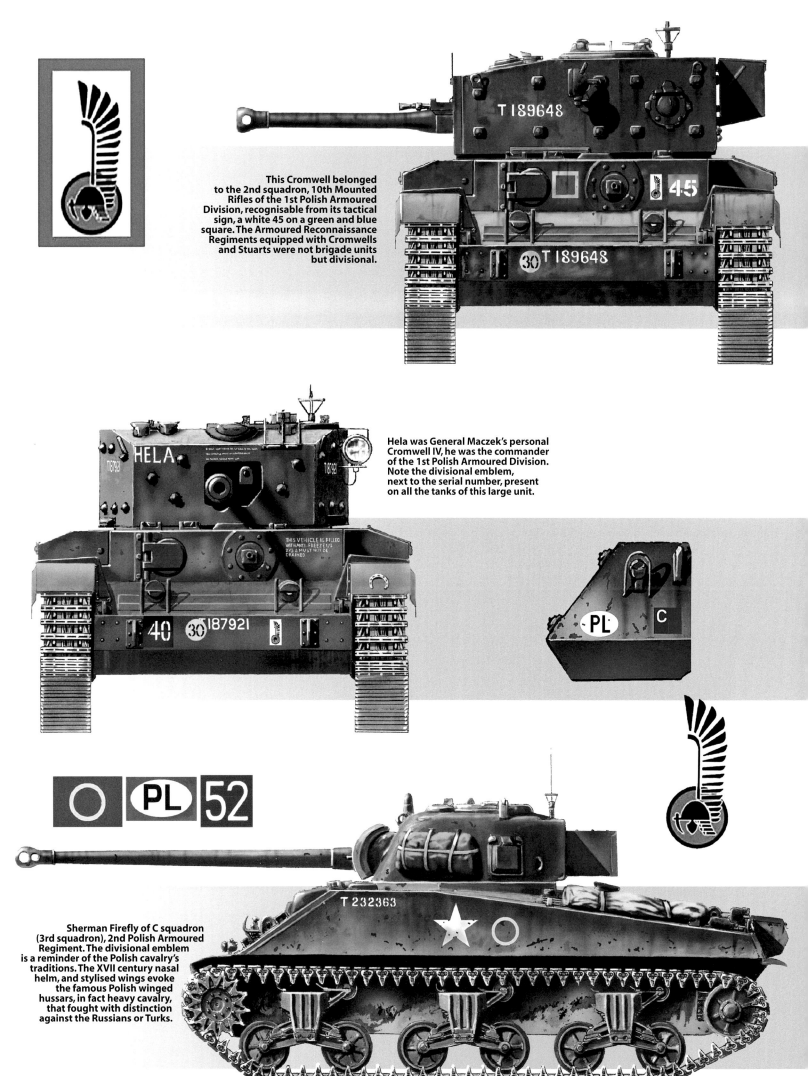

This Cromwell belonged to the 2nd squadron, 10th Mounted Rifles of the 1st Polish Armoured Division, recognisable from its tactical sign, a white 45 on a green and blue square. The Armoured Reconnaissance Regiments equipped with Cromwells and Stuarts were not brigade units but divisional.

Hela was General Maczek's personal Cromwell IV, he was the commander of the 1st Polish Armoured Division. Note the divisional emblem, next to the serial number, present on all the tanks of this large unit.

Sherman Firefly of C squadron (3rd squadron), 2nd Polish Armoured Regiment. The divisional emblem is a reminder of the Polish cavalry's traditions. The XVII century nasal helm, and stylised wings evoke the famous Polish winged hussars, in fact heavy cavalry, that fought with distinction against the Russians or Turks.

T-34/76 model 1943 of the 1st Polish
Armoured Brigade, Eastern Front,
autumn 1943.

T-34/85 of the 4th Armoured Brigade,
1st Army Corps, destroyed at Niesky
in Czechoslovakia on April 17th 1945.

T-34 of the 4th Heavy Tank Regiment,
1st Polish Army, Eastern Front, 1944-45.

JS 2M of the 4th Heavy Tank Regiment,
1st Polish Army, Poland 1945.

Rumania

On the eve of the invasion of the Soviet Union, Rumania had 35 Skoda R1 type tanks, 126 R2 (Skoda 35), 73 Renault R 35 and 60 old FT-17 tanks. Three armoured units were available, these were the 1st and 2nd regiments part of the 1st Armoured Division (the 1st was entirely equipped with R2 tanks and the 2nd with the R 35), and the 1st Cavalry Division that used type R1 light tanks. The 1st regiment was severely weakened in one year, mainly after the extremely tough fighting for Odessa and the breakthrough towards the Don.

Losses at the end of the 1941 campaign seem to be due to the High Command's tactical misuse where they were incapable of carrying out large mobile operations. However, the Division was able to leading operations in liberating the Rumanian province of Bessarabia, annexed by the Soviet Union in 1940, playing an essential role in pushing enemy troops out of this province and suffering light casualties. It was, however, more difficult on the Dneister. They were also badly supported by the infantry and artillery, incapable of coordinating joint operations, the tanks suffered heavy losses against the fortified Soviet positions at Odessa. Added to this was the lack of dive Royal Rumanian Air Force bombers which rendered null and void the principle of lightning war. Despite these difficulties, the German Military Mission was full of praise for the unending courage of the Rumanian tank crews of the 1st Armoured Division, summed up by the words of the German general, von Knobelsdorff : "Poorly equipped but well trained and improving with every day."

Despite receiving eleven Panzer II and III tanks and as many Panzer IV to compensate for the inferiority of Rumanian tanks of the 1st Armoured Regiment that was preparing to go into the lines in the Stalingrad sector in November 1942, the unit could not fight the enemy on equal terms. It did, nevertheless, launch countless counter attacks, causing much damage to the Soviets. By November 25th, 1942, the 1st Armoured Division had lost 70% of its strength. The unit was reformed with fifty German Skoda 38 (t).

The Rumanians, however, had to wait until November 1943 before receiving, at last, tanks capable of taking on their Soviet counterparts. At this time, 129 Panzer Iv and 114 StuG III tanks were delivered. The 1st Armoured Division would fight on until August 23rd, 1944, the date at which the Marshal Antonescu, the country's strong man, was ousted from power.

Going over to the side of their old adversary, the Rumanians fought with them to the gates of Vienna in 1945. As well as continuing to use German tanks, they received T 34/85 tanks from the Soviets.

The Praga R-1 tankette was the cavalry's only tank in 1941-1942. Each brigade had a motorised reconnaissance squadron with, in theory, six R-1. Poorly armed, and without a radio, the only asset of this tank was its mobility. This R-1 has the silhouette of Saint George on the turret, the patron saint of Rumanian cavalry.

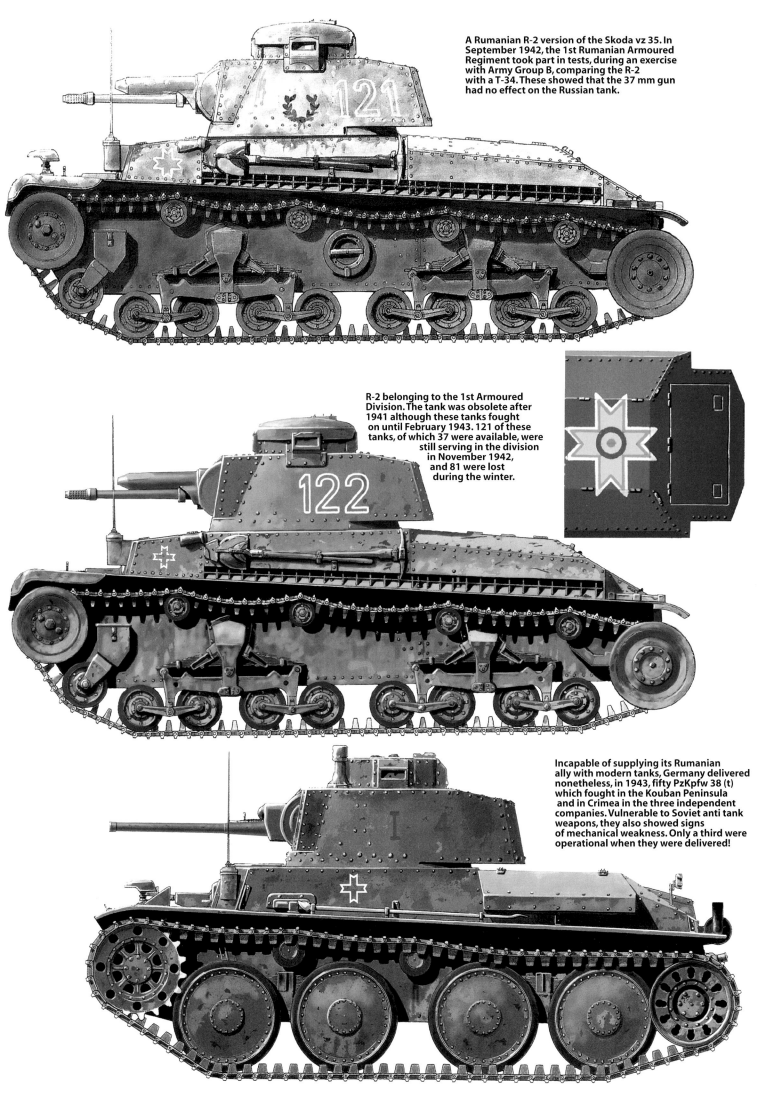

A Rumanian R-2 version of the Skoda vz 35. In September 1942, the 1st Rumanian Armoured Regiment took part in tests, during an exercise with Army Group B, comparing the R-2 with a T-34. These showed that the 37 mm gun had no effect on the Russian tank.

R-2 belonging to the 1st Armoured Division. The tank was obsolete after 1941 although these tanks fought on until February 1943. 121 of these tanks, of which 37 were available, were still serving in the division in November 1942, and 81 were lost during the winter.

Incapable of supplying its Rumanian ally with modern tanks, Germany delivered nonetheless, in 1943, fifty PzKpfw 38 (t) which fought in the Kouban Peninsula and in Crimea in the three independent companies. Vulnerable to Soviet anti tank weapons, they also showed signs of mechanical weakness. Only a third were operational when they were delivered!

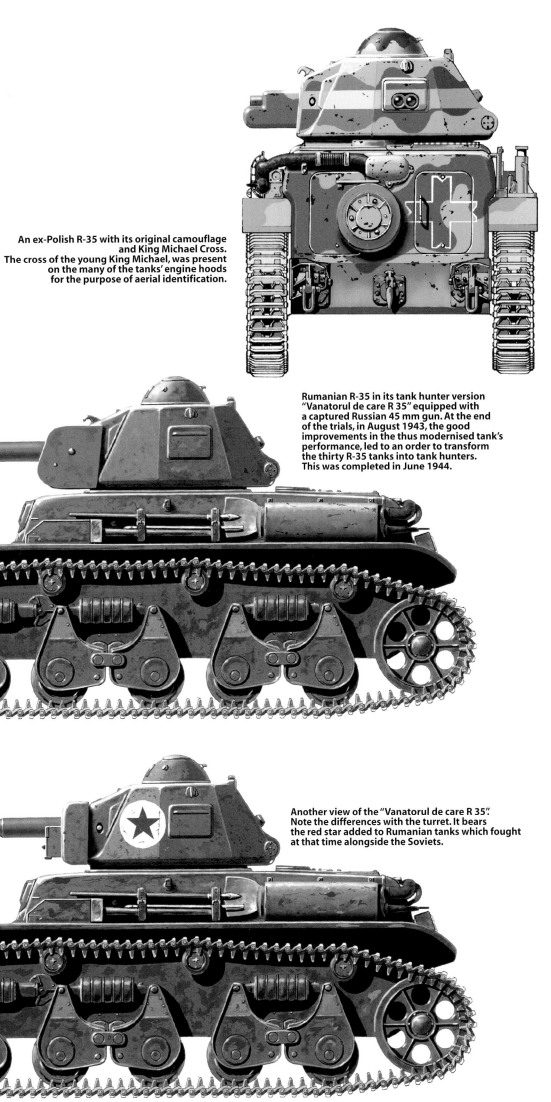

An ex-Polish R-35 with its original camouflage and King Michael Cross. The cross of the young King Michael, was present on the many of the tanks' engine hoods for the purpose of aerial identification.

Rumanian R-35 in its tank hunter version "Vanatorul de care R 35" equipped with a captured Russian 45 mm gun. At the end of the trials, in August 1943, the good improvements in the thus modernised tank's performance, led to an order to transform the thirty R-35 tanks into tank hunters. This was completed in June 1944.

Another view of the "Vanatorul de care R 35". Note the differences with the turret. It bears the red star added to Rumanian tanks which fought at that time alongside the Soviets.

153

On October 17th, 1942, the 1st Armoured Division received 10 Panzer III N like the one seen here. These Panzers substantially increased the small Rumanian tank force, but all were lost during the winter campaign.

Decimated during the winter of 1942-43, the 1st Armoured Division was rebuilt thanks to a few deliveries of modern German tanks, such as the PzKpfw IV- T4 for the Rumanians. These tanks served during the Soviet offensive of August 1944, then within the 2nd Armoured Regiment, against the Germans in 1945. They kept their German type camouflage, as seen here.

T-34/85 tank fighting with the Soviet Army. In many cases, Rumanian units were forced by the Russians to go into the front line with their old, obsolete tanks.

Slovakia

In March 1939, when Slovakia gained independence, there was only one armoured regiment in the ex-province, at Turciansky sv. Martin.

It was, therefore, only logical that this unit, the old 3rd Armoured Regiment of the ex-Czechoslovakian army, was reformed, becoming the only armoured unit of the brand new national army.

79 LT vz 34 and 35 light tanks out of the 298 used by Czechoslovakia, were thus gained and organised into a single battalion. The latter was transformed into a regiment in 1940. A combined group from this regiment (30 LT vz 35, 10 vz 38 and seven LT vz 40s) was sent to the Eastern

Front in 1941 where it fought alongside the Germans in the sectors of Sanok and Lipovec. Despite the urgent demands of the Mobile Division and the Security Division, who wanted to have a tank battalion within their divisions, no other tank unit was formed until August 1942. This was probably due to those in charge of the repairs workshop who were opposed to the regime, saying that the tanks placed in their care were beyond repair, which discouraged for a while any attempts to develop tanks. Nevertheless, in August 1942, the Minister of Defence decided to reinforce field divisions with tanks, which included a few LT 40s tanks. These companies were progressively brought back to Slovakia in the first half of 1943. This same year saw the Armoured Regiment, also brought back from the Eastern Front, reinforced with thirty eight LT vz 38, five Panzer III N with short 75 mm guns (delivered in March 1943) and twenty Panzer II that were delivered in January 1944. Eighteen Marder III were also delivered in mid 1944. On May 23rd, 1944, the Armoured Regiment, an elite unit, was made up of the following tanks : Forty nine LT vz 35, fourteen LT vz 40, sixty one LT vz 38, sixteen Panzer II, five Panzer III and twenty seven LT 34. It was then stationed on Slovakia's eastern border to defend the country. Note that a platoon of five LT 38 tanks was attached to the President of the Slovakian State, Monseignuer Tiso's Guard.

The fighting was finished on the Eastern Front, but the last large scale operation, where Slovakian tanks were in action, was the insurrection started by the Resistance on August 29th, 1944. This was crushed by German units and the rare Slovakian units that remained loyal to the regime.

LT vz 40. Twenty-one of these were delivered to Slovakia by Böhmisch-Mährischen Maschinenfabrik AG. It has the national white-blue-red emblem (Slovakian colours), which replaced the Patriarchal Cross sometime during 1942. The emblem seen here was in use until 1945.

V-3038

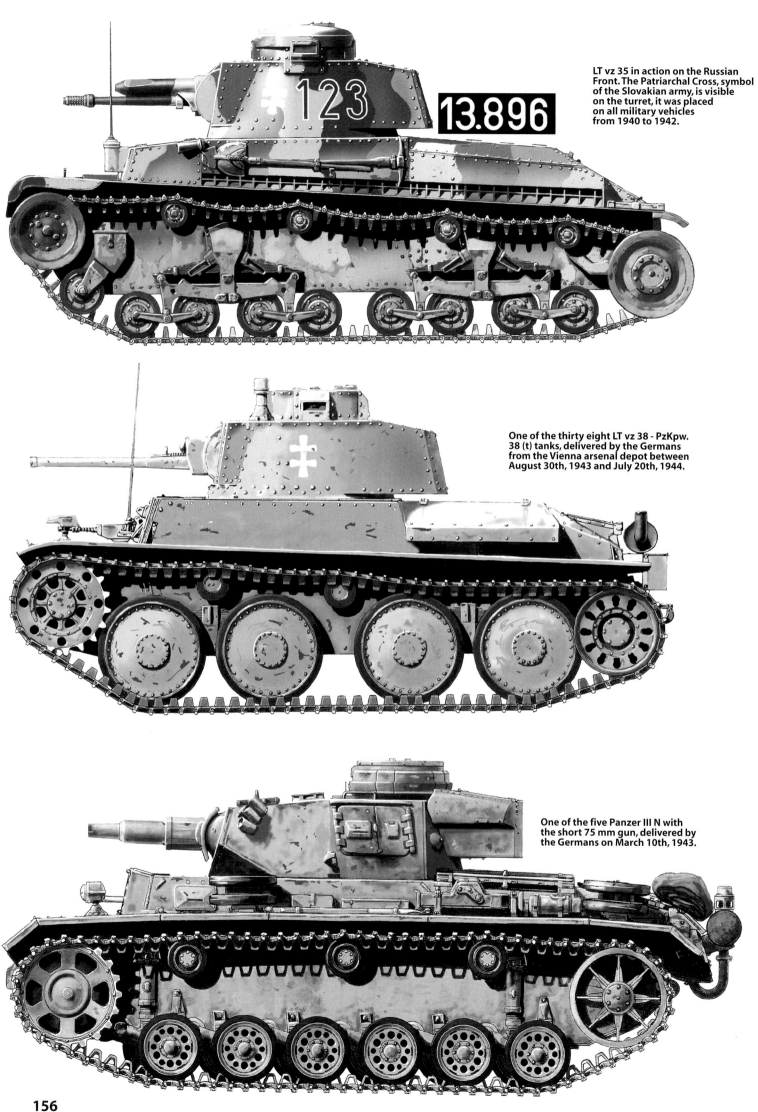

LT vz 35 in action on the Russian Front. The Patriarchal Cross, symbol of the Slovakian army, is visible on the turret, it was placed on all military vehicles from 1940 to 1942.

One of the thirty eight LT vz 38 - PzKpw. 38 (t) tanks, delivered by the Germans from the Vienna arsenal depot between August 30th, 1943 and July 20th, 1944.

One of the five Panzer III N with the short 75 mm gun, delivered by the Germans on March 10th, 1943.

JS-1 and 2, the total is 3,984 tanks between 1942 and 1945. To this impressive force must be added the thousands of tank hunters and assault guns, such as the SU-122, SU-85, SU-100, SU-152, JSU 122-152 and finally the SU-76.

Faced with the vastness of Russia, the Wehrmacht had great logistical problems. After a promising beginning, the lightning attack was stopped after six months of fighting in increasingly harsh weather conditions. The Soviet Army, thanks to the tenacity of the Russian soldier, helped by "General Winter", won the decisive battle of Moscow. A year later, it inflicted a severe defeat on the invader when it encircled Stalingrad, where 200,000 German soldiers perished or were captured. The Russian tanks had, however, played a vital role, even if 2,000 had been lost. It was at Kursk that the Russians proved their strategic worth by partly countering the German attack, and turning it to their advantage in the north and not only gaining the ground lost, but also breaking through the German defensive lines. Here too, what is little known is that the Russians paid a heavy price, losing nearly 6,500 tanks throughout the battle. The StuG III tanks alone, destroyed 1,800 for a total loss of 180 !

The scales, however, inexorably tipped in favour of the Soviets, producing 4 to 5 more tanks than their adversary. Lend Lease gave the Red Army large quantities of Anglo Saxon tanks of lesser quality, which meant that they did not wear out their best tanks like the T-34.

The German heavy tanks, the Panther and Tiger I, forced the Russians to use better guns and thicker armour. The T-34/85 and the first Josef Stalin tanks were introduced in the second half of 1943 and later on in large quantities. The Germans were now only on the defensive, a role that they excelled in until the end of the war, but nothing could stop the Soviet steamroller.

According to some historians, the Russians had considerably reduced their tank losses in the last six months of the war compared to those of the Germans, putting forward the number of one German tank destroyed for 1.2 Soviet tanks. However, the numbers quoted by the Soviets themselves amount to more than 10,000 losses (T-34, JS 1-2, JSU 122-152 and other SU tanks) for this same period. The Germans would have, therefore, lost at least 8,500 tanks to the Red Army. This number is ridiculous when one knows that they only had, at the very most, 1,200 tanks on the Eastern and Western Fronts. The bloodiest battle was without a doubt the final battle for Berlin, on its outskirts and within the city itself.

The last Soviet innovation was the JS-3 which came into service in Berlin but did not take part in the fighting. The chassis of the T-34, T-43 and T-44 being superior, were used as a foundation for the new generations of Communist Bloc tanks. Most of these are still being used in most of the countries in the world.

During the Great War, Russia, as was the case with Germany and the Austro-Hungarian Empire, only had at its disposal armoured cars with machine guns. It is even more surprising that this nation, after the October Revolution and the terrible crisis that followed it, was able to put together in barely more than two decades (in the light of the sad state of its infrastructure), the world's most formidable armoured force. It was not just a case of quantity, with more than twelve thousand T-26 and several thousand BT tanks, but also one of quality with the latest T-34 and KV, two types of revolutionary tanks. But where did the money, the machines and technology necessary to this sort of heavy industry come from ? Why was such an impressive number of tanks made when the population was dying of starvation in its millions, as was the case of the artificially created Ukrainian famine of 1932 to 1933. There are many different answers. However, according to some historians, operation Barbarossa did not destroy a weak peace-time army, weakened by Stalin's purges, unprepared for war and finding itself by chance on the border, but a powerful army, taken by surprise at the most delicate time of assembly and in full preparation for a huge offensive in the West that would certainly not have stopped in Germany. The Germans, however, were fifteen days in advance of them.

The tanks used by the Soviets were mainly BT-2 and 5 tanks (5,000 were made), the BT-7 (7,000) and several variants of the T-26 (nearly 13,000 were made including 1,549 still made in 1940). Added to this were several more 'exotic' tanks (T-28 and T-35). The T-34 was late in leaving the factories, but the Red Army already had 117 of them in 1940, then 3,014 in 1941. For the KV I, there were respectively 141 and 102.

Up to 1944, 35,119 T-34/76 were made, complemented by nearly 11,000 T-34/85. To this you have to add 18,300 T-34/85 that rolled off the production lines in 1945, for a total of 64,519 tanks made in six years. The undisputed world record for tank production !

For the KV-I, KV II and KV-I S tanks, the total is 4,581 made between 1940 and 1943. For the KV-85 (130), the

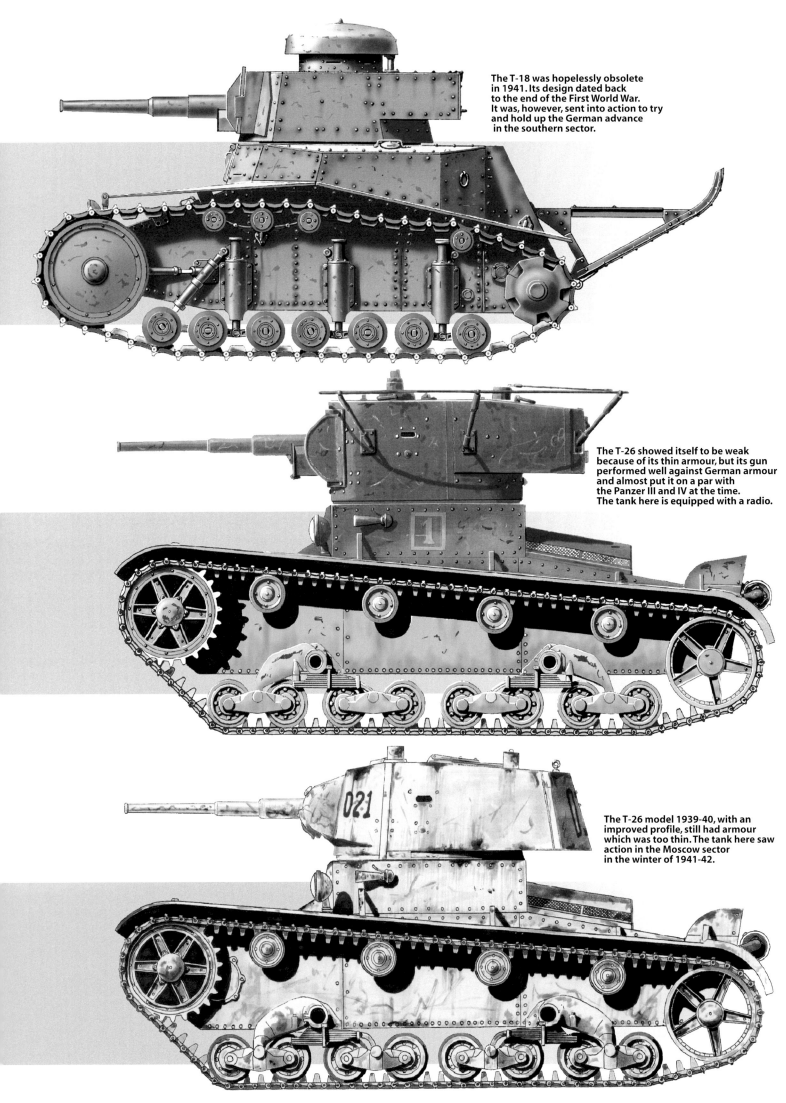

The T-18 was hopelessly obsolete in 1941. Its design dated back to the end of the First World War. It was, however, sent into action to try and hold up the German advance in the southern sector.

The T-26 showed itself to be weak because of its thin armour, but its gun performed well against German armour and almost put it on a par with the Panzer III and IV at the time. The tank here is equipped with a radio.

The T-26 model 1939-40, with an improved profile, still had armour which was too thin. The tank here saw action in the Moscow sector in the winter of 1941-42.

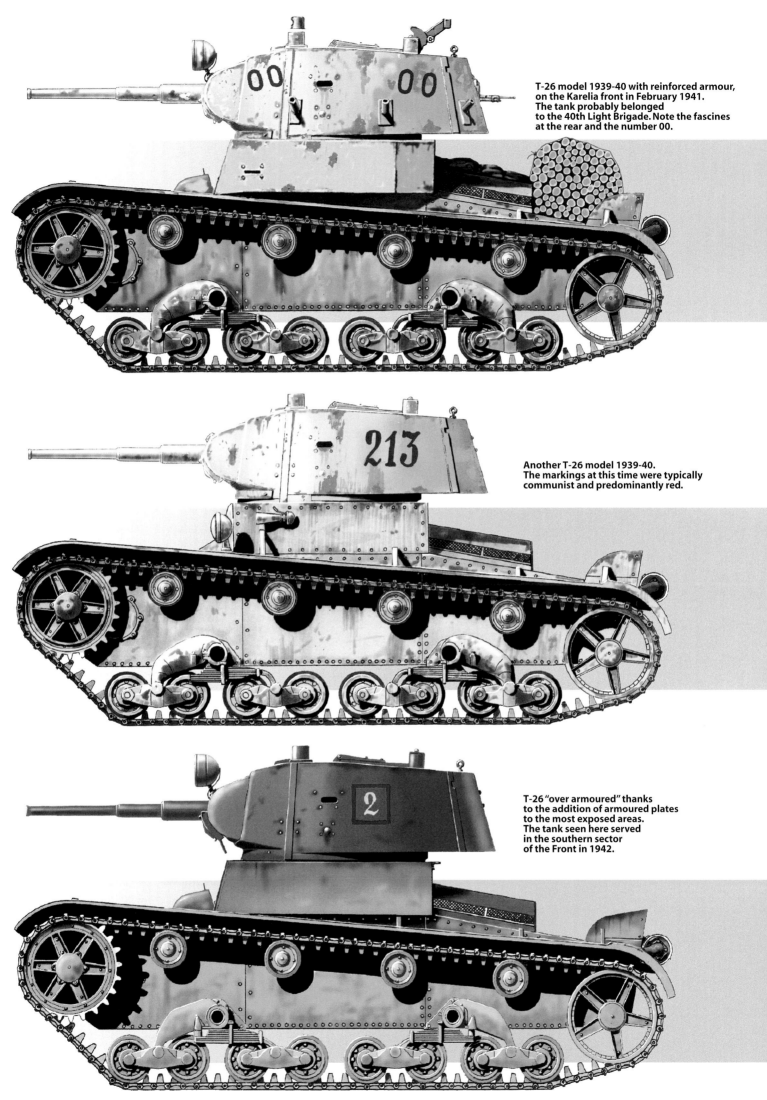

T-26 model 1939-40 with reinforced armour, on the Karelia front in February 1941. The tank probably belonged to the 40th Light Brigade. Note the fascines at the rear and the number 00.

Another T-26 model 1939-40. The markings at this time were typically communist and predominantly red.

T-26 "over armoured" thanks to the addition of armoured plates to the most exposed areas. The tank seen here served in the southern sector of the Front in 1942.

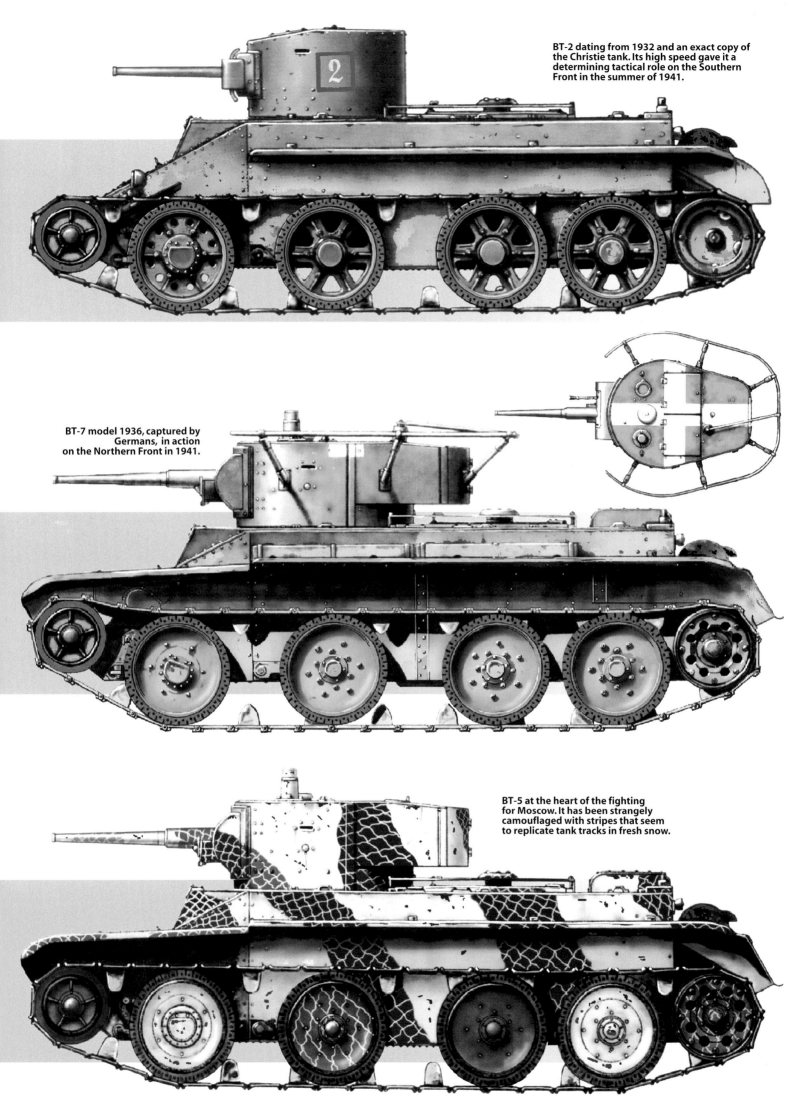

BT-2 dating from 1932 and an exact copy of the Christie tank. Its high speed gave it a determining tactical role on the Southern Front in the summer of 1941.

BT-7 model 1936, captured by Germans, in action on the Northern Front in 1941.

BT-5 at the heart of the fighting for Moscow. It has been strangely camouflaged with stripes that seem to replicate tank tracks in fresh snow.

BT-5 with winter camouflage. As with the Germans, the Soviets did not always have time to add markings to their vehicles.

This tank is painted in a three tone camouflage scheme, dating from the beginning of the conflict and still in use until 1944.

BT-7 in action in the central sector of the Front in 1942, bearing the name of the supreme commander, "Stalin", on the turret.

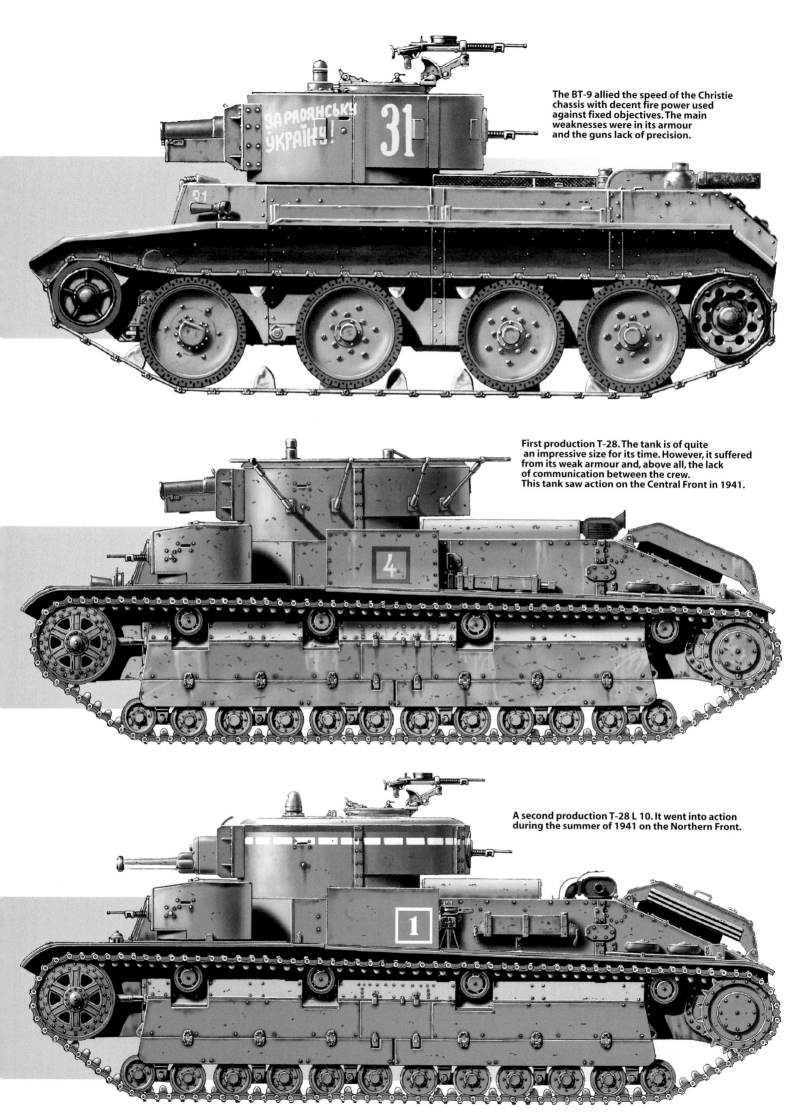

The BT-9 allied the speed of the Christie chassis with decent fire power used against fixed objectives. The main weaknesses were in its armour and the guns lack of precision.

First production T-28. The tank is of quite an impressive size for its time. However, it suffered from its weak armour and, above all, the lack of communication between the crew.
This tank saw action on the Central Front in 1941.

A second production T-28 L 10. It went into action during the summer of 1941 on the Northern Front.

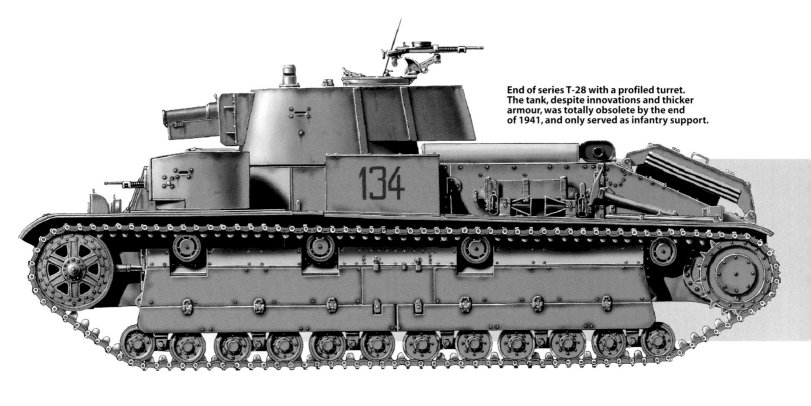

End of series T-28 with a profiled turret. The tank, despite innovations and thicker armour, was totally obsolete by the end of 1941, and only served as infantry support.

Central Front in 1941. Weighing 50 metric tons, this "wheeled fortress" (or with tracks) did not fulfil its tactical expectations. Too heavy, not mobile enough and under powered, it would be easy prey due to its misuse as a solitary tank.

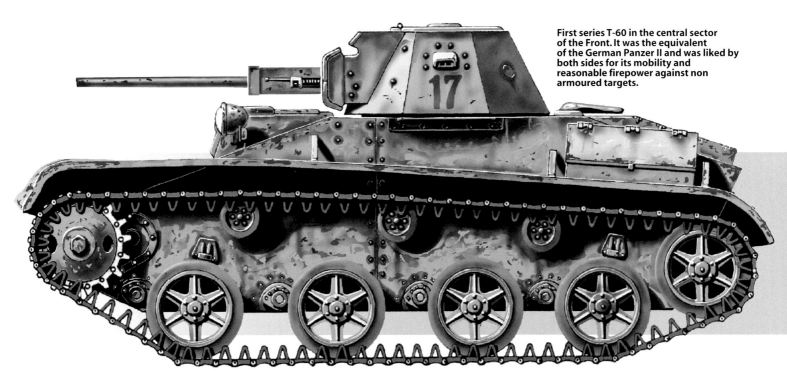

First series T-60 in the central sector of the Front. It was the equivalent of the German Panzer II and was liked by both sides for its mobility and reasonable firepower against non armoured targets.

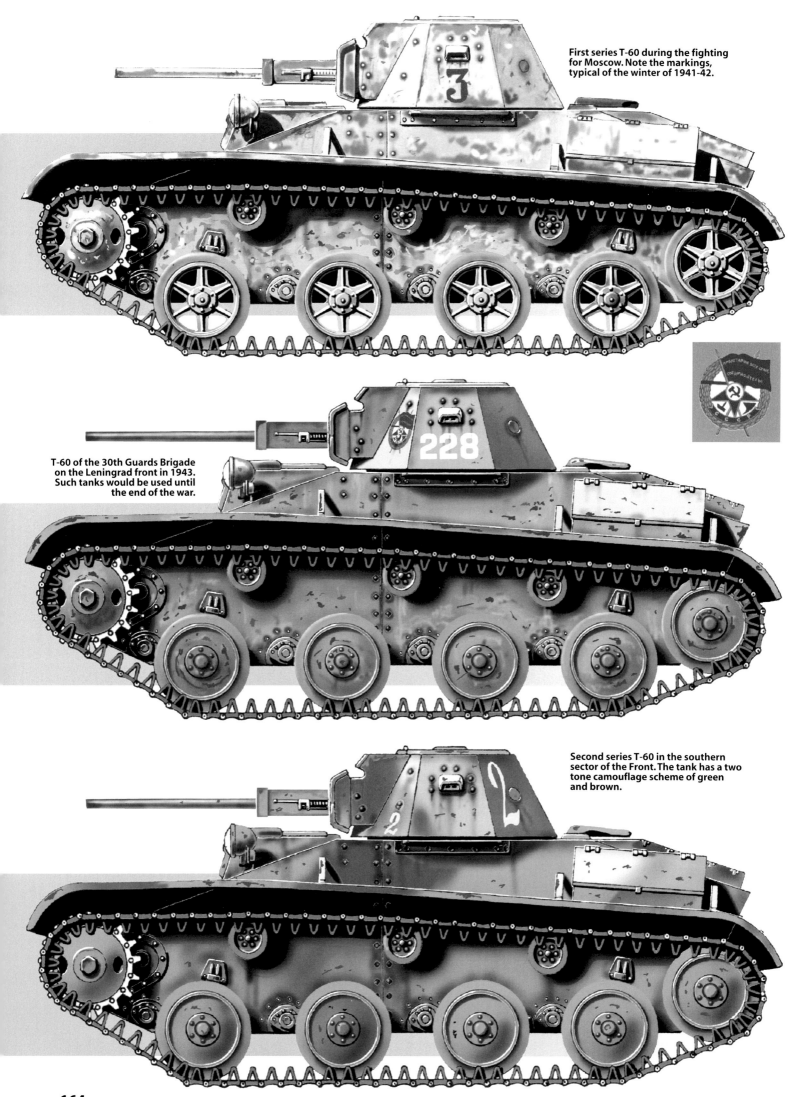

First series T-60 during the fighting for Moscow. Note the markings, typical of the winter of 1941-42.

T-60 of the 30th Guards Brigade on the Leningrad front in 1943. Such tanks would be used until the end of the war.

Second series T-60 in the southern sector of the Front. The tank has a two tone camouflage scheme of green and brown.

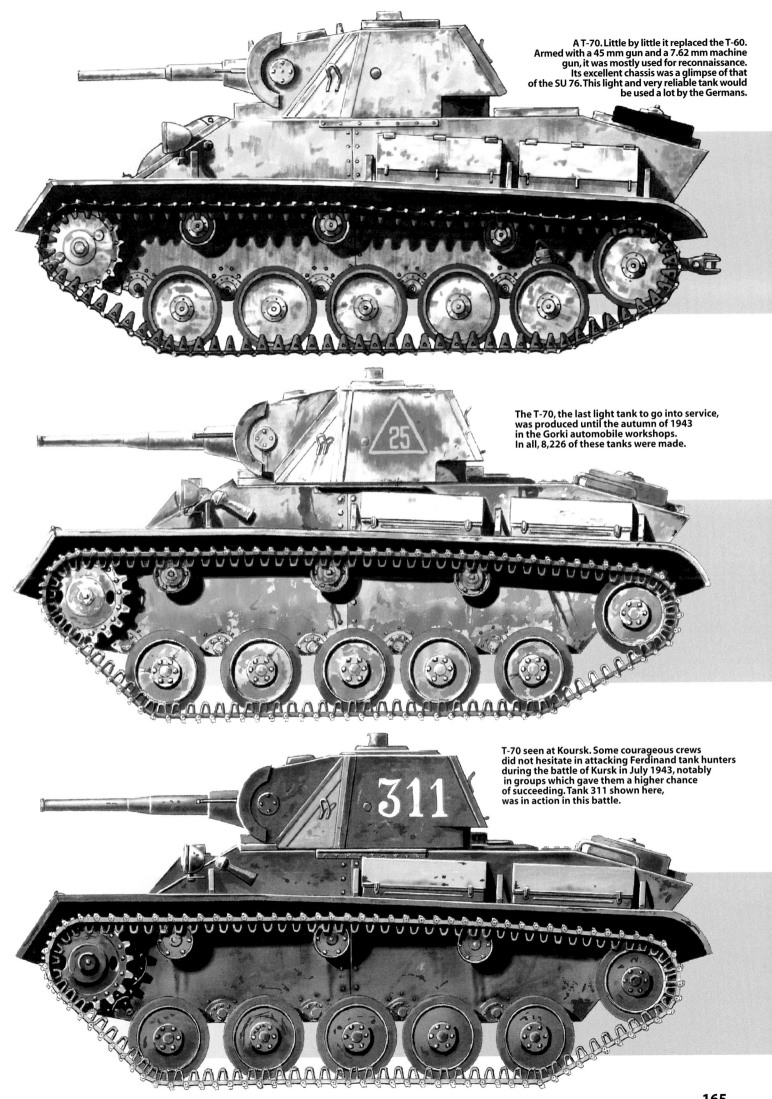

A T-70. Little by little it replaced the T-60. Armed with a 45 mm gun and a 7.62 mm machine gun, it was mostly used for reconnaissance. Its excellent chassis was a glimpse of that of the SU 76. This light and very reliable tank would be used a lot by the Germans.

The T-70, the last light tank to go into service, was produced until the autumn of 1943 in the Gorki automobile workshops. In all, 8,226 of these tanks were made.

T-70 seen at Koursk. Some courageous crews did not hesitate in attacking Ferdinand tank hunters during the battle of Kursk in July 1943, notably in groups which gave them a higher chance of succeeding. Tank 311 shown here, was in action in this battle.

T-70 of the 57th Guards Armoured Brigade during the fighting of operation Zitadelle, northern sector of Kursk, July 1943.

The T-70 had the same chassis as the T-60, but was slightly reinforced to cope with the increased weight. The traction was moved from the rear to the front. The gun, mounted in a new welded turret, was provided with 70 shells.

The T-80 that made its appearance in 1943, just in time for the battle of Kursk.

The streamlined T-50 which, along with the BT tanks, prefigured the type of Soviet tank, the T-34. It was, however, made in small numbers compared to the T-34 as it was not reliable enough.

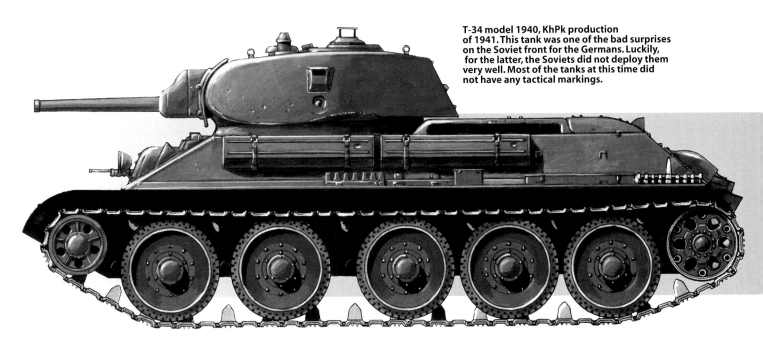

T-34 model 1940, KhPk production of 1941. This tank was one of the bad surprises on the Soviet front for the Germans. Luckily, for the latter, the Soviets did not deploy them very well. Most of the tanks at this time did not have any tactical markings.

T-34 model 1940 KhPk with a long, higher performance gun. The red inscription means "For the USSR".

T-34 model 1940. It was, when it came out of the factories, a remarkable balance between the three main factors that defined the quality of a tank. Armour, mobility and armament.

T-34/68B or model 1941. It was characterised by a heavier armour and a F34 41.5 calibre gun. Approximately 9,000 of these tanks were made.

T-34 model 40 hybrid, having undergone modifications such as the addition of handles for infantry.
The tank was in service in the summer of 1943 in the Kursk sector. During the fighting of the summer of 1943, several units adopted a light camouflage.
It would seem that it was painted over the standard tank green. Other sources mention the use of a light clay.

T-34 model 41/42 ST 2 Barrikady. This tank is also a hybrid. Southern sector of the Front, March, 1943. The shape of the gun shield is badly designed, as shells could lodge themselves between it and the upper hull which would immediately tear off the turret.

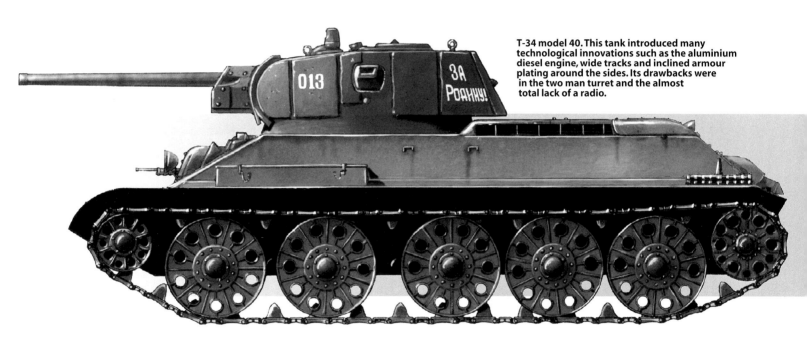

T-34 model 40. This tank introduced many technological innovations such as the aluminium diesel engine, wide tracks and inclined armour plating around the sides. Its drawbacks were in the two man turret and the almost total lack of a radio.

T-34/76 model 1940 with a small sized turret. As is often the case, the wheels are a mix, some having a rubber covering whilst others did not.

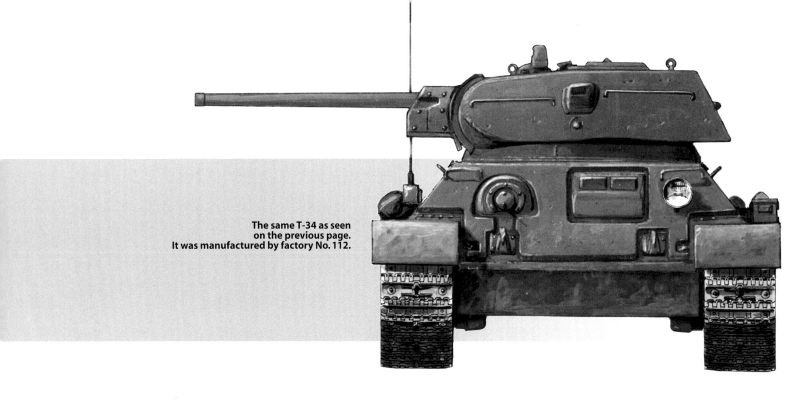

The same T-34 as seen on the previous page. It was manufactured by factory No. 112.

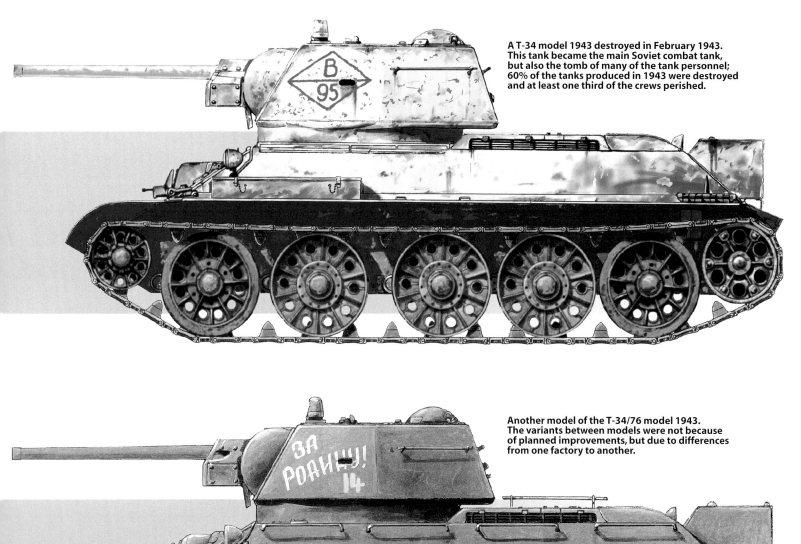

A T-34 model 1943 destroyed in February 1943. This tank became the main Soviet combat tank, but also the tomb of many of the tank personnel; 60% of the tanks produced in 1943 were destroyed and at least one third of the crews perished.

Another model of the T-34/76 model 1943. The variants between models were not because of planned improvements, but due to differences from one factory to another.

A version of the T-34/76 that appeared
at the end of 1942. This tank
was commanded by Lieutenant I.I. Ivanov.

A T-34/76 destroyed in the sector
of the 19. Panzerdivision. It is a model 1943 with
a better armoured and more streamlined turret
than on the previous 1940/41 versions.

Model 1943 T-34, often called the T-43 in German
reports. This was the last version of the T-34/76,
with an improved turret compared to previous
models. Note the green wheel taken from another
tank. This tank was destroyed by a Panther
of Panzer Abteilung 51 during the battle of Kursk.

The T-34/85 began to massively replace the T-34/76 from 1944 onwards, and progressively equipped all the tank corps. Its main advantage over its predecessor lay in its 85 mm gun which gave it a clear edge on the Panzer IV. The T-34/85 also equipped the Polish, Czech and Yugoslavian armoured units formed in the USSR.

T-34/85 of the 23rd Armoured Corps, 39th Armoured Brigade, 2nd Battalion, during the fighting in Hungary at the beginning of 1945.

T-34/85 model 1944 of the 9th Armoured Corps, 95th Armoured Brigade, Berlin, May 1945.

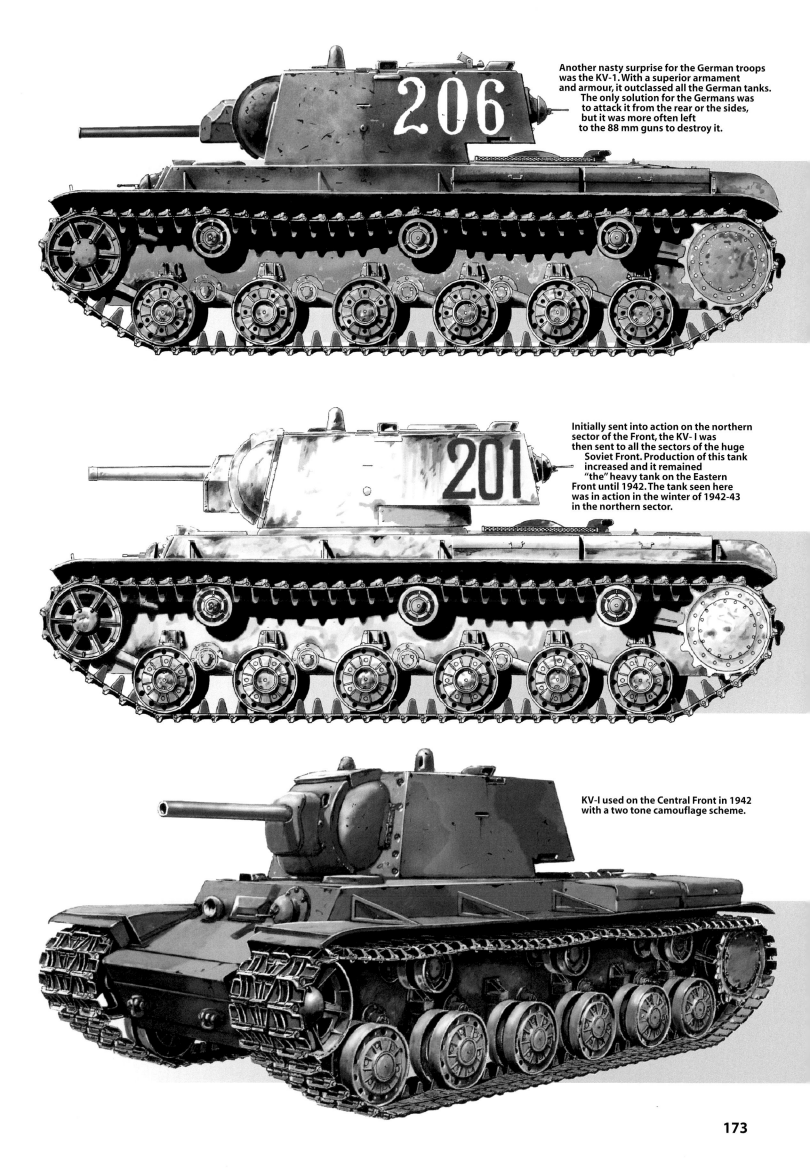

Another nasty surprise for the German troops was the KV-1. With a superior armament and armour, it outclassed all the German tanks. The only solution for the Germans was to attack it from the rear or the sides, but it was more often left to the 88 mm guns to destroy it.

Initially sent into action on the northern sector of the Front, the KV- I was then sent to all the sectors of the huge Soviet Front. Production of this tank increased and it remained "the" heavy tank on the Eastern Front until 1942. The tank seen here was in action in the winter of 1942-43 in the northern sector.

KV-I used on the Central Front in 1942 with a two tone camouflage scheme.

KV-1 S with a three tone camouflage scheme.
It was the last version of the KV-1, lighter
and with a more streamlined turret,
it was not, however, fundamentally better
than the previous versions.

KV-1 S during the fighting of operation Zitadelle
in July 1943. The Soviets had several hundred
of these tanks in the northern and southern sectors
of Kursk. The losses in tanks were very high, despite
being numerically superior. This tank was destroyed
by a Tiger during operation Zitadelle.

KV-S (S = Skorostnyi = fast) which is a lighter
version of the KV-I. The turret is slightly smaller
and the commander of the tank no longer
had the role of loader as had been
the case with previous models.
The gun is the redoubtable 7.62 mm ZIS.5.

A KV-I S in service
at the end of 1944 beginning of 1945.

KV-I S of an unidentified brigade, seen in Berlin
in April 1945. In six months of fighting,
the Soviet Army lost approximately 12,000 tanks
and was forced to use old models.

KV-85. This tank only appeared in small
numbers. It signified a stage and a link
between the KV-I and the JS-2, which
would be much superior to it.
Only 130 were made
by the autumn of 1943.

Although they were of a similar weight to the Panther, the JS-2 was considered as being the Red Army's heavy tank. Approximately 3,800 JS-2 tanks were made during the war compared to 489 Tiger II.

JS-2 in action in the "Grossdeutschland" Division's sector at the end of 1944, where it was knocked out. The tank was equipped with the excellent 122 mm gun whose rate of fire was reduced because of the separation of cartridges and charges on board the tank.

JS-2 M of an unidentified brigade during the battle of Berlin. The last version had the same projectile problem. Another drawback was the poor quality of the steel used in the armour.

T-44, one of the last of the Soviet arsenals, in action during the last fighting in the Reich. It was a taste of Soviet tanks to come in the 1950s, the T-54/55.